# Riding with Ivan Tsarevich

## Mystery Wisdom

## in

## Russian Folktales

### Friedel Lenz

The original Russian of the folktales in this book is all in the public domain. The English translations with the translator named at the top of the folktale are known or believed to be public domain. The translations of the other folktales are by Clopper Almon and are hereby placed in the public domain. The German original of the front material and the interpretations by Friedel Lenz is copyrighted by J. Ch. Mellinger Verlag, Stuttgart, 1968, and is translated and published here in English with permission of this firm. The translation is by Clopper Almon, and is hereby placed in the public domain when the original goes into the public domain.

Title of German original: *Sinndeutung zu Iwan-Johannes: Dreissig der schönsten russischen Märchen.*

Internet source for the Russian original of the folktales:

https://ru.wikisource.org/wiki/Народные_русские_сказки_(Афанасьев)

The Internet source for the translations by Irina Zheleznova is the multilingual folk tale database:

http://www.mftd.org/index.php?action=story&id=3054

The Leonard A. Magnus translation of Afanasyev is at:

https://babel.hathitrust.org/cgi/pt?id=mdp.39015019057895;view=1up;seq=19

The text of Friedel Lenz's German translation of these folktales is on the Internet. The Contents page with links to individual tales is at:

http://maerchen.arpa-docs.ch/SedWEB.cgi?BookSel=49&Alias=Marchen&Lng=1&View=1&PrjName=Marchen

The picture on the front cover is a portion of *Ivan Tsarevich Riding the Grey Wolf,* by Viktor M. Vasnetsov, 1889, Tretyakov Gallery, Moscow. Image source: Wiki Commons.

# Table of Contents

Translator's Introduction..................................................................5
Foreword..............................................................................................7
Towards Understanding Folktales..................................................13
    Secrets of the Soul and Spirit.....................................................15
        Names in the Folktales.........................................................22
    On Secrets of the Soul..................................................................22
        The Three Realms..................................................................22
        The Baba Yaga and the Three Yaga Sisters.....................23
        Nurses and nannies..............................................................25
    The Animals.................................................................................26
        The Horse................................................................................26
        The Dragon.............................................................................28
    Landscapes in the Folktales.......................................................29
    Other Features..............................................................................32
        Bones........................................................................................32
        Numbers..................................................................................33
1. Dawn, Evening and Midnight (A 140)......................................34
2. The Three Kingdoms – Copper, Silver and Gold (A 129)....42
3. The Realms of Copper, Silver and Gold (A 128)...................60
4. The Three Realms (A 130)..........................................................66
5. The Immortal Boneman (A 157)................................................75
6. The Maiden Tsar (A 233)............................................................92
7. The Tale of Ivan-Bogatir, the Peasant's Son (A 571).............103
8. Sivka Burka and the Simpleton (A 182)..................................114
9. Ivan from the Ashes - Ivan Popyalov (A 135)........................127
10. Vasilisa of the Golden Braids and Ivan from the Pea (A 560)........132
11. The Two Ivans, Soldier Sons (A 155).....................................143
12. Ivan Cowson (A 137).................................................................159
13. The Chrystal Mountain (A 162)..............................................176
14. Ivan Tsarevich and Byely Polyanin (A 161).........................180
15. Alyonushka and Ivanushka (A 261).......................................189
16. The Witch (A 108)......................................................................194
17. The Witch and the Sister of the Sun (A 93)..........................200
18. The Bear Tsar (A 201)...............................................................205
19. Legs of Silver, Arms of Gold (A 285)....................................215
20. Golden Legs, Silver Arms (A 284).........................................221
21. Marya Morevna (A 159)...........................................................229

22. Milk of Beasts (A 204)...................................................................242
23. Ivashko-Medvedko and the Three Bogatirs (A 141).......................256
24. Ivan Tsarevich, his Sister, and the Ironskin Bear (A 202)..............266
25. The Clairvoyant Dream (A 240).....................................................273
26. Ivan Tsarevich, the Fire-Bird and the Grey Wolf (A 168)..............285
27. The Tale of the Frog and Ivan Bogatir (A 570).............................297
28. Rejuvenating Apples, and Living Water (A 173)...........................309
29 The Water of Life and the Sweet Apples of Youth (A 174)............320
30. The Sea Tsar and Vasilisa the All-wise (A 222).............................326

# Translator's Introduction

Friedel Lenz (1897 – 1970) is known to those who treasure folktales for her masterful 1971 book *Die Bildsprache der Märchen* in which she intersperses her commentary with a telling of the story for 25 of the Grimm folktales. I had the privilege to translate this book, and it is now available in English as *The Picture Language of Folktales.* Nine years before the publication of *Bildsprache*, Friedel Lenz had published in 1962 *Iwan – Johannes,* her translation into German of thirty of the Russian folktales published by A. N. Afanasyev in the 19th century.

She often told these stories to adult audiences as well as to children. To the adults she would add her commentary on the spiritual meaning of the stories, a commentary that was based on the anthroposophy of Rudolf Steiner. She was frequently asked to put these interpretations into print, and she did so in 1968 in a slim publication of 48 pages of fine print on A4 paper, saddle-stitched, with no binding. It carried the title *Sinndeutung zu Iwan–Johannes.* The word *Sinndeutung* means something like "explanation of the meaning." This *Sinndeutung* is now long out-of-print and is held by only four of the 72,000 libraries participating in Worldcat, none in the USA.

Having been fascinated by her interpretations of the Grimm stories, I was eager to see what she had to say about the Russian stories, which I had long enjoyed reading in the original language. I was fortunate to obtain through the Interlibrary Loan service of the University of Maryland a scan of *Sinndeutung* from the Württembergische Landesbibliothek in Stuttgart. As I began work on a translation of the *Sinndeutung*, I expected to be able to refer the reader to an English translation of the story itself in *Russian Fairy Tales*, translated by Norbert Guterman in 1945 and available inexpensively. This assumption turned out to be wrong on two counts. First, I could often not identify from the title alone which story the commentary applied to. I found the text of Lenz's translation (which is now on the Internet) and from it identified the Russian text of the story – which is also on the Internet. So the first problem – identification – was solved.

The second problem was bigger: for a number of the stories there was no English translation in *Russian Fairy Tales*. That should not have been surprising. That book has just under 200 stories, while Afanasyev's Russian books from which Friedel Lenz selected her stories have have a total of 627. Not surprisingly, therefore, many of the stories she selected were not in the Guterman translation. They are in the seven-volume *Complete Russian Folktales* translated by Jack V. Haney, but the cost of these university-press volumes puts them beyond the reach of most individuals and school libraries.

The only solution to this problem seemed to be to include in this book translations of all of the tales covered in the *Sinndeutung*. In the case of the Grimm stories, every one of them is on the Internet in public domain translation. That proved to be true of only a few of the Russian stories used by Lenz. For the others, I have made translations using both the Russian original and the Lenz translation into German.

This was slow but congenial work; I had studied Russian in college, used it intensively during two years in the army, and kept it up in recent years while working with the Institute of Economic Forecasting of the Russian Academy of Science in Moscow. I have seen and loved old Russia from Pskov and Novgorod to Vladirmir and Suzdal. The Afanasyev versions of the Russian folktales are in the words of the tellers from whom he collected the stories. The language is often not typical standard Russian, and I often found myself looking at how Friedel Lenz had translated a passage – and at what Google Translate knew about unusual words.

A brief biography of Friedel Lenz may be found in my introduction to *The Picture Language of Folktales*.

# Foreword[1]

The folktales in this book are all without exception taken from the collection *Народные русские сказки* by A. N. Afanasyev, Moscow 1861.[2]

Alexander Nikolayevich Afanasyev (Александр Николаевич Афанасьев) - the Russian Grimm, as he is often called – lived from 1826 to 1871. The expression "Russian Grimm" is appropriate in that his books are the most comprehensive compilation of Russian folktales and that he both collected tales from simple peasant tellers and included in his publication tales collected by others. But there is an important difference between his work and that of the Grimm brothers. They often worked several slight variants of a single tale into a unified tale told in their own words. They were men of letters, and their words were beautifully simple, deeply expressive standard German. Afanasyev gives us the tales as collected in the words of the peasant teller. The language is thus often far from the standard literary Russian being defined at roughly the same time by Pushkin, Turgenev, Lermontov, Tolstoy, Chekhov and others. Thus, through the work

---

1   This foreword is translated from the German of the book *Iwan – Johannes* by Friedel Lenz with minor extensions by the translator.

2   This was the best Russian edition at the time of publication of this book in German (1962). In 1984-85, a scholarly edition with footnotes, several indexes and standard Russian equivalents of dialect words was published in Moscow by Nauka. Frequently the same name is given to several, sometimes quite different, stories. In this 1984 edition, tales with the same name are grouped together, and the all the tales are numbered from 1 to 579 – with 48 more in a supplement. In this translation, these numbers – preceded by the letter A (for Afanasyev) – are given in parenthesis following the name of the folktale. Using these numbers, one can easily find the Russian text at https://ru.wikisource.org/wiki/С_(Афанасьев). The text of the German translation by Friedel Lenz can be found at http://maerchen.arpa-docs.ch/SedWEB.cgi?BookSel=49&Alias=Marchen&Lng=1&View=1&PrjName=Marchen (Tht is all one line.)

of Afanasyev we gain direct access to the enormous treasure of the Russian folktales that had remained largely unaltered in the vast, lonely expanses of rural Russia. It is an ancient cultural heritage, and it is precisely here that the original form of the folktale can be found.

Afanasyev writes, "The folk did not arbitrarily invent these stories; they told about what they believed in, and that is why they emphasized repetitions in their stories of the supernatural and did not allow their fantasy to cross the border and loose itself in a world of unreal pictures. There is much similarity in many of these folklore traditions, but they also contain much true poetry and many moving scenes."

Afanasyev calls the folktales narratives of the supernatural. At that time many could still recognize something that was latter largely lost in the age of materialism: *folktales tell of the supersensible nature of mankind.* They come from a time when mankind lived in a a world of inner pictures. The folktales present a sequence of these images; they speak in a picture language.

In ancient prehistoric time, this inner picture vision was the common property of all peoples, but the ability to understand and work with the physical world was limited. As consciousness began to turn towards the physical world, awareness of the spiritual and soul worlds began to fade. Memories of the picture vision were first expressed in myths. They depict the creation of the world, its development and continual change, in which Man – as a psychic-spiritual being – was actively involved, in the inner pictures.

One could also call this clairvoyant consciousness of nature "consciousness of essence," for as long as it lasted, man was more connected with the inner essence of things than with their exterior. Some primitive peoples still partly live in this consciousness. A last remnant of that ancient ability is still present in us, too: the nocturnal dream. Of course, the dream is usually a chaotic copy of the events of the day, but every now and then deeper layers of consciousness are touched, and a true image is created. As rare as the reality dream has become today – it is not yet extinct and is a significant pointer to that almost-extinct capacity for imagination.

The imaginative consciousness of nature receded when thought awakened, and finally ceased altogether when it had become abstract and had become more and more a one-sided intellect. But thinking was still pictorial for long periods of time. Myths and legends laid down in imagery what had once been seen in a dreamlike way. As man became more and more aware of his personal nature and understood its development, the folktales were born. While the **myth** speaks of the Divine Overworld, and the heroic **saga** tells of the fate of a people and its leaders, the **folktale** speaks of the fate of the individual. Folktales are soul paths in pictures.

We should, however, differentiate between two different types of folktales: (1) rigorously structured parables of soul experiences and paths of inner development and (2) other folktales derived from jesting and teasing and related to the fable.

Afanasyev: "Like all folk creations, these folktales breathe poetic purity and truthfulness. With childlike naivety and simplicity they speak with honest sincerity and tell their stories without hidden irony or false sentimentality. This is true of the folktales of the oldest origin. In some of the later ones, the folktale is adapted to new requirements related to a new way of life and becomes an obedient tool of popular humor and satire and loses the original simplicity of the heart."

These folktales of "the oldest origin" clearly show that they have not sprung from naive pictures alone. Without gaps they display picture after picture. Inner soul-paths are described with such precision, and changes and developments emerge from such a comprehensive knowledge of the human being, that one recognizes with reverence the hand of the initiate. And so it can be said that these folktales originated with those who knew, who had complete command of the inner vision, and who, from comprehensive knowledge, grasped the special faculties and tasks of the Russian people. In their folktales they showed the ways that this folk soul, and with it every single soul within that folk, has to go, so that it can make its contribution to the great developing being of "humanity."

Afanasyev's Russian folktales have the advantage, which can not be overestimated, that many of them show the original form of the folktale, where image and word are one and the same. Their peculiar woodcut-like style, which precisely by its simplicity gave the translator no little trouble, shows us the old simile speech in rare purity. Every sentence is a picture. One could speak of a picture canon. Hence the perpetual repetition of the full name, rarely replaced by a personal pronoun; hence the action which progresses in brief, one-clause sentences; hence the absence of relative clauses and of decorative words. Hence the uniformity of exposition, the rhythmic word-for-word repetitions, and the frugal expression.

We are accustomed to a certain folktale style from the warm, comfortable language of the Grimm brothers and are tempted to consider it the only right one for folktales. But the Brothers Grimm were both men of letters and romantics and - as they themselves say – they shaped their stories in their own way and worked long and hard to give them the form they wanted. It was above all Wilhelm who relaxed the old allegory canon and introduced elaborate sentence structures and winding poetic expressions. Jacob, the mythologist, saw in the folktales "documents of a past epic poetry", and this epic poetry was to him the unity of image and word in the most concise language. *The Original Version of the Folktales Based on the Original Manuscript of the Abbey of Ölenberg in Alsace*", edited by Josef Lefftz, and *The Brothers Grimm's Edition of the Children and Household Tales in their*

*Primal Form*" by Friedrich Panzer[3] show us that the style of the German folktales was originally the same as that of those in Russia, where this ancient form was preserved longer than in the West. Indeed, in Russia there are still tellers of folktales who tell from tradition, not from literary sources.

In preparing (the original German) edition of this book, the challenge was to transfer the pictures to the German language with absolute fidelity. For this purpose, it was necessary to work out the inner pictures, as well as to elaborate the described soul paths and their significance. There could be no relaxation of the language to make it more pleasing to modern ear. The unity of word and image was preserved as far as possible. In addition, the right German word had to be found for every picture, so that the inner picture is re-created in the German reader. For that reason, expressions were dispensed with which from the outset gave the tales a Russian character on the cheap. The concept of the inner kingdom, the royal dignity of the human being, is formed more quickly in the German reader by the words *König, Königin, Königssohn* (king, queen, prince) than by *Tsar, Tsarina, Tsarevich*.[4] But in order to do justice to those who also demand the Russian version for typical Russian names, it was left in some folktales. Any reader can use

---

3  *Die Urfassung der Märchen nach der Originalhandschrift der Abtei Ölenberg im Elsaß*, herausgegeben von Josef Lefftz, and *Die Ausgabe der Kinder- und Hausmärchen der Gebrüder Grimm in ihrer Urgestalt* von Friedrich Panzer.

4  In translating into English from the Russian, I found I could not adhere to this practice. It was not a matter of creating a Russian atmosphere by using the Russian terms *tsar, tsarina, tsarevich, tsarevna* for *king, queen, prince* and *princess* but of fitting in with the Russian atmosphere already created by the story itself. I have also kept the Russian word *bogatir* rather than giving a misleading translation as *hero* or *knight*. A bogatir is a strong man who rides forth on a mission or in search of adventure. Heavy, full-body armor and a knightly code of conduct are not part of the bogatir figure. There is a splendid picture, "Three Bogatirs" by Kuznetsov in the Tretayakov Gallery in Moscow. It is on the Internet in Wikipedia. The Baba Yaga also has no corresponding western figure. She is discussed below in the Introduction. – Translator

them or not as he wishes. What is truly Russian in these folktales lies in their content.

In many – but not all – of the Afanasyev stories the central figure is Ivan, the name which corresponds to Ιωαννης in Greek, Johannes in German and John in English. The exploration of these folktales leads to a unique experience: *the spiritual knowledge and the soul paths of the Johannine Christianity are expressed in these folktales.*

To help the reader have this experience, the *Sinndeutung* or *Interpretation of Meaning* – originally published separately and only several years after the translations – is now included in the present book. But it cannot be overemphasized that these sketches are intended as an aid *only to adults*. They do not belong in the hands of a child. To a child one must not interpret folktales, for children still live to some degree in picture consciousness. In it, humanity's early epochs are repeated; truths appear not yet as thoughts but as pictures. The child, unencumbered by the intellect, is able to experience the images of the genuine folktale in their inner truth. But it is very important that the folktale be genuine and not "processed" and not mutilated. One who, for example, complains of "cruelty" in the folktale and modifies the tale to reduce it only shows that he no longer understands the language of pictures. (In ordinary speech we may say that someone is "empty-headed" or "casts his eye" on something – images that are gruesome if taken literally but harmless if accepted as pictures.) If pictures from the folktale are omitted or added arbitrarily, the inner truth suffers. Such folktales ultimately harm the soul of the child, while real truths nourish and build up in real images. Through these Johannine folktales, the child is able to incorporate a treasure of Christian wisdom into his mind in a completely nondogmatic way.

Friedel Lenz

# Towards Understanding Folktales[5]

These hints for the understanding of folktales in general and of those in this book in particular have originated from the wishes of many people to whom the stories have been told. But the hints are only just that; they are in no sense complete expositions. For folktales are truths from the mysteries. They become deeper and deeper the more one ponders them. The most that can be hoped for here is to make their exterior somewhat more accessible.

One who begins to enter the picture world of folktales often feels afloat on water with no firm earth beneath his feet. Coming to them from thinking in the sense world, one is accustomed to have a firm standpoint; but here the standpoint dissolves beneath one's feet, for the pictures are in constant motion. One must pay attention to *every* picture, one must see how one picture works on another; a detail sometimes changes the whole thing. Above all, one must ask oneself: what sets the drama in motion? Who wants what? When and why does he want it? In what state of mind is he? In what condition? One must experience the sequence of pictures as a *Process*. If one interprets a single picture, one gets no further. The sequence of events is decisive. Language itself is a great help. It is full of pictures; we just need to learn to notice them.

One who on a first reading supposes the same motif is repeated over and over in different stories will, on more careful reading, notice what many-sided ways and events are described, and that he is precisely thereby forced to become more active and attentive in his inner visualization.

After some general remarks, the interpretive comments on each folktale follow the tale itself. However, what is found after one tale is often applicable to understanding others as well. The tales repay re-reading and pondering. The whole of the

---

5   The translation of the *Sinndeutung* begins here

commentaries may also. In my book on the Grimm stories, *The Picture Language of Folktales,* the interpretation of each tale was complete in itself at the cost of some repetition. The folktales and their interpretation could be read in any order. The same is explicitly ***not*** true of this book. Points made for one tale may be very applicable to one later in the book but are not repeated. Their application is, so to speak, " left to the reader as an exercise."

I repeat what was said in the Foreword: ***Do not interpret a folktale to children!*** But one *tells* the story with greater devotion and responsibility when one begins to sense its wisdom.

## *Secrets of the Soul and Spirit*

If one wants to understand the content of folktales, one must begin from a different understanding of the nature of the human being than is common today. If one begins from a two-way division between body and soul, one will not be able to interpret properly any of them. Rather one must turn to the structure of the human being as found in the works of Aristotle. When the Aristotelian teaching about the human being as composed of body, soul and spirit had been forgotten in the outer world, it was still preserved in the schools and circles in which the folktales originated.

In Aristotle's account,[6] the lowest member of the human being is the physical, mineral body. The second is the threptikon, the vegetative body that awakens this physical body to life and lifts it to the level of the plant. The next member, the aesthetikon, lifts the human to the level of the animal. The human experiences pleasure and pain internally and can open himself to the outer world through both perception and action, just as can the animal. These three members members have, as it were, a root in the physical body and are referred to in the spiritual science of Rudolf Steiner as the physical body, the life or etheric body (also formative force body) and the sensation body.

The soul nature of the human being was also seen by Aristotle to have a threefold structure: *oretikon, kineticon*, and *dianeticon*. These correspond to the sentient soul, the intellectual or mind soul, and the consciousness soul in Steiner's description.

In modern man, these three soul components are not sharply separated; they play constantly into one another. Nevertheless, they

---

6 Aristotle names the θρεπτικον, αἰσθητικον, ὀρεκτικον, κινητικον, and διανοητικον in *De Anima*, Book 2. section 3, just above the beginning of standard reference page 414b. Lenz interprets them as corresponding to the etheric body, soul body, sentient soul, intellectual soul, and consciousness soul in the anthroposophical terms of Rudolf Steiner. See his *Theosophy* or *Esoteric Science*.

came into being in humanity one after another, and in the individual human they are developed one after another.

The child becomes aware of the world with his senses and responds to the awareness directly with its feeling. Pleasure and pain are expressed without constraint; sense impression becomes soul sensation. Action follows pleasure or pain directly without deliberation. At this point in its growth a child is repeating the Age of the Sentient Soul, the Heroic Age, the age of which the Greek myths and epics tell. This childhood age of mankind is repeated by the individual, the age before "the native hue of resolution is sicklied o'er with the pale cast of thought."

As the child grows, the understanding develops and thinking awakens. The soul examines its sensations, chooses between pleasure and pain, at first chooses the pleasant and useful but later more and more chooses the judicious. Sympathy and antipathy become regulated by thought. The child is repeating the Age of the Intellectual Soul, the which, in human history, began in the Graeco-Roman period and continued well into the Middle Ages.

A third component of the soul, deeply rooted in the mankind, has awakened since since the Middle Ages: the Consciousness Soul, the *Dianoetikon*. It no longer suffices for a thinking human being to affirm what his own reason prescribes for him, or what laws and commandments teach him. It also no longer suffices for him to carry all this inwardly. He begins to search for Truth itself, for the eternal laws of existence, and to seek to be in harmony with them. He strives for objective knowledge of the All-That-Is. Although today still only the sense-perceptible world and its laws are grasped, nevertheless this process is underway. The Consciousness Soul seeks the eternally Beautiful, True and Good for their own sake, independent of sympathies and antipathies and independent of subjective thinking. This trinity in the aspirations of the soul correspond to its three capacities: Feeling, Thinking and Willing.

The Man of an earlier time experienced his three-fold soul not so narrowly personally as we do today. He experienced himself as a "microcosmos within the macrocosmos" and so also his soul as participating with the divine powers in the World Soul. The Egyptians spoke of the three-fold Isis. The Germanen saw her weaving destiny in the image of the three Norns. The human soul beings were for them born from these higher beings like a daughter from a mother – a threefold daughter from a threefold mother. We know them as the three daughters in our folktales.

(In antiquity the three mothers were revered in countless sanctuaries. They were the regents of the human soul beings in the spiritual world contained all the archetypes of everything existing or coming into existence. Goethe called this world the Realm of the Mothers.[7])

The farther back we go in the development of mankind the more pronounced was the division of the soul activity into feeling, thinking and willing. The I was still not strong enough to pull the three into a unity. Only in the mystery centers and later also in the school of Pythagoras did such a unity begin to be formed in some students by exercises and schooling. Everything connected with passions and drives had to be cleansed from the soul. One had to live only to strive for eternal truth. The soul then went through a katharsis, a purification. The purified, unified, renewed soul was always characterized as virginal and was called by the Greeks the Virgin Sophia, meaning Virgin Wisdom. The Virgin Sophia is the higher soul, the "Eternal Feminine" as Goethe called it.

In the picture language of all peoples the soul appears in a feminine figure:

– as a little girl when the undeveloped, young, child-like soul is meant

---

[7] In Goethe's *Faust*, the Mothers are first mentioned on line 6215, which is in Part II, Act 1, Scene 5: Finstere Gallerie (Gloomy Gallery).

- as a virgin when she has matured and is able to unite with the spirit and to be awakened and fructified to the life of the spirit
- as a mother when she makes manifest the soul or spiritual seedling
- as a grandmother when she has become old and wise.
- as a stepmother (or witch) if she has turned to the material world and fallen away from unity with the spirit.

All soul forces, all forces turned more inwardly than outwardly are represented by feminine figures.

Together with the mysteries of the soul work the mysteries of the spirit. In the age of the development of the I one could also call them the I-mysteries. For the human spirit, the eternal entelechy in each of us, is on the way to understand itself as an eternal spiritual being, to become an individual[8] in the truest, most profound sense of the word. The eternal spiritual being in each of us appears in the folktales as a masculine figure. Just as a man tends to be outwardly active, so is the spirit always active, always striving. He wants to be something, to become something, to develop, to learn. He is more turned to the other world than is the above all inwardly working soul. All spiritual forces are represented by masculine figures in the folktales.

Here also we often that from an old, unified spiritual consciousness (the old king) there go forth in the course of development the three basic forces – feeling, thinking and willing – and go their own ways. In the folktale they are the three sons of the old king, the three brothers. They represent the three spiritual forces in contrast to the three soul forces represented by the three daughters or sisters. And just as the human soul being is called to

---

8   I have translated the author's word *Personlichkeit* as *individual* rather than *personality* because *personality* inevitably brings to mind its origin in the *persona*, the mask worn by actors in Roman plays. The mask included a small megaphone which the actor "sounded through" – *per sona*. Since a mask is the very opposite of what is intended, I have avoided the use of "personality."

develop to the Eternal Feminine, so is the human spirit called to develop to the Eternal Masculine. It must fill itself with the divine forces of the world spirit just as the soul, the Virgin Sophia must fill herself with the forces of the world soul. Thereby is accomplished the Royal Wedding. The divine-spiritual fructifies the eternal soul, and a new Man – the true Man – comes into being. As Plato says, only the initiate is a true Man.

The Middle Ages knew only the Mystical Wedding, not the Royal Wedding. The Mystical Wedding involved an inner experience of the soul. The soul grasped the spirit in a subjective, personal inner life, much as nuns experience the Christ, who works into their higher being, as a spiritual bridegroom. The Royal Wedding of the folktales is something else. To understand it, we must turn to the experiences and way of initiation of the Rosicrucians.

In the course of the Graeco-Roman period, the mystery centers from which the spiritual guidance of young mankind had come declined. At the same time, the bonds of kinship loosened and the experience of the family group soul faded. The individual awoke as an independent being who must now more and more take in hand his own self direction. But because spiritual vision had largely come to an end – the Twilight of the Gods had begun – the individual lacked the force and wisdom needed for self direction. At this very point in time, as Man turned outward instead of inward and to the lower world rather than to the higher world – at this very point the Christ event as the greatest divine mystery entered Earth evolution. The true, full Man as bearer of the divine Christ Spirit walked the earth. Through His healing deed every human being was given the possibility to become a "True Man."

Within the transient, temporal I-consciousness which is formed in the course of life another, higher I can be born, and this higher I can become the master and shaper of the lower I. This higher I can see into the spiritual world just as the physical eye sees into the physical world. Christians who set their sights on the development of this higher I and brining it into connection with the Christ may be called Johannine Christians, Christians inspired by John, the beloved disciple. They give special attention to *how* this inner awakening, this initiation can be brought about. Especially in the John Gospel they see the forces which lead to this awakening. John, the beloved disciple who was next to the Master in knowledge and understanding – for that is what the tern means – was also the only one who stood with Him during the death on the cross and the one who above all bore the forces of awakening. The Johannine Christians saw his being as a living spiritual impulse working forward in history. Indeed, his eternal being was present before them. He was for them the one of whom it was said: this disciple dies not. Through their work they sought to prepare a future age of mankind in which the steadily unfolding wisdom of Christianity would awaken the highest power for attaining knowledge: Love.

That is why the hero of many of these Russian folktales is Ivan, for Ivan in Russian is Ιωαννες in Greek, Johannes in German and John in English.

Whoever one now enters into the Sophia of Christianity is called upon to come to know progressively both the wisdom of the lower world, the sense world, and the wisdom of the higher world. That means to grasp in thought the whole of creation. But where one thinks thoughts that grasp the world as a spiritual whole, there the thinker is transformed and becomes an initiate through the Sophia of Christianity, a "True Man." Through the marriage of the Johannine I with the soul that has become the Virgin Sophia are body and soul transformed and the whole Man achieved. This is the Rosicrucian "chemical wedding".

In the course of this "wedding" from the three bodily members of the human being and the three soul members there unfold the three purely spiritual members. In all, there are nine.

From feeling, thinking, and willing is the human being is progressively transformed into a ninefold being. In many of the folktales in this volume, Ivan is told to seek "beyond the three times nine lands."

If the seeker grasps himself as the eternal I in the totality of his nine members, then he surpasses the nine and comes to ten – in the three times ten land.[9]

When the hierarchies of exalted spiritual beings were still a reality to mankind, the lowest hierarchy, the angels, were counted as the ninth hierarchy, that is, the numbering began from the top. To come into the tenth realm therefore also meant to be worthy to takes one's place as an eternal being just below the angelic rank, to have reached the goal desired by God for Man. One could also say, to come into the thrice tenth realm means to find the spiritual world during earthly life. (The Pythagoreans considered ten the all-encompassing, all-bounding mother.)

In the Russian folktales, with deep humility the teller often concludes his story with words like: "And I was at this wedding – took mead and wine, but it flowed over my beard and nothing came into my mouth." That means, "I was invited to the royal wedding. I was offered the strong wine of ego-hood, but I have not grasped the secret itself and been able to realize it in myself."

---

9   If you still don't understand where the *three times* nine comes from, be assured that I don't either. Maybe it is just to stress the nine.

*Names in the Folktales*

In the school of Dionysius the Areopagite[10] the sentient soul was called Mary Magdalene, the intellectual soul, Mary. In the Russian folktales the sentient soul is called Magdalena or Helen. The intellectual soul is Maria, and the consciousness soul is Helen (Elena) the Beautiful (Wunderschöne).

The spiritual force corresponds to the feeling and the sentient soul is called Basilius (king). The name is almost the epitome of Russian monasticism – church father Basilius, order originator Basilius, not to mention St. Basil's on Red Square – and the name of the leader of the age of the sentient soul. Demetri or Peter designates the spiritual forces that correspond to the intellectual soul and appear here as the regent of the next age, the intellectual soul. The spiritual force corresponding to the age of the consciousness soul bears the name Ivan, Ιωαννες, John.

# On Secrets of the Soul[11]

**The Three Realms**

In these folktales the different soul forces are connected with three different realms: the copper, the silver and the gold. In the medieval alchemical tradition stemming from the Rosicrucians,

---

10 Dionysius the Areopagite (Denis of Mars Hill) in mentioned in Acts 17:34. Writings bearing his name appeared in the late 5$^{th}$ and early 6$^{th}$ centuries. Because internal evidence shows that actual date of writing these documents was about then, the author is called the Pseudo-Dionysius. Rudolf Steiner, however, points out that the teachings were written down only when the oral tradition was in danger of dying out. It would have been presumptuous of the writer to sign his own name to what he had learned from a tradition reaching back to Dionysius the Areopagite. Ironically, his modesty has led to his being considered an impostor.

11 It is a good idea to read the first two of the following sections – the three kingdoms and the Baba Yaga – before starting the tales and their interpretation. The later sections can wait. The author will apply what is in them to the interpretation of the individual tales as appropriate.

copper characterized the condition of piety. In this tradition, copper is related to the planet Venus. It is a very beautiful metal, similar to gold in its warm radiance. And indeed, the pious feeling of the sentient soul wisdom is similar to the gold of true wisdom. Silver, characterizing the second realm, is related to the moon. Just as the silver moon does not have its light from itself but reflects the light of the sun, just so the force of the intellect shines not from itself. The light of the intellect is but a reflection of true wisdom.

It is the consciousness soul that penetrates into the laws of the universe themselves and selflessly seeks the pure gold of wisdom that characterizes the third realm. Gold is like the sun; it radiates, warms, gleams and awakens life.

**The Baba Yaga and the Three Yaga Sisters**

The Baba Yaga is often erroneously confused with a witch. The witch is the imagination for a magical evil soul consciousness. The Baba Yaga is no witch. To be sure, under certain circumstances one can loose one's head by her, but that only means that one does not know how to behave when meeting her. She lives in the forest; her hut stands on chicken feet. Why chicken feet? Observe a hen and feel the warm, living body which has within itself the egg and its life coming into being. Then observe how she stands on seemingly dead, hardened, horny three-toed feet. And now look at the shelter of this old soul force: though sheltering secret life it no longer stands alive in earthly existence. "The hut turned like the wind." This realm is no long accessible to just anyone; it spins in a cosmic whirlpool and opens only to one who knows how to master such forces. "Turn round with your door to me and your back to the forest; put yourself like your mother put you," meaning "be accessible for me, as this realm once was open when when the oldest soul, the primal mother, was active." Today one must find the entrance through Will, cleanse oneself (the bath), nourish oneself, and pass the "night." She herself, the mysterious old woman, often has a "bone leg". That means she no longer stands in the midst of life, has hardened and turned to bone. "Her lips are in bed." That means she is silent; her speech sleeps. Or "she lies on the beam above the door": there where one comes from the outside into the inside. On the threshold rests speech and must be awakened again. "Her nose reaches up to the roof." Everywhere that a long nose is mentioned –- also in the case of trolls in the Norse tales – there is a reference to a time when Man lived in a very different way in the breath. For this earlier Man, air was the spirit itself. (In ancient Greek, pneuma = air = spirit.) the long nose also means to live completely in the weather, in the atmosphere. The older the Baba Yaga is, the longer her nose, for in the most ancient times everything spiritual was given by nature. Sometimes her nose is stuck to the roof, for formerly one received the spirit effortlessly from above, something now no longer possible. We also encounter "She has her feet on the ceiling and spins." In German we have an expression for someone who is always sunken into his own thoughts, who never turns loose of a thought. We say he "spins." There is no activity that better represents thinking than spinning. We also say, "I've lost the thread," The picture of the Baba Yaga with her feet against the ceiling and spinning says that she stands in a higher world and thinks. In the cathedral of Chartres in France there is on a column capital a figure of a grown man lying on his back with his feet in the air. His feet appear to flat against some invisible surface. Could a sculptor show more clearly standing in the cosmos, in a higher world? Also for the Baba Yaga, it is an image of Man in the stage before he had fully reached the earth, when still at the stage of the infant that lies on its back, lifts its feet into the air and still largely belongs to another world.

The Baba Yaga represents a mighty soul power, but one of the past. She is the picture of the soul naturally bound to the spiritual world that is still clairvoyant and at home in the cosmos. In many of the folktales there is not one but three Baba Yagas, sisters. This three-fold Baba Yaga is the oldest aspect of the sentient soul, intellectual soul and consciousness soul. In the age of I-development, Man must again open this realm of old soul forces, but now out of free will. Therefore the oft-repeated question from the Baba Yaga: "Do you come of your own free will or from compulsion?" To one who comes not seeking to renew old atavistic clairvoyant wisdom but would eat of the bread of knowledge, to such a one she shows the way or gives a ball with words like "Follow it where it rolls; it will lead you to my elder sister." The ball is the same as the thread that Ariadne gave to Theseus so that he could find his way out of the labyrinth. It is a thread of inner logic that can lead farther, or again, it is a destiny that rolls ever onward. To advance from one soul realm to the next requires us to de-velop.[12] The Baba-Yaga that as a motherly archetype stands behind the consciousness soul is in some sense the oldest because it has taken the consciousness soul the longest to develop.

## *Nurses and nannies*

In the outer world – from which the picture in the folktale is tale is taken – is the Russian folk like no other *the* folk of nurses and nannies – мамки и няньки. In large households or courts a nurse may remain for a lifetime. It was also to the nurses and the maids that the upbringing of the children was entrusted. It was they who brought the children spiritual nourishment in the form of folktales and heroic legends. Pushkin erected a monument to his nursemaid which was also really a monument to the countless women who with forces of body and soul nourished and formed each young generation. In the inner world, the nurses are the picture of those soul forces that nourish the seedling of the soul or spirit; the nannies are a picture of those forces that protect and care for them.

---

12  The original meaning of both the German word *entwickeln* and its English translation *develop* is to unwind, to unfold. Do we not speak of destiny unfolding? It does so as we follow the Baba Yaga's ball.

## *The Animals*

MAN is the crown of creation and has in his evolution surpassed the animal world but he still bears it within himself. It works in him as instincts. Good, natural, wise instincts serve Man, they belong to human evolution and can help to find the spiritual goal. They appear in the folktale as good animals. But when lower instincts get the upper hand, then other instincts appear, dangerous and evil. They become destructive driving forces that destroy both ourselves and others. We can therefore dream that animals pursue us. In reality it is some driving forces that arise within us and work outwardly, so that we experience them as external to us. They harm our own being, so we see them in the dream as pursuing us.

Each animal embodies in a unique and one-sided way a very particular nature, a particular instinct. One must recognize this if one wants to understand picture. Objective observation of nature helps develop pictorial thinking. Our speech is also full of pictorial expressions: the capricious goat, the sly fox, the wise owl, the stubborn donkey. If an instinctive force serves a human for some time, it may momentarily a spiritual force imparting knowledge. In this case, the tale says, "Then spoke the animal with human voice …." If an instinct is brought up out of the dull subconscious of the animal-like soul into the clear light of knowledge, then it is no longer an instinct but a force for understanding. And because Man is capable of knowing spiritually, the folktale says the animal form was taken off and th human form put on.

### **The Horse**

The taming of the horse is one of the most important cultural achievements of mankind. Elephants, camels and asses are beasts of burden and require a driver[13]. That man became a rider was an

---

13  One may feel that the author undervalues somewhat the elephant, camel and ass for riding, but high-spirited they are not. The union of horse and rider that one sees in races and hunts or circus performance is scarcely

important step forward. Early Man did not know this experience, for it presumes the presence of an I-conscious individuality. Therefore the horse with its higher intelligence, tamable and steerable, becomes the symbol for that force, the intelligence, the understanding that awakens in Man at about the same time and that also can be directed: the instinctive understanding. This force works in all areas. As radiant wisdom it appears in the sun horses of Apollo. But it is also the patient draft horse that helps Man work the earth.

In visions and folktales, the type and the color of the horse indicate the type of understanding it represents. In the Apocalypse of John (the book of Revelations), four ages of mankind are represented in the form of horses and riders. The King crowned with the crown of wisdom sits on the white horse. Here the understanding serves as the innocent, pure force completely in the service of the highest in Man. The second horse is red and the rider has a sword in his hand. Here the understanding is in the service of the egotistical blood nature. In the age of the black horse the understanding is entirely in the service of dark, material world that is understood in terms of mass, number and weight – so the rider carries a scale. But where the understanding serves only the forces that lie, deceive, lame and destroy, there Death rides the pale green[14] horse.

Sivka Burka, the great gray horse is the image for that understanding which grasps two worlds, the over world, light and white and the under world, dark and material. It is therefore the understanding directed at both the supersensible and the sense worlds. The gray horse is the horse of the Rosicrucians. And

---

imaginable with the other animals.
14 The word generally translated as *pale* is χλωρος (chloros), a pale green. To the modern ear, the word calls to mind chlorine, so called because of its pale green color with a slight yellowish tint. It is both highly useful, necessary for life, and in elemental form deadly poisonous.

indeed, in the word *Burka* there is a hint of the color red. Burka is the color of the reddish brown cossack coat.[15]

*Stallion and Mare:* There is an intelligence that is more masculine, intellectually inclined, and another that is more feminine, intuitive and fantasy inclined.

### The Dragon

Dragons are often bad but not always. In tale 6, *The Maiden Tsar (A 233)* the dragon is one of the three beasts freed from the tower by the tsarevich, and he serves the tsarevich well and rules well in his own realm. In tale 3, the dragon helps find the way in the soul world. In tale 2, the thirsty dragon-snake is given something to drink and then opens the way. On the other hand, in other tales the dragon is the great persecuting power; the hero must cut off his many heads and rescue the maiden. The image changes like the inner process. Behind the dragon hides that spiritual power that in earliest times took hold of mankind and called his not yet independent nature to self awareness – a Luciferic spiritual power. Man should become an independent being (*Eigenwesen*) – an I – and so long as he remained in childlike innocence this power worked as an impulse to awakening the I-consciousness. Therefore the dragon was respected as a divine being in early times. He abounds in early Christian churches; in East Asia he still holds a place of honor.

But if selfhood becomes egoism, then the fire of spiritual inspiration becomes the fire of desire and takes hold of the lower senses. Healthy self respect becomes egoism, pride and vanity.

---

15 Here the author adds a strange parenthetical comment. "In 'Ciwa Burka, the all-knowing Black Horse', Bd. II, Nr. 25, during the first night light colored horse is won; during the second, the fox [colored], and during the third, the black." I at first thought that this might be a reference to an Afanasyev story other than our Number 8 = A 182. Siva Burka appears also in the rather similar story A 564, but it does match this comment, nor have I found any story matching it.

Lucifer becomes the dragon of the lower sense nature. The dragon captures the maiden; the lower sense nature rules the soul and drives it into an isolation without love. He forces her to serve him; the soul confronts this lower power and cannot free herself. The dragon threatens to swallow her; the lower egotistical sense nature overcomes the higher.

From age to age, the power of the dragon grows: from the three-headed dragon comes the six-headed; from the six-headed comes the nine-headed, and from him the twelve-headed, when he rules the whole Man in all his members and potentials. The stronger the I development, the stronger the dragon. Therefore, in the Occident, where this development is most advanced, the dragon slayer appears even in antiquity. Apollo kills the python snake; Siegfried, the dragon. In the center of the coat of arms of the Russian Empire was a picture of St. George slaying the dragon. In the Age of the Consciousness Soul, Ivan is such a dragon slayer.

*Coat of Arms of the Russian Empire*

## *Landscapes in the Folktales*

Landscapes in the folktales are inner landscapes. Recognizing them is not hard if one begins from language.

*The Land:* We say, "one must stand firm on the earth", one should have "one's feet on the ground" and have a "firm standpoint." In *material sense knowledge* we stand on the firm ground of facts. In the folktale, to walk means to make progress in mastering this material sense world. The tale often says, "he walked and walked." To ride (horseback) over the land means to use one's intellect to advance steadily.

*The Sea:* One can "sink" or "go under". It is a world of uncertainty where one looses the ground from under one's feet. It symbolizes a soul consciousness which goes beyond the limits of the sense world. Like the ebb and flow of the tides or of waves, so our soul life alternates between attachment to the material world and to the spiritual world.

*The River:* streaming, flowing forces in the soul world.

*The Meadow:* the realm of sprouting etheric life forces in us. They include orchards (called "tree meadows" in German). In former times there were carefully cared-for lawns around the tsar's castle. To walk on them uninvited or to pitch a tent on them was an open challenge. In the folktales they are specially guarded areas of sprouting life forces in the vicinity of the inner ruling power.

*The Forest:* Its green shades awaken an anticipation, a suspicion, and can send a shivers down the spine. It is a picture for an inner transition, where one feels surrounded by secrets, where one can easily go astray but can also find the right path. When one is in a situation where there seems to be no right way out, one may dream of being lost in a forest. Children often experience their own inner growth forces, their vegetative inner life as a recurring forest dream. In this area ways of development are sought. A long forgotten sense of a primeval certainty can arise in us. The ancestor approaches us, or the all-knowing Old One: soul and spiritual forces which we had not known before. As the hunter hunts in the outer forest, so the spiritual seeker seeks in the inner. He experiences and hunts out.[16] He kills the wild desires and recognizes the instincts that can serve him.

*The Tree:* a picture of growth and life forces in us. We grow like a tree: our nervous system and our circulatory system divides and branches like a tree. So also etheric, life-giving forces arise within us like sap in the tree.

*The Garden:* A region of many-fold etheric growth forces where germinating life can be planted and cared for and grow, where inner fruit ripens. The opposite of the garden is:

*The Desert, Wasteland, Steppe:* expressions like "to live in an inner wasteland" mean to be uncreative, lonesome, and inwardly poor.

*The Swamp:* where one begins to loose the ground under one's feet, where one becomes unsure of one's own senses. There is also the expression "to be swamped" or "to mire down".

*The Mountain:* the inner heights. We speak of being "in high spirits", or of "the highpoint of my day" or of "getting an overview" or of "breathing the rarefied atmosphere."

*The Open Field* plays a significant role in the Ivan folktales. It means the sphere of freedom. In the age of development of the consciousness soul we must strive for truth out of inner freedom. *How* this sphere of freedom is perceived, as good or ill, is shown by action in the folktale. In the open field can begin either development or envelopment. Often the key to the whole drama of the folktale lies in this decisive event. It is very revealing to follow this image in its mobility through the folktale.

*The Wide World* is related to the Open Field but is not yet the sphere of freedom itself.

---

16   The pithy German is: *Er erlebt und erjagt.*

*Village and City:* These are pictures of social cooperation. The city, the largest human settlement, means in the picture speech the largest social community.

*The Whitestone Palace:* Stone is the picture of material hardening; whitestone[17] means enlightenment that penetrates into the physical. In Russian icons, whitestone houses can sometimes be seen behind the holy figures.

## Other Features

### Bones

The periosteum[18] has the ability to replace bone substance. New blood cells are created in the bone marrow, so that one may say that the whole action of the blood begins in the bones. Therefore the bones with their living marrow a picture for renewing and awakening forces. "You Russian bone, whence come you here?" means "You Russian awakener, whence come you here?" In some tales, Ivan is killed and his bones strewn in the open field until he is re-awakened: the totality of the Johannine impulse is cut to pieces before its final action. The brothers take its content for themselves. But even in the pieces live awakening forces. They work everywhere until he arises again from the dead and can work again. In A 158 (not included here) we find "Beyond the thrice nine lands, in the thrice tenth kingdom, there sits in a tower Vasilisa Kirbityevna and out of one little bone the marrow flows into another little bone." With her Ivan overcomes the boneman.

---

17  The white limestone churches that survive from before the Mongolian invasion in Vladimir, Suzdal and a few other places uplift the soul in a way that cannot be forgotten.

18  The periosteum is a thin membrane covering many bones. It both protects and nourishes the bone.

The boneman is, however, a different picture. He is the skeleton that has fallen out of the living organism. (See tales 5 and 23.) The boneman is the picture of death.

## *Numbers*

Numbers must be interpreted according to their inner quality, not quantitatively. The subject is too vast to be entered into here. The book *Die Geistigen Grundlagen der Zahlen* by Ernst Bindel is a good introduction.

# 1. Dawn, Evening and Midnight (A 140)

Translation by Irina Zheleznova

In a certain realm there once lived a king who had three daughters so beautiful as cannot be described. The king treasured them as the apple of his eye and had underground chambers built where they were kept like birds in a cage that the wild winds might not blow on them or the bright sun burn them with its rays. One day the three princesses read in a book about the wonders of the great wide world, and when the king came to pay them a visit, they began pleading with him with tears in their eyes to let them out of their chambers. "Please, Father, you who are our king and ruler, let us out for a walk in the green garden that we may see the light of day!" they said. The king tried to talk them out of it, but they would not listen to him, and the more often he entreated them to think better of it the more they badgered him and the louder they begged him to do as they wished. It could not be helped, and the king gave in.

The beautiful princesses came out for a walk in the garden, they saw the bright sun and the trees and flowers and took great joy in being free and out in the fresh air. They ran about and played, marveling at every blade of grass and every flower, when all of a sudden the wild wind caught them up and carried them off none knew where. Their nurses and maids were greatly alarmed and ran to tell the king about it, and the king at once sent his many faithful servants to all parts of the realm, promising that he who found some sign of them would be richly rewarded. But though the servants searched far and near, they came back with nothing to show for it. The king then called together the highest of his courtiers and asked them if there was not one among them who would undertake to try to find his daughters. And he said that he who found them would get whichever one he chose of the three in marriage and a dowry that would make him rich for the rest of his life. He addressed the courtiers once, and they were silent; he addressed them a second time, and they said nothing; he addressed them for a third time, and they uttered not a word! The king burst into tears. "It seems I have no friends or defenders to help me in my trouble," he said. And he had it heralded throughout the realm that he was waiting for someone from among the ordinary folk to come forward and offer to find his daughters.

Now, at that selfsame time, in a certain village there lived a poor widow who had three sons, strong and fearless lads all three. They had been born on one day: the eldest son in the evening, the middle son at midnight, and the youngest son at dawn, and because of that were named Evening, Midnight and Dawn.

Hearing of the call put out by the king, they asked their mother's blessing, made ready and rode off for the king's own city. They came to the palace, bowed low before the king and said: "May you prosper for many years to come, Sire! We have not come here to feast but to serve you. Allow us to go to seek the princesses." "May good luck attend you, brave youths! What are your names?" "We are brothers, and our names are Evening, Midnight and Dawn." "Is there anything I can do for you before you go?" "We want nothing for ourselves, Sire, but do not leave our mother in her old age; help her if she should be in want." The king did as they asked. He had their mother brought to the palace to live there for as long as she desired, and he gave orders that she should share of his board and be given clothes to wear from his own coffers.

The three brothers set out on their way, they rode for a month, and another, and a third, and they came to a great and empty plain. Beyond it stretched a dense forest, and they were halfway through it when there before them they saw a little hut. They knocked at the window, but there was no reply; they came inside, and there was no one there. "Well, brothers, let us stay here awhile and rest from our journey," they said. They took off their clothes, said their prayers and went to bed, and on the following morning Dawn said to his elder brother Evening: "Midnight and I will go off to hunt, and you must stay home and prepare our dinner for us." To this Evening agreed, and there being a shed full of sheep near the hut, he slaughtered the best one he could find among them and roasted it. Then, everything being ready, he lay down on a bench for a sleep. All of a sudden there came a great thumping and banging, the door opened, and a bearded old man the size of a thumb stepped into the hut looking glum as glum. "How dared you play the master in my house, how dared you slaughter my sheep!" he cried. "First grow a wee bit so a man can tell you from a bug!" Evening said. "You don't want me to drown you in a spoonful of soup, do you!" The little old man became angrier still. "I'm small but bold and can knock you out cold!" he cried. And grabbing a crust of bread, he began hitting Evening over the head with it and gave him such a walloping that he was all but dead by the time he got through with him. Then he thrust him under the bench, ate up the roasted sheep and went away. And as for Evening, he came to after a while, tied a rag round his head and lay there moaning. The two brothers came back, and, seeing him in so sorry a state, asked what had happened. "Well, you see, brothers, I lit the oven and got such a terrible headache from the heat that I lay around all day in a half-swoon and could not cook anything."

On the following day Dawn and Evening went off to hunt, and they left Midnight at home to prepare the dinner.

Midnight lit the oven, slaughtered the fattest sheep he could find in the shed and, having roasted it, lay down on the bench for a sleep.

All of a sudden there was a great thumping and banging, and a little old man the size of a thumb came into the hut looking glum as glum. He fell on Midnight, gave him such a walloping that he was all but dead by the time he was through with him, and, having eaten the roasted sheep, went away. And Midnight tied a rag round his head and lay moaning under the bench. Dawn and Evening came back, and Dawn asked him what had happened to him. "I lit the oven and got such a headache from the fumes that I had to lie around all day and could not cook anything," Midnight said.

On the third day the two elder brothers went off to hunt, and Dawn stayed home. He slaughtered the best sheep he could find in the shed, skinned and roasted it, and, this done, lay down on the bench for a sleep.

All of a sudden there was a great thumping and banging, and a little old man the size of a thumb came into the yard looking glum as glum can be. He had a whole stack of hay on his head and a large tub of water in his hands, and having set the tub of water down on the ground and strewn the hay over the yard, began counting the sheep. Seeing that one sheep was missing, he flew into a temper, ran into the hut, threw himself at Dawn and gave him a sharp knock on the head. But Dawn jumped up, clutched the little old man by the beard and began dragging him over the floor, saying as he did so, "Look before you leap if it's whole you would keep!"

"Have mercy on me, brave youth!" cried the little old man. "Spare my life and let me go!" But Dawn dragged him out into the yard and up to a pillar of oak, and, using a wedge of iron, stuck his beard into a split in the wood. Then he came back into the hut and sat there waiting for his brothers. The brothers were soon back and they marvelled to see him unharmed. "Come out into the yard with me, brothers, and you'll see your 'headache'," said Dawn with a laugh. They came out into the yard, but the little old man was gone, and all they saw was a part of his beard sticking out from the split and a trail of blood on the ground.

The trail led the brothers to a deep pit, and Dawn went to the forest, stripped some bark off a tree, made a rope out of it and told Evening and Midnight to let him down into the pit on it. This they did, and, finding that he was in the netherworld, Dawn untied himself and set off along a road that stretched before him and led he knew not where. He walked and he walked, and there before him was a palace of copper. He stepped inside, and the youngest of the princesses, a maid as lovely as a flower, came toward him. "Is it of your own free will or at another's bidding that you have come here, brave youth?" she asked. "It was your father who sent me to seek you and your sisters," Dawn told her. The princess at once seated him at a table, dined and wined him and then gave him a phial of strong water. "Here, drink this water, and it will make you very, very strong," said she. Dawn drank the water and at once felt himself to be filled with a great strength. "Now I can get the better of anyone!" said he to himself.

All of a sudden a wild wind began to blow, and the princess was frightened. "The three-headed dragon is coming!" she cried, and she took Dawn by the hand and hid him in her chamber. The dragon now came flying up, and he struck the ground and turned into a man. "I smell Russian flesh!" he cried. "Is anyone here?" "How could there be!" the princess said. "You have been flying over Russ and must have brought the smell of Russian flesh with you." The dragon asked her to give him food and drink, and she brought in a plate of food and a goblet of wine, and, first having added a sleeping powder to the wine, offered it to him. The dragon ate and drank, and, feeling very sleepy, placed his head on the princess's lap and fell fast asleep. The princess at once called Dawn, who came out of his hiding-place and smote off all of the dragon's three heads with one stroke of his sword. He then made up a fire, burnt the dragon's body and strewed the ashes over the plain.

"And now I must bid you goodbye, Princess," said Dawn, "for I am off to seek your sisters. But I will come back for you as soon as I find them."

He set off on his way, he walked and he walked, and there before him rose a silver palace in which the middle sister was kept captive by a six-headed dragon. Dawn killed the dragon, freed the princess and went on. Whether a short or a long time passed nobody knows, but he came at last to a palace of gold where the eldest princess was kept captive by a twelve-headed dragon. He killed the dragon, and the princess was overjoyed and prepared to set out for home. She came out into the courtyard and waved a red kerchief, and the kingdom of gold turned into a golden egg. This she put in her pocket and went with Dawn to where he had left her sisters. Then after the middle princess had turned her kingdom into a silver egg and the younger sister had turned hers into a copper egg, the four of them made for the bottom of the pit. Evening and Midnight dragged Dawn and the three princesses out of the pit, and they all went back together to their own realm.

The princesses sent the eggs rolling over the plain, and at once the three kingdoms, one of copper, one of silver and one of gold, appeared before them. They came to the palace, and so happy was the king as cannot be told! He married his youngest daughter to Dawn, his middle daughter to Evening, and his eldest daughter to Midnight, and he made Dawn his heir.

## Interpretation

Sentient soul, intellectual soul, and consciousness soul as the daughters of a kingly spiritual consciousness live in the still unconscious depths of the soul. When they come out into open, wide-awake consciousness that is seeking freedom and self-enlightenment they fall prey to a wild, unbridled spirituality. (Note: *pneuma* in Greek means both air and spirit.) Three mighty sons grow up – three active spiritual forces. Two, by their names – Evening and Night – relate to long-ago times when Man was night creature. Time was then reckoned by moon periods and nights. A trace remains in the use of months (moon periods) and in the English expressions fortnight (14 nights) and the now rare sennight (7 nights). Man received the wisdom needed for life in inspirations during sleep. The third son is Dawn. Dawn precedes the sunrise.

The name points to age when day-consciousness, I consciousness begins – roughly the middle of the Roman period.

Before any one of the three heroes can free the princesses, they must deal with those forces which have previously led and protected mankind. As the ancient clairvoyant wisdom came to an end, there arose everywhere the great shepherds of the people, who through law and commandment led the peoples who had lost their inner guidance. Examples are Confucius and Moses. Their time is now past. Each human being must now take in charge his or her own direction through the force of the spirit-bound I. But many still want the shepherd. Only the Johannine spiritual force that hides behind the name Dawn is able to deal with this shrunken but in old age still everywhere active shepherd-like force. The hardened remains of a spiritual knowledge that was formerly the bread of life dazed the other brothers, but Dawn grabs the old one by the beard. – The beard, which grows downward and is also a sign of age, points to a relation with the earthly. Earth dwarfs appear in the imagination with long beards. As a sign of his earthly power, the Egyptian pharaoh would fasten on beard. In German we say "So ein Bart ..." (Such a beard ...) when we mean that something is out-dated. (There is a variant of the tale in which Dawn beats the Old Man on the ground until the beard comes off and says, "Not from the fumes of the oven but from this beard have you become sick.")

When old, decadent forces yield place, blood flows, but the trail is found. Out of free will, not by law or compulsion must I-conscious spirituality come to the rescue of the soul life. Then is the lower nature that had taken possession of the soul overcome. The dragon falls asleep and is destroyed. The soul that has been free becomes active – waves the red kerchief – and is able to transform her whole soul realm into a life force germ – an egg. The soul forces then rise into the consciousness and in the sphere of freedom now won unroll the copper realm of the sentient soul, the silver realm of the intellectual soul, and the gold realm of the consciousness soul.

# 2. The Three Kingdoms – Copper, Silver and Gold (A 129)[19]

Translation by Irina Zheleznova

In a certain kingdom, in a certain realm there lived a tsar by the name of Bel-Belyanin who had a wife named Nastasya the Golden Plait and three sons, Peter Tsarevich, Vasily Tsarevich and Ivan Tsarevich. One day the queen and her women and maids went for a walk in the garden. All of a sudden a great whirlwind arose and it caught up the queen, which God forbid should happen to anyone, and carried her off none knew where.

The king was very sad and woebegone and did not know what to do, but when his sons had grown to manhood he said to them: "My dear sons, my beloved sons, will not one of you go to seek your mother?" The two elder sons did not delay but set off at once, and the third and youngest son began pleading with his father to let him go too. "No, my son, you mustn't leave me, an old man, all alone," said the king. "Please let me go, Father! I do so want to travel over the world and find my mother." The king reasoned with him, but, seeing that he could not stop him from going, said: "Oh, all right then, I suppose it can't be helped. Go and God be with you!"

Ivan Tsarevich saddled his trusty steed and set forth from home. Whether he was long on the way or not nobody knows, for a tale is quick in the telling and a deed is slow in the doing, but by and by he came to a forest where stood a most beautiful palace. Ivan Tsarevich rode into the yard, and a large yard it was, and, seeing an old man coming toward him, said: "Good morrow, old

---

[19] Afanasyev placed three different tales under the title *Три царства — медное, серебряное и золотое*. In the 1984 edition by *Наука* they are distinguished by number. Friedel Lenz discusses them in the order 129, 128, and 130.

man, and many long years of life to you!" "Welcome, welcome, my brave lad! And who may you be?" "I am Ivan Tsarevich, son of King Bel-Belianin and Queen Nastasya the Golden Plait." "Then you are my own nephew! Whither are you bound?" "I am seeking my mother. Do you know where she is to be found, Uncle?" "No, my lad, I don't. But I'll do what I can for you. Here is a little ball. Throw it down before you, and it will start rolling and bring you to a tall, steep mountain with a cave in it. Go into the cave, take the iron claws that you will see there, fit them on to your hands and feet and climb the mountain. You may well find your mother on its top."

Well and good. Ivan Tsarevich bade his uncle farewell and threw the ball before him. On the ball rolled, and he rode after it. Whether a short or a long time passed nobody knows, but by and by he came to a field and whom should he see there but his brothers Prince Pyotr and Prince Vasily surrounded by a host of fighting men. The brothers rode forth to meet him. "Where are you going, Ivan Tsarevich?" they asked. "I got bored staying at home and thought I would go to seek our mother. Send your men home and come with me." The brothers did as he said. They sent the men home and joined him, and the three of them followed the ball together.

By and by they saw the mountain, and so tall and steep was it that it touched the sky with its peak! The ball rolled up straight to a cave, and Ivan Tsarevich got off his horse and said to his brothers: "Stay here and look after my horse, brothers, and I will climb the mountain and try to find our mother. Wait for me for three months, and if I am not back by then, you will know that it's no use waiting any longer." "A man can break his neck climbing a mountain like that!" thought the brothers, but they said to him: "Very well, then, go with God and we will wait for you here."

Ivan Tsarevich came up to the cave, gave its door of iron a mighty push and sent it flying open. He came inside, and the iron claws jumped up and fixed themselves to his hands and feet. But it took all of his strength to climb the mountain, and a whole month passed before he at last reached its top. "God be thanked, I'm here at last!" said he. He rested awhile and then went on. He walked and he walked, and, standing before him, saw a palace of copper. Chained to the gate with copper chains were the most fearful of dragons, while close by was a well with a copper dipper dangling at the end of a copper chain. Ivan Tsarevich scooped up some water and gave the dragons a drink, and, thus having quietened them, passed on into the palace where he was met by the Princess of the Copper Kingdom.

"Who are you, brave youth?" she asked. "I am Ivan Tsarevich." "Is it of your own free will that you have come here, Ivan Tsarevich, or at another's bidding?" "Of my own free will. I am seeking my mother, Nastasya the Golden Plait, who was carried off by Whirlwind. Do you happen to know where she is?" "No, I don't. But my middle sister the Princess of the Silver Kingdom, lives nearby, and she may know." And she brought out a copper ball and a copper ring and gave them to him. "This ball," said she, "will lead you to my middle sister, and in this ring is the whole of my Copper Kingdom. When you have vanquished Whirlwind, who keeps me captive here and comes to see me every three months, do not forget me, unhappy soul that I am, but deliver me from captivity and take me with you to where I can be free." "Very well, I'll do that," said Ivan Tsarevich. He cast the copper ball down on the ground, started it rolling and went after it.

He came to the Silver Kingdom and saw before him a palace that was made of silver and was even more beautiful than the copper one. Chained with silver chains to the gate were fearful dragons, and close
by was a well with a silver dipper. Ivan Tsarevich scooped up some water and gave it to the dragons to drink, and they lay down on the ground and let him pass on into the palace where he was met by the Princess of the Silver Kingdom. "It will be three years soon

that I have been kept here by Whirlwind, and I have not seen a Russian face or heard Russian speech in all that time, and now a Russian spirit appears before my eyes," said she. "Who are you, brave youth?" "I am Ivan Tsarevich." "Have you come here of your own free will or at another's bidding?" "Of my own free will. I am seeking my mother whom Whirlwind seized when she was out walking in the garden and carried off none knows where. Do you know where I can find her?" "No, I don't. But my elder sister, Elena the Fair, the Princess of the Golden Kingdom, lives nearby, and she may know. Here is a silver ball for you. Send it rolling and follow it, and it will lead you to the Golden Kingdom. And when you have killed Whirlwind do not forget me, unhappy soul that I am, but deliver me from captivity and take me with you to where I can be free. For Whirlwind keeps me captive here and comes to see me every two months." She gave him a silver ring and said: "My whole Silver Kingdom is in this ring." And Ivan Tsarevich sent the silver ball rolling along and went after it.

Whether a short or a long time passed nobody knows, but by and by he saw before him a palace of gold that flamed like fire. Fearful dragons, chained to the wall with chains of gold, guarded the gate, and close by was a well with a dipper of gold dangling at the end of a gold chain. Ivan Tsarevich scooped up a dipperful of water and gave the dragons a drink, and they quietened and lay down on the ground so that he was able to pass on into the palace. Elena the Fair met him there and asked him who he was. "I am Ivan Tsarevich." "Have you come here of your own free will or at another's bidding?" "Of my own free will. I am seeking my mother, Nastasya the Golden Plait. Do you know where I can find her?" "That I do. She lives nearby, and Whirlwind comes to see her once a week and me, once a month. Here is a gold ball for you. Send it rolling along and go after it, and it will lead you wherever you wish to go. And take this gold ring, too; in it is the whole of the Golden Kingdom. But mind this, Ivan Tsarevich: when you have vanquished Whirlwind, do not forget me, unhappy soul that I am, but take me with you to where I can be free." "I'll not forget you, " said the Prince.

He sent-the ball rolling along and went after it, he walked and he walked, and he came to a palace that flamed like fire so many were the diamonds and other gems studding its walls. By the gate were six- headed dragons that hissed as he came near, but Ivan Tsarevich gave them water to drink and they quietened and let him pass on into the palace.

Many were the chambers he passed through, and in the last one, sitting on a high throne, he found his mother. She was garbed in royal garments and had on a gem-studded crown. She glanced up as he came in, and seeing who it was, cried: "Dear God in Heaven, is it you, my beloved son? How did you get here?" He told her all about everything and then said: "1 have come for you." "It is a hard task you have set yourself, my son," said she. "For .the ruler of this mountain is Whirlwind who is as mighty as he is evil and who holds all the spirits in his sway. It was he who carried me off, and it is with him you will have to grapple! Now come down into the cellar with me."

They went down into the cellar, and there were two tubs of water there, one standing near the right wall and the other, near the left one. "Drink some water out of the tub that is near the right wall," said Nastasya the Golden Plait. Ivan Tsarevich did as she told him. "How strong do you feel?" she asked him. "So strong that I know I could turn this whole palace round with one hand if I chose!" "Take another sip from the same tub." Ivan Tsarevich bent down and took another sip. "And how strong do you feel now?" "So strong that I know I could turn the whole world upside down!" "That makes you very strong indeed! And now move the tub that is near the right wall to the left wall, and the one near the left wall to the right one." Ivan Tsarevich did as she told him. "The tub you drank from is filled with strong water, my dear son," his mother said, "and the other, with strengthless water. He who drinks of the first will become very, very strong, and he who drinks of the second, very weak. Now, Whirlwind always drinks out of the first tub, which he keeps near the right wall, and if we are to get the better of him we must trick him."

They climbed the cellar stairs and were soon back in the self-same chamber, and his mother told Ivan Tsarevich that Whirlwind would soon be coming home. "Hide under my mantle that he might not see you," she said. "And as soon as he flies in and begins embracing and kissing me, grab hold of his cudgel and don't let go of it. He will rise high into the air and carry you over mountains and seas, but you must never loosen your hold. He will tire after a while, and, wanting to drink of the strong water, come down into the cellar and rush to the tub we have put near the right wall. He will drink from it, and you must drink from the other one. When you see that he has lost all of his strength, you must seize his sword and smite off his head with one blow. When you have done that, you will hear voices telling you to smite again. Do not heed them but say in reply: 'A true knight never smites but once!' "

No sooner had Ivan Tsarevich hidden himself under his mother's mantle than it grew dark outside, everything around them began to shake and to tremble, and Whirlwind came flying up. He struck the ground, turned into a tall and handsome man and came into the palace, a great cudgel in his hand. "Fee-fo-fum! I smell Russian flesh. Has anyone been here?" "No, and I don't know what makes you think so," the queen said. Whirlwind threw his arms around her and began kissing her, and Ivan Tsarevich grabbed hold of his cudgel. "I'll soon do away with you!" Whirlwind cried. "That remains to be seen. You might and then again you might not." At this Whirlwind flew out through the window and soared to the sky, and he bore Ivan Tsarevich away with him. They flew over a mountain, and Whirlwind said, "I'll dash you to the ground and kill you!" They flew over the sea, and he said, "I'll throw you down and drown you!" But he could not make good his threats, for Ivan Tsarevich held on to the cudgel and would not let go of it.

Whirlwind flew all round the world, and at last, feeling weary, he came down to the ground and into the cellar. Not knowing that it was filled with strengthless water, he rushed to the tub that stood near the right wall and began drinking from it, and Ivan Tsarevich let him do it and himself drank from the tub that stood near the left wall and that was filled with strong water. Very soon Whirlwind lost all his strength while Ivan Tsarevich became the strongest man that ever lived. Snatching his sabre from him, he smote off Whirlwind's head, and the moment he had done so he heard voices calling from behind him: "Smite again, smite again or he will come back to life!" "No," said Ivan Tsarevich, "a bogatir's hand never smites but once." He made up a fire, burnt Whirlwind's head and his body and cast the ashes into the wind. Nastasya the Golden Plait was overjoyed. "Let us now make merry and eat and drink, my son," said she, "and then make haste and set out for home, for this is a dull place with no one even to talk." "Who is to serve us, then, if no one lives here?" "That you shall see." And before another word was said the table was covered with a cloth, and all sorts of foods and drinks appeared on it. And as they ate, the sound of music fell on their ears and someone they could not see sang to them. They ate and they drank and had a rest, and Ivan Tsarevich said: "It is time to go, Mother! My two brothers are waiting for us at the foot of the mountain, and I still have to free the three princesses whom Whirlwind has been keeping captive."

They took every thing they needed and set out on their way. They freed the three Princesses and taking away a length of cloth as well as many of the fine and costly things they found in the three palaces, went on and soon came to the place where they could begin their descent from the mountain. Ivan Tsarevich tied his mother to the cloth first and let her down on it, and then he let down Elena the Fair and her two sisters. His two brothers stood below watching and said: "We'll leave Ivan Tsarevich on the mountain top, and we'll take our mother and the three princesses to our father and tell him that it was we who found and freed them." "I will marry Elena the Fair, and you the Princess of the Silver

Kingdom," said Prince Pyotr to Prince Vasily, "and the Princess of the Copper Kingdom will have to be content with a general."

It was now the turn of Ivan Tsarevich to let himself down from the mountain, but his brothers seized the bottom end of the cloth and ripped it off. Ivan Tsarevich was left on the top of the mountain and there was nothing he could do. He burst into tears and went back along the road, but though he walked all over the Copper Kingdom, the Silver Kingdom and the Golden Kingdom, not a soul did he see. He came to the Diamond Kingdom, but there was no one there either, and he felt so lonely he wanted to die. Then, lying on the window sill in one of the palace chambers, he saw a pipe. "I think I'll play a little tune just to keep boredom away," said he picking it up. He put the pipe to his lips and blew, and as if out of nowhere there appeared before him a lame man and a one-eyed man. "What can we do for you, Ivan Tsarevich?" asked they. "I'm hungry. Bring me something to eat." And lo!— quick as lightning the table was set and the best of foods and drinks appeared on it. Ivan Tsarevich ate and then he said to himself: "And now I wouldn't mind having a rest." He put the pipe to his lips and blew, and the lame man and the one-eyed man appeared. "What can we do for you, Ivan Tsarevich?" they asked. "Make a bed for me." No sooner were the words out of his mouth than the bed was made, and it was the softest he had ever slept on.
He had a good sleep and then blew upon his pipe again. "What can we do for you?" asked the lame man and the one-eyed man. "Does that mean that I can ask for anything and it will be done?" asked Ivan Tsarevich. "Yes, anything at all, Ivan Tsarevich. All you have to do is blow upon the pipe. Just as we were ready to serve Whirlwind before, so are we ready to serve you now. Only you must have the pipe with you always." "Good!" said Ivan Tsarevich, and he added: "I wish to be back in my own realm." And no sooner had he said this than he found himself in his own realm, at a market-place. He walked along, and there, coming toward him, he saw a shoemaker, as jolly a fellow as ever lived. "Where are you

going, my man?" asked Ivan Tsarevich. "To sell a pair of boots. I'm a shoemaker." "How would you like me to work for you?" "Can you make shoes?" "Yes, and clothes, too. I can do anything." "Good! Come along, then!"

They came to the shoemaker's house, and the shoemaker said: "Now, then, make me a pair of boots out of this piece of leather, and it's fine leather, believe you me. I want to see what you can do." He showed Ivan Tsarevich into the room he was to live in and left him there. Ivan Tsarevich got out his pipe and blew upon it, and the lame man and the one-eyed man appeared before him. "What can we do for you, Ivan Tsarevich?" they asked. "I want you to make me a pair of boots, to be ready by tomorrow." "It shall be done!" "Here, take this piece of leather." "A poor piece, if ever there was one! It ought to be thrown out." Morning came, Ivan Tsarevich rose, and there on the table stood a beautiful pair of boots! The shoemaker too got up from bed. "Are the boots ready?" he asked. "They are," said Ivan Tsarevich. "Well, then, let me see them!" Ivan Tsarevich brought out the boots, and the shoemaker took one look at them and gasped in wonder. "I have found myself a master shoemaker, a man with magic fingers!" he cried. And he took the boots and made for the market-place with them.

Now, at this same time preparations for three weddings were under way in the palace: Prince Pyotr was marrying Elena the Fair, Prince Vasily, the Princess of the Silver Kingdom, and a general the Princess of the Copper Kingdom. Finery of all sorts was being purchased for the brides and grooms, and Elena the Fair said that she needed a pair of boots. Now, as no boots better than the ones the shoemaker was offering could be found, he was at once brought to the palace. And Elena the Fair took one look at them and said: "Such boots can only have been made in Whirlwind's palace!" She paid the shoemaker a large sum of money and bade him make her another pair. "They must be ornamented with diamonds and other precious stones," said she. "And I will not have you measuring my feet. Just remember this. If they are not ready by breakfast-time tomorrow, you shall be hanged!"

The shoemaker took the money and the gems with which the boots were to be ornamented and left the palace with hanging head. "Unhappy man that I am! What am I to do?" he said to himself. "How can I have the boots ready by tomorrow? It's the gallows for me and no mistake! I think I had better have a drink or two with my friends before I die." He stepped into an inn where he found some of his friends, of whom he had many, and, seeing him, they asked why he was so glum. "Ah, my friends, I'm to be hanged tomorrow!" "Hanged? What for?" The shoemaker told them about the boots he had been ordered to make. "It's no use trying to work!" said he. "Let's drink and make merry instead." They drank and made merry, and by the time the day was drawing to a close the shoemaker could hardly stand on his feet he was so drunk. "I think I'll take a keg of wine home and go to bed," said he. "And when they come for me tomorrow, I'll down a half of it. A man can't feel the rope round his neck when he's dead drunk." He came home and said to Ivan Tsarevich: "See what those boots of yours have done, curse you! I'm to be hanged. Wake me when they come for me tomorrow morning."

Night came, Ivan Tsarevich got out his pipe and blew upon it, and the lame man and the one-eyed man appeared. "What can we do for you, Ivan Tsarevich?" they asked. "You are to make me a pair of boots to be ready by morning," said he, and he told them what kind of boots were wanted. "It shall be done!" Ivan Tsarevich went to bed and to sleep, and in the morning, there were the boots standing on the table, the gems on them sparkling and glittering. "Time to get up, Master!" he called to the shoemaker. "Have they come for me, then? Bring the keg of wine and pour me a cupful, let them hang me drank." "But the boots are ready, Master." "What! Where are they?" He rushed into Ivan Tsarevich's room, and, seeing the boots, said: "When did you and I manage to make them?" "During the night, Master. Don't you remember?" "No, I'm that fuzzy. I don't."

He took the boots, wrapped them up and ran to the palace, and when Elena the Fair saw them she at once knew that it was Whirlwind's two servants who had made them. "How ever did you manage to make these boots?" asked she of the shoemaker. "I can do anything!" "If that is so, then make me a wedding dress sewn with gold and studded with diamonds and other precious stones. And it must be ready by tomorrow or I'll have you put to death!" The shoemaker left the palace with hanging head. His friends, who had been waiting for him, greeted him and asked how he had fared. "It's cursed I am!" he told them. "Elena the Fair will drive all us good Christians to our grave! She's ordered me to make her a dress sewn with gold and studded with precious stones, and what sort of a tailor am I! I'm sure to be put to death." "Let's have a drink or two now, friend, and then you can go to bed. Night is the mother of wisdom, don't forget."

They went to an inn and drank and made merry, and by and by the shoemaker was so drank he could hardly stand. He dragged a keg of wine home with him and said to Ivan Tsarevich: "Wake me tomorrow and I'll down this whole keg of wine. I want to be drank when they chop off my head. For never in my life can I hope to make a dress like the one demanded of me." He went to bed and was soon snoring loudly, and Ivan Tsarevich put his pipe to his lips and blew. The lame man and the one-eyed man appeared and asked him what they could do for him. "I want a dress to be made by tomorrow, and it must be as fine as the ones Elena the Fair wore when she lived in Whirlwind's palace." "It shall be done!" Ivan Tsarevich woke at dawn, and there was the dress lying on the table and sparkling so brightly that it lit up the whole room. So he went and roused the shoemaker who rubbed his eyes and said: "Have they come for me, then? Hurry and bring the wine!" "But the dress is all ready." "Is it? When did we make it?" "During the night. It was you did the cutting." "Did I? I'm that fuzzy I don't remember." And taking the dress, the shoemaker ran to the palace.

Elena the Fair gave him a large sum of money and said: "You are to build a kingdom of gold in the middle of the sea and also a bridge of gold that will connect this palace with it. The bridge is to be carpeted with the richest of velvets, beautiful trees are to grow on either side of it, and songbirds are to sit in them and sing away for all they are worth. And if it is not ready by breakfast-time tomorrow, I shall have you quartered!" The shoemaker left the palace with hanging head. "Well, how was it?" his friends asked him. "It's the end of me, I am to be quartered tomorrow. She's set me such a task that the devil himself could not cope with it!" "Now, now, let's go and have a drink and then you can go to bed. Night is the mother of wisdom, don't forget." "And why not! A man should have a little pleasure before he dies."

They went to an inn and drank much wine, and so drank was the shoemaker by evening that his friends had to drag him home. "Goodbye, my lad!" said he to Ivan Tsarevich. "I am to be put to death tomorrow." "Have you been set another task?" "Yes." He told Ivan Tsarevich what it was, went to bed and was soon snoring away. And Ivan Tsarevich went to his own room and blew upon his pipe. The lame man and the one-eyed man appeared and asked him what they could do for him. He told them what it was he wanted done, and they said: "That is no easy task, Ivan Tsarevich, but never fear, everything will be done by tomorrow morning." Ivan Tsarevich woke just as day broke, he looked out of the window, and lo and behold!—there stood the palace of gold flaming like fire. Ivan Tsarevich roused the shoemaker who jumped to his feet with a start. "What is it? Have they come for me? Bring the wine, quick! I want to be put to death drunk." "But the palace has been built." "It has?" And the shoemaker glanced out of the window and gasped in wonder. "When was it built?" he asked. "Don't you remember? You and I worked very, very hard." "I must have slept so soundly I forgot all about it."

They hurried to the golden palace and found it to be full of treasures such as no one had seen or heard of before. Said Ivan Tsarevich: "Here is a feather duster for you, Master. Go and dust the railings, and if anyone comes and asks you who lives in the palace, don't say a word but just give them this note." Off went the shoemaker and began dusting the railings, and Elena the Fair, who had just risen from bed, saw the golden bridge and hurried to tell the king about it. "Just look, Your Majesty!" she cried. "A palace of gold has been built in the middle of the sea, and a bridge too that connects it with your palace. And on either side of the bridge grow the most beautiful trees in which sit songbirds that fill the air with their music."

The king, who feared that some great warrior was about to lay siege to his kingdom, at once sent envoys to ask what it all could mean. And the shoemaker being on the bridge, the envoys addressed all their questions to him. "I know nothing, but here is a note you can take to your king," the shoemaker said. Now, in the note Ivan Tsarevich had told his father all about everything, about how he had freed his mother and Elena the Fair and about how his elder brothers had tricked him. And he sent coaches of gold for the king and queen, asking them to pay him a visit together with Elena the Fair and her sisters. He invited his brothers too, but said that they were to travel in an ordinary peasant sled.

The king and queen and the rest did not delay but set off at once, and Ivan Tsarevich welcomed them with great joy. The king wanted to punish his two elder sons for what they had done, but Ivan Tsarevich pleaded with him not to and he forgave them. A great feast was then held, and Ivan Tsarevich married Elena the Fair. He gave the Princess of the Silver Kingdom in marriage to Prince Pyotr, and the Princess of the Copper Kingdom, to Prince Vasily, and he had the shoemaker made general.

I was at the feast too, and I drank mead and wine, but all of it ran down this beard of mine.

Interpretation

Once long ago the spiritual consciousness of Man was still little connected with the earthly element; it remained in a bright higher world. Bel-Belyanin means White-the-White. White is the color of the super earthly, just as black is the color of the earthly. The soul was gifted with a primeval whiteness, given to her by grace without effort on her part. The enlightened state of her head appears in the picture of the golden hair. But this most inner soul being, the enlightened, inspired, spiritually connected "Mother" is seized by a wild nature spirit and carried off to a distant height. Man had no longer any access to her.

Three brothers, representatives of developmental epochs, grow over long ages. Basilius, Peter and Ivan. From his uncle, thus in the realm of old spiritual forces accessible through kinship not through the intellectual soul, Ivan finds guidance. He is given the guiding ball: spherical, cosmic forces lead him. The spirit brothers "are lying" in the sphere of freedom. (There is a variant: they have fallen into the desert.) With iron will forces in growth and action, Ivan attains the inner height and enters the realm of the Sentient Soul. Devout feeling must dip down into the spring of life and be the vessel to lift from it the forces to still the burning fires of desire of the sense nature. By the copper ring the spiritual seeker binds himself with this soul being and wins a new guide: the copper ball that leads the way.

In the Silver realm, the forces of the intellect must reach into the well and draw out the forces to calm the dragons. The intellectual soul knows of the mission of Johannine Christianity in Russia; therefore the greeting: "Now a Russian spirit appears befor my eyes." With the help of cosmic forces of understanding – the silver ball – he finds the consciousness soul. She of course guides to the Mother who is in the diamond realm.

A diamond is pure carbon, and carbon is the Earth element. Its purity, its radiance, and its beauty make it the symbol for most pure, the highest Earth force, the Christ Force. For indeed the Christ Being has united with the Earth and is its highest element.

Whirlwind always drinks the strength-giving water from the right side. Wild nature spirituality strengthens itself through activity; it lives in thoughtless action. Ivan, however, moves the strength-giving water to the left side, the side of the heart. As heart forces of Ivan grow, Whirlwind fades. But in the hand of Ivan, the cudgel of Whirlwind (wild striking power) becomes I-conscious, spirit-directed activity. Who can use this club is master of the wild forces. (Recall the club of Hercules.)

A hero's hand strikes but once. A second blow would awaken the defeated forces to new life. And they have in the meantime assembled the forces of opposition. Without the second blow, the evil spirit is consumed in its own fire.

The spirit seeker becomes again "son" of the mother. And in the world of harmony of the spheres he nourishes himself with heavenly food. Now must the soul queen be led from the realm of the Ideal – that is no longer accessible – into the free world.

We have already met spinning as picture language for thinking. Weaving is the further development of this process. The intentional, planned working together of thoughts is like weaving. We speak of weaving thoughts together, of the web of thought. Weaving appears in the picture of the cloth Ivan Tsarevich uses to let his mother and the three sisters down into the human world. On this fabric of thought the soul queens glide "down".

But the leaders of the past ages who have not developed through contending with Whirlwind selfishly grab the souls and tear the fabric of thought connecting to the higher world. The Johannine impulse is thwarted in its mission, and for the moment the elder brothers prevail. Ivan must acquire new abilities while still remaining in the spiritual world. He gets the magic flute and becomes master of the forces that had formerly served Whirlwind. (Also in Mozart's *Magic Flute* the flute constrains the forces that would block the way of the spiritual seeker to initiation.) One who learns to live in harmony and rhythm is master of the flute. To one who can make cosmic harmonies sound in life and in art the spirits of the cosmos serve. They appear as the lame man and the one-eyed man.

[There follow here two paragraphs seemingly intended to explain why one of the spirits of the cosmos appears in the form of a one-eyed man. Partly they are factually wrong (Archimedes did not invent the right angle) and partly they are incomprehensible to your translator. Perhaps it will suffice to say that the one-eyed man has no depth perception, everything is equally close – and equally distant – and thus perhaps his consciousness could be said to be cosmic.]

In the lame man, something else is expressed. He is the spirit of earthly weight, restraint and constriction, the enemy of progress. He limps. Under his influence alone, Man would become dried up, shriveled, lamed. But if he is bound to the cosmic consciousness – the one-eyed man – then the cosmic gets the necessary earthly weight and together they can work in the right way in earthly existence.

What was won above in the realm of the spirit must now be applied in ordinary life. In the market, in economic life, Ivan meets the shoemaker. He represents the spiritual force through which this relation to the earth can be developed. Just as we must outwardly stand on the earth in shoes, so we inwardly need to get ground under our feet. We must stand firmly on the ground of facts. Just how we do that is shown by the color and nature of the shoes. The Johannine spiritual seeker knows that Christianity is no one-sided, other-worldly religion. The divine appeared and worked on earth. Ivan knows that everything found in the ideal world of the spirit must be brought into the earthly world. He serves the shoemaker, the lower I, who the whole day long concerns himself with the earthly. First of all, the purified consciousness soul must work out of the realm of wisdom into the earthly: she needs golden shoes. The shoemaker in us cannot unaided make them, because he is always devoted to everyday tasks and gets drunk on the wine of egohood. Ivan's cosmic forces work during the night: when in sleep we dip into the world of morality (from which we have come) in order to acquire strength from the cosmos, then there are formed in us forces to work wisely in the earthly element. One who cannot form these abilities falls into one-sided, intellectual thinking and looses the ground under his feet: he hangs. ("The man," – that is, the intellectual in us – "will hang himself," says the devil in the Oberufer paradise play.) For this shoe, no measurement may be made; such wisdom is without measure.

We know from Mathew 22 that at the heavenly wedding the wedding garment is mandatory. By this garment is meant the supersensible human sheath, the soul aura. It should shine radiantly like the sun. (We say that someone has a radiant face and glowing soul warmth.) If one in everyday life looses this ability, he will gradually loose his previous consciousness and become more and more "headless" in the truest sense of the word.

Just as our lower I needs the "house" of the body, so the higher soul need a spirit house in which it can live, the wisdom enlightened spirit body, the golden palace. It must stand "in the sea" – that is, be grounded in the soul world. The bridge is seven versts wide – the medieval path of initiation had seven steps through which the spiritual student built up spiritual being. Who cannot build this spiritual being must live in only the *four* lower members, the physical body, the life or etheric body, the astral body and the lower I. He is *quartered*. The shoemaker does not remember what happened during the night. How can the ordinary sense man grasp these mysteries?

At the end of the tale, "A great feast was then held, and Ivan Tsarevich married Elena the Fair [of the Gold Kingdom]. He gave the Princess of the Silver Kingdom in marriage to Prince Pyotr [Peter], and the Princess of the Copper Kingdom, to Prince Vasily, and he had the shoemaker made general."

The Johannine spirit becomes the leader of the Consciousness Soul age. Each spiritual brother gets the corresponding soul bride: Peter, the regent of the Intellectual Soul Age gets Intellectual soul; Basilius, regent of the Sentient Soul age, gets the Sentient soul; and Ivan-John, regent of the Consciousness soul age, gets the Consciousness soul.

But the shoemaker, the lower I who has learned much working with the Johannine spirituality, has now attained a certain authority. He can exercise, command and direct. He is made a general.[20]

---

20 At the end of her commentary, notes the existence of a slight variant, Vol. 1, No. 5 in the old edition from which she was working. I have not been able to identify it in the current edition of Afanasyev. She does not add any interpretive material because of it.

# 3. The Realms of Copper, Silver and Gold (A 128)

Translated by Leonard Arthur Magnus

Once upon a time there was an old man and his old wife, and they had three sons. One was called Egórushko Zalyót (bold flier); the second was called Mísha Kosolápy (curved-foot) and the third was called Iváshko Zapéchnik (behind the stove). The parents wanted to secure wives for them, and sent the eldest son out to seek a bride. He went for a long time, and saw many maidens, but he took none to wife, for he liked none well enough. On the way he met a three-headed dragon, and was very frightened.

The dragon asked him, "Whither are you going, brave youth?"

"I am going a-wooing, but I cannot find a bride."

"Come with me; I will take you where you may find one."

So they journeyed together till they came to a great heavy stone; and the dragon said to him: "Lift that stone off, then you will find what you are seeking." And Egórushko endeavored to lift the stone away, but he failed. Then the dragon said: "I have no bride for you here!"

So Egórushko went back home, and he told his father and mother all he had gone through. And the parents reflected for a long time. And they at last sent Mísha Kosolápy on the same journey. He met the dragon after many days, and asked him to show him how he should get a bride. The dragon bade him go with him. And they came to the stone. Mísha tried to lift it away, but in vain; so he returned to his parents and told them all he had gone through.

This time the parents were at an utter loss what they should do. Iváshko Zapéchnik could not have any better luck! But still

Iváshko asked his parents' leave to go to the dragon, and after some reluctance he obtained it.

Iváshko met the three-headed dragon, who asked him: "Where are you going, sturdy youth?"

"My brothers set out to marry, but they could find no brides. It is now my turn."

"Come with me; perhaps you may win a bride."

So the dragon and Iváshko went up to the stone, and the dragon commanded him to lift the stone up, and Iváshko thrust the stone, and it flew up from its bed like a feather, as though it were not there, and revealed an aperture in the earth, with a rope ladder.

"Iváshko," said the dragon, "go down that ladder; and I will let you down into the three kingdoms, and in each of them you will see a fair maiden."

So Iváshko went down, deeper and deeper, right down to the realm of copper, where he met a maiden who was very fair.

"God greet you, strange guest! Sit down where you may find room, and say whence you come."

"Oh, fair maiden, you have given me nothing to eat and drink, and you ask me for my news!"

So the maiden gave him all manner of meat and drink and set them on the table.

Iváshko had a drink, and then said: "I am seeking a bride; will you marry me?"

"No, fair youth! go farther on into the silver kingdom. There there is a maiden who is much fairer than I." Thereupon she gave him a silver ring.

So the young boy thanked her for her kindness, said farewell; and he went farther until he reached the silver kingdom. There he saw a maiden who was fairer yet than the former, and he prayed and bowed down low.

"Good day, fair maiden!"

"Good day, strange youth! Sit down and tell me whence you come and what you seek."

"But, fair maiden, you have given me nothing to eat or drink, and you ask my news!"

So the maiden put rich drink and food on the table, and Ivàshko ate as much as he would. Then he told her that he was seeking a bride, and he asked her if she would be the bride. "Go yet farther into the golden realm; there there is a maiden who is yet much fairer than I!" the girl said, and she gave him a golden ring.

Ivàshko said farewell, and went yet farther, went deeper still, into the golden realm. There he found a maiden who was much, very much fairer than the others, and there he said the right prayer, and he saluted the maiden.

"Whither art thou going, fair youth; and what do you seek?"

"Fair maiden, give me to eat and drink, and I will tell you my news."

So she got him so fine a meal that no better meal on earth could be wished, and she was so fair that no pen could write and no tale could tell.

Ivàshko set to valorously, and then he told his tale. "I am seeking a bride; if you will marry me, come with me!"

So the maiden consented, and she gave him a ball of golden thread. Then they went on and on together, until they reached the silver realm, where they took the maiden who was there; and they went on and on and on from there to the copper realm, and took this maiden with them as well. And then they came to the hole through which they were to climb out. The rope ladder stood all ready, and there there stood the elder brothers, who were looking for him. Iváshko tied the maiden out of the copper realm to the ladder, and the brothers lifted her out, and they let the ladder down again. Then Iváshko laid hold of the maiden from the silver realm, and she was drawn up, and the ladder let down again. This time the maiden from the golden realm came, and was also drawn up. When the steps were let down again, Iváshko sat on them, and the brothers drew it up into the height. But when they saw that this time it was Iváshko Zapéchnik who sat on it, they began to reflect: "If we let him out perhaps he will not give us any of the maidens." So they cut the steps down, and Iváshko fell down. He wept bitterly, but it was no good. He went down farther, and he then came across a tiny old man, who sat on a tree-stem and had a long white beard. Iváshko told him how it had been.

The old man advised him once more to go on. "You will come to a little hut. Enter it and you will see a long man lying in it from one corner to the other. Ask him how you shall reach Russian land once more."

So Iváshko went up to the hut, stepped in and said: "Strong giant, spare me, and tell me how I shall get home again."

"Fi, fo, fum, you Russian bones!" said Ídolishche, "I did not summon you, and still you have come. Go to the thrice-tenth sea, there there stands a hut on cocks' legs in which the Bába Yagá lives. She has an eagle who will carry you."

So the young boy went on and on, a far way, to the hut, and he stepped in.

The Bába Yagá cried out at once, "Fi, fo, fum, Russian bones, why have you come here?"

"Oh, mother, the giant Ídolishche sent me to ask you to lend me your mighty eagle to carry me to Russia."

"Go," said Bába Yagá, "into the garden. At the gate there stands a watchman; take his keys and pass through seven doors, and when you open the last the eagle will flap his wings. Sit on his back if you are not afraid, and fly away. But take meat with you and give him to eat whenever he turns round."

Iváshko did as he was bidden, sat on the eagle and flew away. The eagle flew on, flew on; then he soon turned his head round, and Iváshko gave him a bite of flesh. Then the eagle flew on afar, and turned round again, and Iváshko fed him. And he fed him until he had nothing more left, and Russia was still far off. Then the eagle turned round, and as he had no flesh, he tore a fragment out of Iváshko's withers and ate it up. But they had already reached the aperture. When Iváshko parted from the eagle, he spat a bit of flesh out and bade Iváshko lay it on him. And Iváshko did so, and his body healed; and Iváshko went home, took the maiden from the golden realm from his brothers; and they then lived happily, and may still be living if they are not dead.

I was there and I drank beer; I drank the beer, and it flowed up to my whiskers, but none of it reached my mouth.

## Interpretation

The first brother, the bold flier, is a spiritual force too little bound to the earth. The second, the curved-footed, shuffles along, too much bound to the earth, and cannot free himself from it. The third holds the middle ground. The picture of the stove, the warm center of the house, points to the warmth center of the body, the heart. Only the spiritual force hidden behind the heart is able to lift the stone of materialism from the entrance to the soul world and to court the soul brides.

The spirit seeker nourishes himself in the soul realm, only then can he by asking form a connection with maiden soul and receive assurance to advance to the next realm. Finally the ball of golden thread for wise development is in his hand. But then the Johannine impulse is pushed back by the brothers and must traverse long ways. An ancient spirit force gives good advice; a giant recognizes the awakener and directs him into the realm of the most ancient soul wisdom. There he goes through a sevenfold transformation. (In the Mithras mysteries, the seeker must go through a seven-fold transformation represented by seven doors.) At last Ivan receives for his task in Russia the eagle: the force of thought that flies to the sun.

## 4. The Three Realms (A 130)

In times long past, when God's world was still populated with forest spirits, mermaids and witches, when the rivers were still full of milk and the shores of red groats, and when over the fields the black grouse flew already roasted, at that time Tsar Pea lived with his wife, Anastasia the Fair. And they had three sons.

One day a grave disaster befell the family: a wicked spirit abducted the beautiful queen. Then the eldest son said to the father, "Father, give me your blessing, I will go forth and seek my mother!" He rode away, and for three years nothing was seen or heard from him.

Then the second son went to the father and asked: "Father, give me your blessing, I will try my luck and find my mother and brother. Maybe I'll succeed. "The Tsar gave him his blessing, the Tsar's son rode off, and he, too, disappeared as if he had fallen into a deep well.

Then the youngest son, Ivan, spoke to his father: "My father, give me your blessing, and let me go on the long journey, perhaps I will find the mother and the two brothers."

"Go forth, my son," said the father, and the Tsar's son Ivan rode into distant, foreign lands. He rode and rode and came to the blue sea. There he stopped on the bank and said to himself: "Where should I take my way?"

Suddenly thirty-three swans came flying, threw themselves on the damp earth and turned into virgins of great beauty, but one of them was more beautiful than all the others. They threw off their clothes, jumped into the water and bathed. Whether they bathed for a long time or not so long, as they played in the water, Ivan Tsarevich sneaked up, took the girdle of the most beautiful virgin, and hid himself in a hollow in the sand. When the virgins had bathed, they came to the shore to get dressed, but lo, a girdle was missing. "Oh, Ivan Tsarevich, give me back my girdle!"

"Tell me first where my mother is!"

"Your mother lives with my father, and my father is Raven Ravenson. Walk along the shores of the sea, where a silver bird with a golden tuft will fly across across your way. Watch where it flies, and follow it! "

The Tsar's son gave the maiden back the girdle. He walked along the sea, where his two brothers came to meet him. They greeted each other, and Ivan took them with himself, and they walked on the bank. Suddenly they saw the silver bird with the golden tuft flying past, and they followed its course. The bird flew and flew, but suddenly it dropped down and disappeared under an iron plate in a crack in the ground. "Well, brothers," said Ivan, "since Father and Mother are not here, give me your blessing. I will let myself down into that hole and see what that world of foreign faith looks like and if our mother is there." The brothers blessed him, and he started letting himself down on a rope into the deep hole. He went down deep and deeper, and kept going down for three years, no more and no less.

He reached the strange earth and went on his way. He went and went, went and went and suddenly saw the copper empire. There stood a castle, and thirty-three swan maidens sat embroidering in the castle, embroidering the linen towels with ornate patterns, embroidering small towns and suburbs. "Greetings, Ivan Tsarevich, where are you going, where does your way lead?" asked the Tsar's daughter of the copper empire.

"I'm going to look for my mother!"

"Your little mother is with my father, the Raven Ravenson, who is cunning and wise, flying over mountains and valleys, over abysses and clouds. He will kill you brave young man! But here you have a ball, go after it to my middle sister, talk to her and hear what she may say to you. And when you return, do not forget me! "

Ivan Tsarevich rolled the ball and went after it. And so he came to the silver world empire. Thirty-three swan maidens sat inside, and the Tsar's daughter of the silver kingdom said: "To this day I had not seen a Russian spirit with my eyes nor heard it with my ears, and now a Russian spirit appears before my eyes! Ivan Tsarevich, are you you avoiding the deed or are you seeking it?"

"Oh, beautiful maiden, I'm going to look for my mother."

"Your little mother is with my father, the Raven Ravenson, who is cunning and wise, flying over mountains and valleys, over abysses and clouds. Ivan Tsarevich, he will kill you! But here you have a ball, follow it to my youngest sister, who will tell you whether you should go on or turn back. "

Ivan Tsarevich came to the golden kingdom. And there were thirty-three swan maidens, embroidering the linen towels. But bigger and more beautiful than all was the princess of the golden kingdom. So great was her beauty that one can not describe it with a pen, can not tell in a folktale. And she said to him, "Where are you going? Where does your path take you? "

"I'm going to look for my mother."

"Your little mother is with my father, the Raven Ravenson, who is cunning and wise; he flies over mountains and valleys, he shoots over clouds and stars. O king's son, he will kill you! Here you have a little ball, follow it and go into the pearl realm, there lives your dear little mother. When your mother sees you, she will be glad of heart. She will at once call her maids and order them to bring to you the young wine! But you shall not take the young wine; ask for the three-year-old wine, which is in the cupboard, and for a seared bread crust. And one more thing: note that there are two vats in the yard with my father, in one of which there is strong water, in the other less strong. You have to swap the vats and drink quickly from the strong water.

The youngest king's son and the youngest king's daughter talked to each other for a long time and liked each other so much that they did not want to think about parting. But what to do – Ivan Tsarevich had to go on his mission. So he took leave and went on his way.

He went and went and came to the Pearl Kingdom. When his mother saw him, she was very happy and called out, "You maids and attendants, serve my son the young wine!"

"I do not drink young wine," said the King's son John. "Give me the three-year-old and, as a snack, a seared crust of bread!" He drank the wine and ate the bread, and went out into the wide yard. There he changed the vats and drank the strong water.

All at once the Raven Ravenson arrived, brighter than the brightest day. But when he saw Ivan Tsarevich, he was darker than the darkest night. He came down on the tub and began to drink from the weaker water. Ivan Tsarevich jumped swiftly on his wings. The raven Ravenson shot up, up to the sky, carrying Ivan with him. He carried him over mountains and valleys, over abysses and clouds. At last he began to ask, "What do you want from me, Ivan Tsarevich? Do you want my treasure? I'll give it to you."

"I do not want much from you," replied Ivan, "just give me your power feather."

"Oh, no, Ivan Tsarevich" answered the raven, "there you are asking too much!"

And again the raven flew with him over mountains and valleys, over clouds and crevasses. Ivan Tsarevich however, held on tight, lay down with all his weight on the raven and almost broke his wings. "Do not break my wings!" cried the Raven Ravenson. "Better take my power feather!" He gave the power feather to the tsarevich, became a common raven, and flew up into the steep mountains.

Ivan Tsarevich came to the Pearl Kingdom, took his mother and went back. He looked around and lo! the Pearl Realm wrapped itself in a ball and rolled after him. He went on and came to the Golden Empire and then to the silver and finally to the Copper Empire. Everywhere he took the beautiful royal daughters with them, and each of the three empires knotted together and rolled after him. So they all came together to where the rope hung. There, Ivan Tsarevich blew into a golden horn and shouted: "My dear brothers, if you are still alive, then do not betray me!" The brothers heard the horn, pulled on the rope and pulled the king's daughter out of the copper kingdom. When they saw the beautiful maiden, they began to argue, neither wanted the other to have her.

"Why do you argue, brave youths? Below is a maiden who is even more beautiful than I."

The brothers at once lowered the ropes and drew the princess of the silver kingdom. When they saw her, they began to argue again and beat each other. "She belongs to me!" said one. "No, she shall be mine!" cried the other.

"Do not quarrel, brave youths, there is another down there, far better than me!"

Then the sons of the tsar stopped fighting, quickly lowered the ropes, and drew the golden maiden up. As soon as they saw the beautiful princess, they argued much more. But she said: "Stop arguing, your mother is waiting below!" So they immediately pulled up the mother, and then they lowered the ropes once more for the Tsar's son Ivan. But when they had pulled him halfway up, they cut the ropes, and Ivan fell again to the ground. And he smashed himself so badly that for half a year he lay unconscious.

When he finally came to, he looked around and remembered everything that had happened to him. He took the power feather out of his pocket and hit the ground with it. At the same moment, twelve youths appeared and said, "What do you wish, Ivan Tsarevich? Command!"

"Take me up to the free world!"

The youths took him in their arms and carried him out into the free world.

Ivan Tsarevich asked about his brothers and learned that they had both been married long ago. The king's daughter from the copper empire married the middle brother, the king's daughter from the silver kingdom the elder; but his own chosen one, the princess of the golden kingdom, did not want to wed.

But now the father, the old king, had set his mind on taking the virgin out of the golden kingdom. He summoned all his councilors and accused his wife of dealing with evil spirits. And he ordered her to be beheaded. When this had happened, he asked the king's daughter from the Golden Realm, "Will you marry me?"

"Only then will I do it," answered the maiden, "if you make me shoes without taking measurements."

Everywhere the king looked for someone who could make shoes for the maiden, without taking measurements.

Just at this time, the Ivan Tsarevich returned to his kingdom. When he heard of the call, he hired himself to an old man as a craftsman. "Go to the king, Grandfather, and accept the work!" He said to him. "I'll sew the shoes, but say nothing about me!"

The old man went to the king and said, "I am ready to do this work!"

The king gave him material for a pair of shoes and asked, "Are you going to do it to my satisfaction, old man?"

"Do not be afraid, O king, my son is a good shoemaker."

When the old man came home, he gave the tsarevich the material. Ivan took it, cut it into tiny bits and threw everything out of the window. Then, out of the golden ball, he unwrapped the golden kingdom, took out the finished shoes, and said, "Grandfather, take these and bring them to the king!"

The king rejoiced greatly and began to press the bride again: "When shall we marry?" But she answered him, "Only if you make me a dress without taking measure."

The king was all a-bother, summoned all the masters of the kingdom to make a dress for the golden maiden without taking any measure, and offered them much gold for it.

"Grandfather, go to the king," said Ivan to the old man, "get the cloth, and I will sew the dress. But you must not betray me!"

The old man went to the castle, took velvet and silk, returned and gave it to the tsarevich. Ivan immediately took the scissors, cut the material into small bits and threw everything out of the window. Then he unwrapped the golden kingdom out of the little ball, took the most beautiful dress from it, and gave it to the old man. "Here, old man, take it to the castle!"

The king did not know what to do for joy. "Well, my beloved bride, it is time to marry!" But the king's daughter from the Golden Realm answered him, "Only then will I marry you when you give the command to cook the son of that old man in milk!"

The king did not think long and gave the order immediately. On the same day a bucket of milk was brought from each farm, poured into a large copper kettle, and the whole brought to a boil over a strong fire. Ivan Tsarevich was brought in; he took leave of all and bowed low, deep to the ground. Then he was thrown into the cauldron. He dived in, once and again - jumped out and had become such a wonderfully handsome youth that one can not describe it with the pen, nay, not even a folktale can tell.

"Whom shall I marry now?" said the maiden to the king, "thee, old man, or this brave young man?"

The old king thought to himself, "If I bathed in milk, I might come out as an equally beautiful man." He jumped into the cauldron, and lo! he was totally cooked!

Ivan married the princess of the golden kingdom. The wedding was celebrated and they began to live together and they lived and lived and prospered.

Interpretation

The pearl realm is totally different from diamond realm. Whereas the diamond is formed from pure carbon deep inside the earth under great pressure, the pearl is formed in water. Its soft luster appears next to sparkle of the diamond like the glow of moonlight next to broiling sunshine. Pearls are not finished and durables like the hard diamond. They need to be worn in contact with the skin to preserve their luster. They continue to always have something to do with the watery element. Pearls mean tears – says the proverb. An inner dream realm is meant by the pearl realm, for dreams rise and fall, flood and ebb like water. One can experience the pearl realm as the polar opposite of the diamond realm.

In this folktale there is described how the inner moon nature has won control, the motherly soul has been carried away into the realm of dreams. Ivan must go to the seashore and walk along it to find her. And the bird that guides him is silver like the moon.

The picture of the swan points to a higher consciousness that overshadows the human. ("It swans me" is a German idiom meaning "I am afraid.") Hidden, pure, half instinctive soul forces are the swan maidens who advise him. He finds them again as he wanders in the soul realms. There they embroider cities and suburbs into linen cloths. The thirty-three working souls create thought pictures of human society.

Who is the raven, brighter than the brightest day, who, on seeing Ivan, becomes darker than the darkest night? Think of the very special call of the raven, who seems old, wise, relaxed but enigmatic – quite different from the brave eagle. His dark feathers, his often ghostly flight make him the symbol of certain forces of wisdom that have darkened or been enchanted. In this tale we see how formerly bright wisdom forces darken when Ivan appears, for they know their time is at an end.

Milk is formed in connection with birth under the influence of moon rhythms. Cosmic forces of a more moon-like nature express themselves in the picture of milk. There is still an order in India whose members consume only milk. The wish to preserve in themselves a certain child-like consciousness and with it inner forces of clairvoyant experience which they use for healing. To cook milk means to fire up this nature-related, moon-related consciousness with will forces. To be boiled in milk and thereby to become more handsome than before – this was the ultimate test for the spirit that had searching, learning, and redeeming penetrated into the Pearl realm. The old spirit consciousness could not withstand the test and passed away. The tales says "He jumped into the cauldron, and lo! he was totally cooked!"

# 5. The Immortal Boneman (A 157)

In a kingdom somewhere there once was and lived a tsar and a tsarina. The tsarina gave birth to a child, Ivan Tsarevich. The nannies cradled him, rocking him back and forth, but the tsarevich could not sleep. "Tsar, mighty ruler," they called to the father, "come and rock your own son!"

The tsar rocks the cradle: "Sleep, my son, sleep! When you grow up, I'll marry you with the Ineffable Beauty of whom no one can see enough - with the Ineffable Beauty, daughter of three mothers, granddaughter of three grandmothers, sister of nine brothers. "

The tsarevich fell asleep and slept for three days and three nights. When he awoke, he screamed harder than before. The nannies cradled him, but they could not lull him to sleep. They call the Father: "King, magnanimous ruler, come and rock your son!"

The king rocks his son and speaks to him: "Sleep, little son sleep! When you grow up, I'll marry you with the Ineffable Beauty of whom no one can see enough - with the Ineffable Beauty, daughter of three mothers, granddaughter of three grandmothers, sister of nine brothers. "

The tsarevich fell asleep, and again slept for three days and three nights. But then he woke and screamed even more. The nannies cradled him, but they could not lull him to sleep. "King, magnanimous ruler, come and rock your own son!"

The king rocks and speaks to him: "Sleep, little son, sleep! When you grow up, I'll marry you with the Ineffable Beauty of whom no one can see enough - with the Ineffable Beauty, daughter of three mothers, granddaughter of three grandmothers, sister of nine brothers. "

The tsarevich fell asleep and slept again for three days and three nights. Then he awoke and said, "Father, give me your blessing, I must ride forth!"

"What, my child? You are only nine days old!"

"If you give me your blessing, I will ride forth; if you do not give it, I will ride forth anyway."

"Well, go with God's grace," said the king, blessing him. Ivan Tsarevich prepared to travel and went out and took a horse.

When he had already gone a long way, he met an old man who asked, "Where are you going and are you you going voluntarily or involuntarily?"

"I have no desire to talk to you," answered the tsarevich, and went on. But then he thought: Why did I not tell the old man? Old people make you think. "Wait, Grandfather," he said, "What did you ask me?"

"Whither your way, I asked, and whether you go voluntarily or involuntarily?"

"I go voluntarily, but even so twice as much involuntarily. When I was little, my father rocked me in the cradle, promised me the Ineffable Beauty for of my wife, daughter of three mothers, granddaughter of three grandmothers, sister of nine brothers. "

"You are right, and polite is your answer. But you will never reach your destination by foot or on that horse, for the Ineffable Beauty lives far, far from here. "

"How far?" asked the tsarevich.

"At the end of the wide world, in the golden realm, where the sun rises."

"What should I do, Grandfather? I cannot find a horse on which no one has ever ridden, nor a silk whip that no one has yet used."

"You cannot find a horse? Your father owns thirty horses that all look alike. Go home, order the servants to water the horses in the blue sea. The horse which pushes ahead of all the others, goes in up to his head, raises it to drink and makes waves in the blue sea that rise and roll from one shore to the other – that is the horse you should take! »

"Thanks for the good advice, Grandfather," said the tsarevich, did as the old man had taught him, and chose his bogatir's horse. In the night he slept deeply, the next morning he set out, opened the gates wide, and wanted to ride away.

Then the horse spoke in a human voice: "Ivan Tsarevich, throw yourself to the ground, I must first kick you!" The horse then kicked him once, then again, but not a third time: "Were I to kick you a third time, the earth could not bare us both anymore!"

Ivan Tsarevich then took the horse out of the chains, bridled and saddled it, swung himself into the saddle and rode off, just before the king saw him.

He rode far, far away. The day was fading, night was approaching, when there appeared before him a farm yard as big as a city, with a hut as high as a tower. He rode into the yard, straight up to the steps of the hut. There he tied the horse to a copper ring. Then he approached the hut. First he prayed to God, then he asked for bed. "Where is God taking you?" asked the old woman, "stay overnight, good young man."

"Oh, you old ones, you invite so crudely. First give me food and prepare a bed for me. Then you may ask me!"

The old woman did as he asked, gave him food and drink and set up the bed. Then she began to ask again. "When I was a small child, my father rocked me in the cradle. He promised me the Ineffable Beauty for my wife, daughter of three mothers, granddaughter of three grandmothers, sister of nine brothers. "You are a brave young man," she answered politely. The seventh decade I have lived to the end, but I have never heard of the Ineffable Beauty. Next on the way lives my sister, maybe she knows of her. And now sleep, O tsarevich. The morning is wiser than the evening. The tsarevich slept one night. In the morning he got up, washed himself white and clean, led his horse out, saddled it and put his foot in the stirrup. He rode far, far out. He rode up, up high.

The day was getting short, night was approaching. There was a yard before him, as big as a city. There was a hut in it, as high as a tower. He rode into the yard, up to the steps. There he tied his horse to the silver ring. Then he stepped down the way to the hut. He prayed to God and asked for a night's lodging.

"Foo, huh," shouted the Baba Yaga, "I have never smelt a Russian bone, I've never seen or heard of any, and now it's coming to my farm by itself! Where from your way, Ivan Tsarevich? "

"Oh, old woman, what are you saying, 'foo, huh' and why are you asking so rudely? Give me something to eat and drink and a cot for the night, then you can ask me." She seated him at the table, gave him food and drink, and set up a cot. Then she sat down at his head and said, "Where is God taking you?" "Mother, when I was little, my father rocked me in the cradle, promised me the Ineffable Beauty for my wife, daughter of three mothers, granddaughter of three grandmothers, the sister of nine brothers."

"You are right, brave young man," said the old woman,"you speak politely, answer reverently. The eighth decade I have lived to the end, but I have never heard of the Ineffable Beauty. Next on the way lives my oldest sister; maybe she knows about her. She has many who must give her information. The first to give their answer are the animals of the forest, the second the birds in the air, and the third are the fish and beasts of the sea. Everything in the wide world is her subject. Ride to her tomorrow. But now you should sleep, the morning is wiser than the evening."

Ivan Tsarevich slept one night. He got up early, washed himself white and clean, saddled his horse and fort he went. He rode far, far out, he rode up, up high. The day was getting shorter, night was approaching. There was a yard before him, as big as a city, with a hut as high as a tower. He rode into the yard, up to the steps. There he tied his horse to the golden ring. Then he stepped down the way to the hut. He prayed to God and asked for a night's lodging.

"Oh, you so and so," shouted the Baba Yaga, "you are worth an iron ringt, and to the golden one are you tying your horse?"

"That's right, Grandmother, do not scold. You can untie the horse and tie it to another ring."

"Well, young man, did the old one give you one? Fear not, sit on the bench, I want to ask you. Tell me where you came from, from which cities do you come? "

"Oh, my dear mother, first you should give me food and drink, then you may ask me. You see, I come from a long journey, and have not eaten all day. "

Immediately the old woman put down a table, brought salt and bread, poured brandy into the glass, and began to entertain the tsarevich. He ate and drank, threw himself on the couch, and told her everything. "When I was little, my father rocked me in the cradle, promised me the Ineffable Beauty for wife, daughter of three mothers, granddaughter of three grandmothers, sister of nine brothers. Tell me, mother -- do me the great favor – tell me - where lives the Ineffable Beauty and how can I get to her? "

"I do not know that myself, O tsarevich. My ninth decade is over, but I have never heard of this beauty. Now sleep with God!

Tomorrow morning I will call all my servants together, perhaps one of them knows."

The next day the old woman rose early, washed herself white and pure, and stepped over the threshold with the tsarevich. She called like a hero and whistled like a youth over the sea: "You fish and all beasts of the sea, gather here!" Immediately the blue sea began to roll and rock. The big and the small fish and all the animals of the deep gathered and covered the water to the shore. "Where lives the Ineffable Beauty, daughter of three mothers, granddaughter of three grandmothers, sister of nine brothers?" Then all the fish and all beasts of the water answered in one voice: "We never saw her with our eyes, we never heard of her with our ears."

Then the old woman called up to the sky, "Come together, birds in the air!" The birds came flying, covering the sky. "Where lives the Ineffable Beauty, daughter of three mothers, granddaughter of three grandmothers, sister of nine brothers?" "We never saw her with our eyes, never heard her with our ears."

"Now there's no one left to question," said the old woman, taking the tsarevich by the hand and leading him into the hut. As soon as they had entered, the Mogol bird came flying and fell to the ground. It was getting dark, and the lights went out in the windows. "O Mogol, bird of life, where have you been, where have you been flying, how have you been so late?"

"I have decorated the Ineffable Beauty for the Sacred Act."

"I need that now, Mogol Bird, do me a service, carry the tsarevich Ivan thither!"

"I will serve you gladly," replied the Mogol bird,"but it takes a lot of food. "

"How much do you need? "

"Three measures of meat, the measure of forty buckets, and a vat of water. " The tsarevich filled a vat with water. He bought cattle, slaughtered them and filled three measures with the meat and offered it to the bird. Then he went to the blacksmith and had made a long iron lance. Then he returned and took leave of the old woman: "Farewell, mother, feed my good horse, I will reward you for everything."

He sat down on the bird's back, and then the Mogol bird rose into the air and flew away. The bird flew and turned its head ceaselessly. As soon as he looked back, Ivan passed him a piece of meat on the spearhead. They flew for a while, two measures were fed, the third already started. Then the tsarevich said to the bird: "Mogol bird, let yourself fall on the damp earth, little remains for you to eat!"

"What a bad idea," said the bird, "down there are impenetrable forests and groundless marshes. We would suffer until the end of time." The tsarevich had fed all the meat and pushed down the empty barrels. The Mogol bird flew and turned for more food. "What should I do?" thought Ivan. He cut out his two calves and gave them to the bird. The bird devoured them - and flew to green meadows, to silky grasses, to blue flowers. He settled down on the ground. Ivan came down and moved his limbs, but he limped on both legs. "What's wrong, son of man, you are not limping?"

"Yes, Mogol bird, I am limping. I cut out my two calves and fed you. That's why I'm limping." The bird coughed out his calves, laid them on his legs where they had been, and spat on them. His calves grew back, and the tsarevich was again strong and vigorous as before.

He came to a great city. He stayed with an old woman from the outskirts to rest. She said to him, "Sleep, Ivan Tsarevich, at the first stroke of the morning bell I will wake you up!" The tsarevich lay down and fell asleep immediately.

He slept the rest of the day, he slept the night. The bells rang for the early morning service, the little mother comes running and starts to wake him up. She strikes him with everything that comes to her hands. But she does not manage to wake him. The early morning service was over; the bells rang for Mass. The Ineffable Beauty rode to the church. Again the old mother came running and begins to try to wake him up. With everything that comes to her hand, she strikes the sleepy head. At last, she woke him up. Ivan jumped up quickly, washed his clothes white and pure, dressed himself very well and went to the service. He entered the church, praying in front of the images of the saints, bowing in all four directions, and especially to the Ineffable Beauty. So they stood side by side praying to God. At the end of the service she was the first to step under the cross. He followed second behind her. Then he crossed the threshold and looked at the blue sea. There came six ships, six heroes came to free the princess. They beheld the tsarevich Ivan, and began to laugh: "You corpulent peasant, is such a beauty for you? You're not worth her little finger!" They said it once, they said it twice. When they said it for the third time, the tsarevich took offence. He waved one hand and opened an avenue through their ranks. He waved his other hand, and all around was swept clean.

He himself went back to the little woman in the outskirts. "Well, Ivan Tsarevich, have you seen the Ineffable Beauty?"

"I have seen her and will not forget her for all eternity!"

"Well, so go to sleep. Tomorrow she will go to Mass again. At the first stroke of the bell, I will wake you up."

The tsarevich lies down. He sleeps the day, he sleeps the night. The bells ring for early mass, and the old woman from the backyard comes running. She tries to wake him up with everything that comes to hand she beats him – but no, he does not wake up. The bells ring again for midday mass, and again she struck him and woke him. At last he sprang up, washed himself white and pure, threw himself into neat clothes, and ran to the church. He prayed to the images of the saints, bowed to all four directions, but especially to the Ineffable Beauty. She looked at him and blushed. So they stood side by side praying to God. At the end of the service, she stepped first under the cross, he followed second behind her. Then he crossed the threshold and looked at the blue sea. That's where ships come in. Twelve heroes come sailing up intending to free the Ineffable Beauty. They scoff at the tsarevich: "You crude farmer, is such a beauty for you? Not her little finger are you worth!"

Their words offended the tsarevich. He waved one hand and opened an avenue through their ranks. He waved his other hand, and all around was swept clean.

He himself went back to the little woman in the outskirts. "Well, Ivan Tsarevich, have you seen the Ineffable Beauty?"

"I have seen her and will not forget her for all eternity!"

"So sleep, I will wake you up tomorrow morning." The tsarevich lies down. He sleeps the day, he sleeps the night. As the bells ring for early mass, the old woman comes running to wake him up. She strikes and hits him without mercy, but he does not awake. She struggles until the bells ring for the midday mass, and finally she succeeds. Quickly the tsarevich jumped up, washed himself, dressed herself and hurried to the church. He prayed to the images of the saints and bowed in all four directions and especially to the ineffable beauty. She greeted him and put him on her right. She stood on the left. So they stood and prayed to God. This time, at the end of the service, he came first under the cross, and she followed second behind him. Then he crossed the threshold and looked at the blue sea. Ships have come, twenty-four heroes have come, they start to free the Ineffable Beauty. They ridicule the tsarevich: "You corpulent peasant, is such a beauty for you?" They surround the tsarevich, seeking to wrest the bride from him. The tsarevich could not stand it. He waved one hand and opened an avenue through their ranks. He waved his other hand, and all around was swept clean. He had killed them all to the last man.

The Ineffable Beauty took him by the hand and led him into her chambers. She sat him down at the oak tables with the patterned tablecloths. She entertained her guest, called him her bridegroom, and gave him rich hospitality. Then they set out to go to the kingdom of Ivan Tsarevich. They rode on and on. In the open field they stopped to rest. The Ineffable Beauty went to sleep, and Ivan Tsarevich watched over her.

When she had slept well and woken up again, the tsarevich said to her: "Ineffable Beauty, watch over my body, for I too want to sleep!"

"And how long will you sleep?"

"Nine days and nine nights will I not turn from one side to the other. Even if you want to wake me, you cannot. When the time comes, I wake up by myself."

"So long, tsarevich? I'll miss you!"

"Long or not, it must be like that!"

He lay down and slept exactly nine days and nine nights. During this time, however, the Immortal Boneman came and carried the Ineffable Beauty away to his kingdom. The tsarevich awoke from sleep, gazed around, and saw that the Ineffable Beauty was gone. He started to cry. Then he went on without a way or path. Whether it was long or not so long - he finally came into the realm of the Immortal Boneman.

There he asked an old woman to rest. "Why are you going along so sadly?" "Granny, that's the way it has gone. I've owned everything, I've lost everything."

"It looks bad for your cause, Ivan Tsarevich. You cannot kill the Boneman."

"At least I want to see my Bride, the Ineffable Beauty."

"Well, lie down and sleep; tomorrow the Boneman goes to war." Ivan Tsarevich lay down, but thought not of sleep. Early in the morning the Boneman went out into the courtyard. Ivan Tsarevich went into the courtyard, went to the house and knocked on the door. The Ineffable Beauty opened, looked out and cried. Then they went into the room, sat down at the table and started talking. And the tsarevich instructed her: "Ask the Immortal Boneman, where is your death?" "Good, I'll ask him."

Hardly had Ivan left the court when the Immortal Boneman came back. "Here it smells like a Russian bone, surely the tsarevich Ivan was with you!"

"What nonsense, Immortal Boneman! How should I see the tsarevich? He stayed behind in the dark woods, in the groundless swamps, and the wild beasts have certainly torn him to pieces." They sat down to supper. During the supper, the Ineffable Beauty asked, "Tell me, Immortal Boneman, where is your death?" "Do you need to know, you stupid woman? My death is in the bound brushwood broom."

Early in the morning the Boneman rode again into the war. The tsarevich came to the Ineffable Beauty, took the broom, and covered it with bright, pure gold. No sooner had the tsarevich gone than the Boneman came into the yard: "Ah, here it smells like a Russian bone, surely the tsarevich Ivan was with you!"

"What strange things come to your mind, immortal Boneman! You flew through Russia yourself, took the Russian spirit into yourself; you smell like the Russian spirit. How should I see the tsarevich? He stayed behind in the dark woods, in the groundless swamps; the wild beasts have certainly torn him to pieces in the meantime."

The time for supper came. The Ineffable Beauty sat down on a chair, the Boneman left her sitting on the bench. Then he looked to the threshold; there was the gilded broom. "What's that?" asked the Boneman. "Oh, immortal Boneman, you see how I honor you. Since you are dear to me, so also is your death."

"Foolish woman, I only joked; my death hangs out in the oak fence." Early in the morning the bone-man rode off. The tsarevich Ivan came and gilded the whole fence. In the evening the immortal Boneman returned: "Ah, here it smells like a Russian bone, surely the tsarevich Ivan was with you!"

"What strange things come to your mind, Immortal Boneman. Did not I tell you often enough? You yourself flew through Russia and took in the Russian spirit. You smell like Russian spirit! How should I see the tsarevich? He stayed back in the dark woods, in the groundless swamps. Surely the wild animals have long ago torn him apart."

They sat down to supper. The Ineffable Beauty sat down on the bench. She gave him the chair. The Boneman looked out the window. There stood the gilded fence, burning like fire. "What is that?"

"Immortal Boneman, you can see for yourself, as I honor you, since you are dear to me, so is also your death!" This speech pleased the Boneman: "Oh, you stupid woman, I have just joked. My death is in the egg. The egg is in the duckling, the duckling is in the root. and the root floats in the sea."

As soon as the Boneman had gone to war in the morning, the Ineffable Beauty brought good white bread to the tsarevich and told him where to look for the death of the Boneman. The tsarevich Ivan got up and walked. He wandered without a way until he came to the broad, wide sea. He no longer knew where to go. The bread had long since been consumed. There was nothing left to eat.

Suddenly a hawk flew by. Ivan Tsarevich aimed: "Now I have you, hawk, I'll shoot you down and eat you as you are!"

"Do not eat me, Ivan Tsarevich, in the right hour I will be useful to you!"

A bear came by. "Ah! You crooked-pawed Misha, I will kill you, and eat you as you are! "

"Do not eat me, Ivan Tsarevich, at the right hour I will be useful to you!"

"Look, there's a pike trembling on the shore!"

"Oh, you most splendid Pike, I'll eat you as you are!"

"Do not eat me, Ivan Tsarevich; throw me into the sea; at the right hour I'll be of use to you."

Then the tsarevich stood and thought to himself: When will the right hour come? - still I must suffer bitter hunger. Suddenly the blue sea rose, the water surged and poured over the shores. The tsarevich rushed up the mountain. He ran with all his might; but the water chased after him, up to his heels. At last he reached the summit and climbed a tree. After a while, the waters fell. The sea became silent and lay down. On the bank a big tree stump appeared. The bear came running, grabbed the root and struck it against the ground so that it broke apart. A white duckling flew out and swung up into the air. Suddenly the hawk appeared from somewhere, lunged at the duckling and tore it into two pieces. From the duckling the egg fell and fell into the middle of the sea. There the pike snapped it up, swam to the shore and brought it to the tsarevich. He hid the egg in his jacket and went to the Immortal Boneman. When he came into the yard, the Ineffable Beauty met him, kissed him on the mouth and leaned on his shoulder. But the Boneman sat at the window and threatened: "Ivan Tsarevich, if you want to take away the Ineffable Beauty, you are dead!"

"You yourself have taken her from me," replied the tsarevich. He took the egg out of his jacket and held it out to the Boneman.

"What's that?" The light of the day passed out of the Boneman. He fell silent and gave in. Ivan Tsarevich dropped the egg from one hand to the other, faster and faster. Then the Immortal Boneman collapsed and died.

The tsarevich found precious treasures in the house of the Boneman. He harnessed horses to a golden cart, took whole sacks of silver and gold, and drove home with his bride, the Ineffable Beauty, to his birth father. Whether it was long or not so long - they came to the same old woman who could question all the animals, the fish, the birds and the animals of the forest. When the tsarevich saw his horse again, he exclaimed: "God be praised, my black horse lives!" He showered the old woman with gold for the horse's food and care. And if she lived another ninety years, she will not consume it all.

Then he prepared a messenger and sent him with a letter to the king: "Father, come to meet your son, I come with my bride, the Ineffable Beauty!" His father received the letter, read it and barely trusted his eyes. How can that be, Ivan rode away when he was only nine days old! Behind the messenger came the tsarevich. The king saw that his son had written the truth, ran out to the open gate and told his servants to beat the drum and play music.

"Father, bless me for the wedding!" And since kings do not need to brew beer nor to make wine before a wedding, because they already have an abundance of everything, the wedding was celebrated on the same day with a merry feast, and the tsarevich Ivan was married to the Ineffable Beauty. There were big barrels of all sorts of drinks along the way, and anyone could come and drink as much as the soul demanded.

I went to that wedding and drank honey mead and wine. It flowed over my beard, but not into my mouth. But in my soul I became drunk and full.

## Interpretation

In this folktale an inner initiation is particularly clearly described. In nine days the spiritually born Johannine matures and begins the search for the Virgin Sophia. Dante lay for nine days in the mystic sleep and traveled through the spheres of the other world. For nine days Wotan hung on the tree and was rocked by the wind. The ethnologist Richard Karutz (1865 – 1945) reports that formerly there were "swing feasts" in which in the springtime young maidens were rocked above the fields of sprouting grain. Through swinging and rhythm one sought to bring cosmic forces down into the sprouting grain. To rock the king's son means to bring the I into connection with cosmic rhythms. But the nourishing and protecting soul forces alone cannot bring the I into that mystic sleep. That can be done only by the spiritual consciousness in Man.

The inexpressible beauty, Sophia, can look back on three mothers from whom she is born: the sentient soul, the intellectual soul, and the consciousness soul. But these have come from still older beings whom we experience in the threefold Baba Yaga. So this Virgin Sophia is the daughter of three mothers and the granddaughter of three grandmothers. And if we regard the spiritual forces that work in the nine-fold Man as brothers, then is she also as the encompassing, eternal consciousness also the sister of nine brothers. The way to her is long.

The understanding or intellect that serves the spiritual seeker – his horse – is so formed that it brings the whole soul world into motion. Nevertheless, he cannot bear him into that world "where the sun rises." He remains behind and nourishes himself, while the Johannine spirit begins his flight into the heights.

Mighty heroes fight for the possession of the sun-maiden. They arrive from the sea. They are seafarers. They have had the experience of the soul world, the seaway. Once the initiates were "seafarers". They lived in the element of a floating picture wisdom, which was not, however, attained through thinking. Only when the intellect and logical thinking developed did Man become a wanderer and rider. ("He walked and walked" … "he rode and rode" … "he made progress") These seafaring heroes call the spiritual seeker who laboriously works the earth (the hard ground of facts) "you corpulent peasant". But the peasant, the land-man is stronger. In three epochs he defeats the forces of the past, stands under the cross with the maiden – as once did John the Evangelist – and on the third day assumes the spiritual leadership.

But in the age of development of the consciousness soul, the Virgin Sophia cannot be won through inner merit and achievement [Hochflug] alone. For today Man is a citizen of the material sense world. The material world of the past has fallen out of the spiritual-creative world. As steam condenses to water and water, to ice, so is all matter thickening and hardening from the spiritual world. To regard the sense world as only material means experience it as a dead world, like a skeleton is the left-over remains of a once living being. A natural science that, for example, no longer recognizes the powerful creative forces but grasps only the result – what has been created – appeared to the wise ones who created the folktales as the realm of the boneman. And they could say, "The boneman has abducted living wisdom, the Virgin Sophia, to his realm." But to study the material world in such a way that the creative, spiritual forces are experienced and to know Man in such a way that his eternal, indestructible being is grasped means to rescue the Virgin Sophia from the realm of the boneman. There, in the realm of the dead, Man becomes awake.

"My death is in the brushwood broom," says the Boneman. But it is death he brings to others, not his own end, that lies in broom. The broom is made from branches that were once living but are now cut off from the living, green tree and have become dry and hardened in the broom on the doorstep. "My death is in the fence," he says further. Again, it is a death he brings to others. It is the death of limitation, that fences in blooming life, that restricts the free spirit, that denies that knowledge can transcend the limits of the physical world. But the Johannine spirit makes golden even what is dried and dead and transforms limitation into wisdom. "My death is in the egg" – is the egg not the picture of regenerating life, do not cosmic forces live in it? When Man has knows that in him there lives germ that never dies, then he has recognized his immortal I. When this I has become a being of unselfish love, and when it has grasped the law of "die and become" – then it has overcome death. It is a long road until this egg has been won.

"Do not eat me" say the hawk, bear, and pike. In other words, do not incorporate into yourself forces that can better serve you not embodied. These are the forces of the elementary realms, Air, Earth, and Water. Body-free forces help release those of the eternal spiritual consciousness.

In the concluding remark of the teller, the sentence "But in my soul I became drunk and full"[21] has been added from a another version of the same story (A 158) to share with the reader this unique expression. The whole concluding remark means, "I have experienced the mystery of the chymical wedding, but I have not been able to take it into my being. But from the secrets of death in this age of materialism I am drunken and full."

---

21  In Russian, "на душе пьяно и сытно стало."

# 6. The Maiden Tsar (A 233)

In some kingdom, in some state, once lived a Tsar with his Tsarina. They had a son, Vasily Tsarevich, and a servant was assigned to him.

The Tsarina died, and the Tsarevich became a half orphan. The Tsar considered for a long time whether the Tsarevich should marry or whether he himself should take a new wife. Finally he decided that he himself should marry again. He took a young woman, who was soon sole ruler in the house and to Vasily Tsarevich a bad stepmother. The Tsar lived with her for a while. Then he got sick and died. The Tsarina then became intimate with the servant of the tsarevich.

One day Vasiliy Tsarevich said to his servant, "Let's go for a walk along the city wall!" They went, walked back and forth, and went down the wall. Suddenly three voices called out of a stone tower: A lion, a dragon and a raven called to the Tsarevich: "Free us from captivity, Vasily Tsarevich, we will save you from three deaths!"

"Do you hear who calls us? What is happening at the city wall?"

"No, Vasily Tsarevich, I hear nothing."

"If you do not hear it, then you shall not hear it for all eternity!" and they returned home.

In the evening Vasily Tsarevich went to bed early and dismissed his servant. The servant was glad and hurried off to have fun with the stepmother. Vasily waited a while, got up quietly, took an iron staff weighing twenty-five poods, climbed out of the window and went back to the city wall. He struck the tower once and once more and smashed it. The lion, the dragon and the raven came forth, surrounded the Tsarevich and said: "Vasily Tsarevich, listen to what we tell you! When you still had your own father and mother, they looked for a bride for you for a long time. They found her behind the thrice-nine lands, in the thrice-tenth tsar's kingdom, and gave you free service for the queen; You shall not take another bride, and she will not marry another man. Now she has been waiting for you for twelve years. Take your gusli[22] tomorrow, board a ship and head out to the sea! When you are out on the sea and playing on the gusli, the princess will appear soon. But beware, if sleep overpowers you! You must not fall asleep! If you sleep, she cannot awaken you and must leave you again. And one more thing we say to you: beware, Tsarevich, tomorrow a death awaits you!"

"What death?"

"Your stepmother will make three cakes with snake grease and send them to you. Do not eat them, but put them in your pocket, in a short time you will recognize all the evil."

Said and done. The Tsarevich took the cakes, put them in his pocket and went down to the city wall. He reached into his pocket and pulled out a grass-snake, he reached for the second time and pulled out a poisonous snake, he reached for the third time and grabbed a frog.

"The lion, the dragon, and the raven spoke the truth, had I eaten the three cakes, it would have come to life inside me."

The Tsarevitch returned home, took the gusli and said to his servant: "Come on, we'll board a ship and head out to the open sea!" The servant hurried to the stepmother: "The Tsarevich wants to go out to sea and take his gusli with him!"

The tsarina said to him, "Here is a copper needle, stick it in the back of the neck of the tsarevich; then he will fall into a deep

---

[22] A gusli is a plucked stringed instrument similar to the psaltery. There are many different designs.

sleep from which nobody can awaken him, no matter whether they came on foot or in carriage!"

The servant took the needle and went with the Tsarevich to the harbor. They sat down in a ship and went out to the open sea, and Vasily Tsarevich began to play on the gusli. The Queen heard him playing from beyond the three times nine countries. She assembled six regiments, hurried to their fast ships, and sailed towards the Tsarevich. When they had come up to within three versts[23], the Tsarevich saw the white sails, pointed them out to his servant, and asked, "Whose ships are sailing there?"

"How should I know?" answered the servant, taking out the copper needle and sticking it into the back of the the neck of the tsarevich.

"Oh, how I feel so sleepy!" said the Tsarevich. He lay down in a hammock and fell fast asleep. The Maiden Tsar came, ordered a bridge laid from her ship to Vasily Tsarevich's ship, went to him and tried to wake him up. She kissed him and rocked him back and forth in the hammock. She spoke tender words to him. But no, she could not wake him. Finally she spoke to the servant: "Greetings from me to Vasily Tsarevich, tell him to go to sleep in the evening and not grieve over missing me; tomorrow I'll be back." With that she sailed away.

As soon as she had sailed a verst or two, and the servant saw that if called, she would not hear, if waved to, she would not see, he grasped the needle and pulled it out. Vasily Tsarevich awoke: "In the dream it seemed to me as if a bird fluttered around me and twittered so sadly that my heart is still heavy."

"No bird fluttered around you," answered the servant, "but the queen was herself here. She kissed and caressed you, she rocked you back and forth on the tarpaulin, but could not wake you up by ant means. When she left, she wished that you should go to sleep in

---

23  A *verst* is about 0.66 miles or 1.1 kilometer.

the evening, but get up early in the morning and sail out to the sea." They returned home, and the Tsarevich lay down, but he could not sleep with grief. In the morning he got up early, very early, and said to his servant, "Let's go down to the ship!"

The servant hurriedly told the evil stepmother that the Tsarevitch was going out to sea again with his gusli. "Here you have a second needle," said the Tsarina, "do with it the same thing you did yesterday!" The servant took the needle and went with his master to the harbor. They sat in the ship and sailed out to the sea. The Tsarevich played his gusli - he played so tenderly, so sweetly, that one can not describe it. The maiden heard his playing, it no longer held her, she jumped up and shouted in a loud voice: "Get up, you sailors, lift the iron anchors, tighten the light sails, and prepare yourself to rush towards the Tsarevich! We must be there early, before he falls asleep from which he can not be awakened." Their ships flew across the sea like light-winged birds. When they were three versts away, Vasily Tsarevich saw the white sails and asked his servant, "Whose ships are sailing there?"

"How should I know?" replied the servant, taking the needle and putting it in the back of the neck of the Tsarevich. Sleep descended on Vasily Tsarevich. He washed himself with cold water, wanted to stay awake at all costs, but it did not help, the brave youth could not hold out. He lay down on the deck and slept like a dead man. The maiden came up, had a bridge put from her ship to the ship of Vasily Tsarevich, went to him and began to try to wake him. She kissed him, rocked him in the hammock, but he slept and did not wake. She began to sprinkle him with cold water - but no, it does not help, he can not be awakened. Finally she wrote a letter, put it on the chest of the Tsarevich, returned to her ship, and sailed away. The letter said: "Farewell, Vasily Tsarevich, do not expect me a third time. He who loves me will find me himself."

When she was so far away that she could no longer be reached by voice, could no longer see a hand waving, the servant took the needle out. The Tsarevich awoke: "Again it seemed to me that a little bird was flying around!"

"It was not a bird," said the servant."It was the beautiful maiden herself who was around you. She stroked and kissed you, she rocked you in the hammock, she showered you with cold water, but she could not wake you up."

"And what's the letter on my chest?"

"She wrote that letter to you." The Tsarevich opened the letter, read it and cried bitter tears: "Now I see that the lion, the dragon and the raven were telling the truth, I should beware of sleeping. But one cannot escape his fate."

He sailed home in great sorrow, took his rifle in his hands, and went into the garden to deal with his grief. On his favorite apple tree sat a black raven. It croaked: "Krah, krah, Vasily Tsarevich, you did not listen to us, you could not stay awake, now complain about yourself."

Must I, thinks the Tsarevich, endure a bird scoffing at me? He lifted the rifle, squeezed the trigger and broke the raven's right wing. But then he felt even more miserable, and he ran out into the open field. He went and went and came to a horseherd, who was pasturing his steeds.

"God help you to feed the herd!" greeted Tsarevich.

"I wish you well, Vasily Tsarevich," answered the shepherd.

"How do you know me?"

"How could I not know you? For thirty years I have served as a horseherd with your father. My name is Ivashka-white-shirt-with-the-white- cap. I used to be a first voivode, but your father got angry with me and put me among the herdsmen."

"Ivashka-white-shirt-with-the-white- cap, do you not know a good horse for me? If you choose a good horse for me, I will not forget you for all eternity, and if I am here again, I will make you the first voivode again."

"How can I choose a horse for you when I do not know your strength? Here is a willow bush, try to pull it out by the roots!"

Vasily Tsarevich grabbed the willow bush and tore it out by the roots. Under the bush was a hero's armor, sword, lance and shield, and armor for the horse. The bridle weighed three poods[24], the saddle twenty-five poods, the lance one hundred and fifty poods.

"Well, Tsarevich, wait for me here," said Ivashka White-shirt, "tomorrow morning I will drive the horses back here. A mare will run in front and behind her a stallion. They will plunge into the water and swim far, far. When the sun passes it highest point at noon and the heat decreases, the stallion will chase the mare onto green meadows. Then be careful and do not be idle: As soon as the stallion comes to shore, hit him with the lance between the ears!"

Said, done. The next morning Vasily Tsarevich waited for the right hour and struck the stallion with his lance between the ears. Then the stallion fell to his knees, and the young man put on the bridle of three poods and the Tscherkassian saddle[25] and mounted him. When the stallion had recovered from the mighty blow - oh, how he carried the Tsarevich and flew with him through meadows and valleys and over the high mountains! For three days and three nights he carried him without rest, and no sweat, but red blood dripped down on him.

Then the horse spoke in a human voice: "Hey, you, Vasily Tsarevich, release me, let me run three times in the morning. I want to bathe in the blue sea, to roll in the dew, then I will be your faithful servant." The tsarevich let the horse run. It ran around for three days and returned more strong and beautiful than you have

---
24  A pood is about 36.1 pounds.
25  A Tscherkassian saddle is a soft, round cushion with stirrups.

ever seen. Vasily Tsarevich mounted the horse and rode past the thrice ninth country into the thrice-tenth realm. Whether he rode long or not so long, we do not know. He came to the kingdom of the lion. In a loud voice the lion-tsar cried: "Come, my seven little children, bring me the iron pitchforks, put them under my old eyelids and let me see the brave youth!" He saw him, recognized him and was very happy. "I wish you well, Vasily Tsarevich, you have done me a great service, now be with me as guest as long as you want." He gave him food and drink and had a bed prepared for him. The next morning he equipped him for the journey.

The Tsarevich rode and rode and came to the kingdom of the dragon. The dragon-tsar received him kindly and dismissed him lovingly.

The Tsarevich rode on and entered the kingdom of the raven. The Raven tsar came to meet him and said: "Good youth, why have you broken my brother's wing? I should have your head cut off for that. But I will let you pay for it with fear of death!" He grabbed the youth, took off, flew out over the blue sea, soared up high and dropped him right where it was deepest. Vasily Tsarevich plunged to the bottom, but rose again. As soon as he came up, the raven tsar took him and brought him to land."Now ride where you must go!"

The Tsarevich mounted his horse and continued on his way. Then the good horse spoke in a human voice: "Hold on tight, tsarevich. You must ride faster. In three hours and three minutes we have to be in the thrice-tenth reign. There is Ivan, a Russian bogatir. He has a patched face, a plaited nose, a quilted tongue, his feet are calf's feet, his ears are dog ears. If we have not arrived in three hours and three minutes, then he will take the Maiden Tsar for himself."

Vasily Tsarevich rode to the thrice-tenth kingdom of the tsars. Like lightening he flashed past Ivan the bogatir. They rode twenty versts apart, then stormed against each other, beating each other with butcher's clubs. The noise rumbled like thunder. They fought and fought, but neither gained the upper hand. Finally, they tired and arranged a truce for three days. Vasily Tsarevich opened his tent, lay down to rest, and fell fast asleep. When the third night had passed, he was still asleep. The brave horse went to wake him up."Wake up, wake up, Vasily Tsarevich! Now is no time to sleep, you must get up and fight with Ivan, the Russian bogatir."

They rode thirty versts apart. They spurred their horses, clashing and beating each other, but neither defeated the other. Then they made another truce for three days. The Tsarevich lay down again in the tent and fell asleep. At the end of the third day the good horse woke him."Wake up, wake up, Vasily Tsarevich, you have slept enough, you must get up and cut off the Russian bogatir's head!"

Vasily jumped up, quickly saddled his horse, pulled on the straps - not to encourage himself, but to sit more firmly in the saddle - and rode off. Below him, the horse danced. Then Ivan, the Russian bogatir, rode. The horse cried beneath him. They lined up at fifty versts and spurred their steeds. When they hit each other, the whole earth quaked. Ivan, the Russian bogatir, made a mighty stab, but missed and lost his lance, which stuck three fathoms into the earth. Vasily Tsarevich charged his horse straight against the chest of Ivan, threw him backwards onto the naked earth, and cut off his wild head.

"Now the way is no longer denied me! I want to fetch the gusli and play in the Maiden Tsar's garden."

He took the gusli and went into the garden. He played so tenderly and so sweetly that you can not describe it. The Maiden Tsar heard him playing play. She called her maids and maidens, gave them the portrait of Tsarevich and sent them to her favorite garden: "Run like the wind and see if Vasily Tsarevich has come, see if he plays in the garden on the gusli!" The nurses and guards went running down, looked at him, compared him with the portrait and returned again. "Oh, no, it's not Vasiliy Tsarevich who plays the gusli, though he looks like him. Vasiliy Tsarevich is much nicer!"

The Maiden Tsar replies, "Oh, you foolish ones, the Tsarevich is exhausted. He does not resemble his image!" She hurried down to the garden and recognized her bridegroom. She took him by the hands and led him into her high rooms. Then the wedding was celebrated. Then they went home to the kingdom of Vasily Tsarevich. The Tsarevich had the wicked stepmother and his servant killed at the gates of the city. Then he started to live with his young wife, and they lived and prospered many a year[26].

## Interpretation

Vasily (corresponding to Basil in English) is the representative of the Age of the Sentient Soul. He must deal with that soul being that has lost connection with the living spirit and has turned to the earthly-material – the step mother. Moreover, he must deal with his own lower self, the body servant.

Three mighty instinctive forces that up until them had been walled in inside his being are made free by the iron staff of the I-conscious will. They point to the higher, eternal soul which wants to unite with the human spirit. "Go out to sea and play on the gusli!" they say, that is, form a consciousness that is beyond the sense-bound one; let harmony and rhythm work in you. But a prick with a copper needle puts the sentient soul, the lower self, in charge at just the moment when the greatest spiritual wakefulness is needed, and the higher soul disappears,

The German folktales like to tell how the hero forgets the maiden of his true destiny because he lets himself be kissed on the

---

[26] Many tales that do not end with a wedding feast end with the rather materialistic rhyme "стал жить-поживать, добра наживать," "began to live – live-up, wealth pile up." I have softened it as above.

right cheek by the stay-at-home. The German is always in danger of forgetting his ideal when he meets old, conservative forces. His right side – the action side – is too much emphasized; from excessive action he forgets his eternal purpose. In the Russian stories, the danger is sleep – that is, to want to remain passive when active wakefulness is called for. The Slavic soul is deeply penetrated by piety, but it must constantly work to transform itself through active spiritual knowledge.

Vasily must make his way to the Maiden Tsar "on land" and "by horse". The keeper of the horses – which is to say, of the forces for understanding necessary the challenge ahead – is Ivashka-white-shirt-with-the-white- cap. In this long name is hidden a reference to a caul birth[27] in which part of the amniotic sac is still over the face. The German word for the caul is *Glückshaube,* good-luck cap for it allows the pre-birth cosmic forces to work a little longer into the child. With this name the herdsman characterizes himself as a Johannine being gifted with thinking that is still cosmic. From him Vasily gets understanding (a horse) that rises out of the world-wide soul element and in its direction is sun-related. One who can exercise this kind of thinking can experience those instinctive forces that were formerly walled-in but now operate freely as mighty forces for advancing knowledge.

As Vasily Tsarevich approaches his goal – as the spirit seeker reaches the threshold of the spiritual world – he encounters the distorted image of himself,[28] Ivan, a Russian bogatir. He has a face patched together – not developed through organic growth – his

---

27  A caul is a piece of membrane that can cover a newborn's head and face. Birth with a caul is rare, occurring in fewer than 1 in 80,000 births. The caul is harmless and is immediately removed by the physician or midwife upon delivery of the child. – Wikipedia

28  Students of Rudolf Steiner's *Knowledge of Higher World's and its Attainment* will recognize in Ivan the Russian Bogatir the Lesser Guardian of the Threshold.

quilted tongue can speak no consistent truth; his feet, his relation to the earth, are the feet of an animal, between his ears lives dog-like thinking, cynicism and spying. Everything that is base in his own nature Vasily must be reognized and overcome. And that applies to both the individual and the folk. Indeed, the leading spirit of a folk must stand on the threshold of self knowledge before it can unite with the folk soul. When we need a caricature of the German, we speak of "deutschen Michel." The name is a last reference to that spiritual power that was revered in many pictures and holy places as the leading spirit of the Germanic folk: the Archangel Michael. The caricature of the Russian spirit is this bad Ivan. He also has a mighty Intelligence (horse) at his command. The conflict is apocalyptic – the whole earth trembles. Finally, Ivan looses his spear, and Vasily charges his horse against the other horse, knocks Ivan to the ground and cuts off his head. Thus it is superior strength of the horse Vasily received from Ivashka with the white cap that is decisive. Now on a higher plane can Vasily play upon the inner harp and unite with the soul who has remained faithful to him through all conflicts.

# 7. The Tale of Ivan-Bogatir, the Peasant's Son (A 571)

(The tale is also called "I don't know."

In a village there once lived a not-so- rich farmer with his wife. For three years they did not have a child. In the fourth year the woman gave birth to a son to whom they gave the name Ivan. When the boy was five years old, he still could not walk and always sat. Father and mother were sad and prayed to God that he would give their son healthy feet. But as much as they prayed, the boy could not walk and sat for thirty and three years.

One day the farmer and his wife went to church for a midday service. At the same time a beggar came to the window of the hut and begged Ivan, the peasant's son, for alms. Ivan, the peasant's son, replied, "I would like to give you something, but I can not get up from the spot." Then the beggar said to him, "Get up and give me alms, your feet are healthy and healed!" Ivan, the peasant's son, immediately got up from his seat and was indescribably glad, for his feet were healthy and had no more damage. He called the beggar into the hut and gave him food. Then the old man asked him for a drink of honey mead. But the beggar did not drink, but urged Ivan himself to empty the full cup. And Ivan drank it down to the bottom. Then the beggar asked him: "Well, Ivan, how much strength do you feel in you now?"

"Very much," answered Ivan, the peasant's son.

"Farewell, then," said the beggar, and disappeared. Ivan, the peasant's son, remained in great wonder.

When father and mother came home and saw that their son was healthy, they were very surprised and asked him how he was cured of his illness. Ivan told them, and the parents said that it was not a beggar who had healed him of all suffering, but a holy man. And they rejoiced and celebrated a feast.

Ivan, the peasant's son, wanted to test his strength. He went out into the cabbage garden, grabbed a fence post, pushed it into the middle of the garden, and turned it around so that the whole village turned around. Then he came back to the hut and asked the parents for their blessing, because he wanted to say goodbye to them. The old folks began to cry bitterly and begged him to stay at least a little while longer. But Ivan did not pay attention to their tears and said: "If you do not let me go, then I have to go by myself." Then the parents gave him their blessing. Ivan prayed, bowed in all four directions, and bid farewell to his father and mother. Then he left the farmyard, turned to the right, went where his eyes looked, and walked exactly ten days and ten nights until he came to another kingdom.

No sooner had he entered this kingdom than a great noise and a dreadful din rose. The king of the country was so alarmed that he offered anyone who could silence the noise his daughter as his wife and half of the empire as a dowry. When Ivan heard this, he went to the royal court and announced that he wanted to eliminate the noise. The guard went to the king and reported it. The king immediately summoned Ivan the peasant's son and said to him, "My friend, is it true what you have told the gatekeeper?"

"Yes, it is true, I have prided myself on it," replied Ivan, the peasant's son, "and I ask nothing more than that you give me what is causing this noise."

Then the king smiled and said: "I will gladly give it to you, take it if you want it!"

Ivan, the peasant's son, bowed to the king and went out. He came to the gatekeeper and asked for a hundred workers from him. The gatekeeper gave them to him. Ivan led them to the castle and ordered them to dig into the earth. When the workers opened the earth, they saw an iron trap door with a copper ring. Ivan opened the door with one hand, broke it and threw it away. In the ground stood a hero's horse with bridle and saddle, and a full knight's armor was hanging there. The horse saw a worthy horseman, dropped to his knees and spoke in a human voice: "Greetings, you brave young man, Ivan peasant's son! The strong and brave hero Lukopero put me here. I have been waiting here for you for thirty and three years with all my strength. Mount me and ride wherever you must go. I will serve you in faith and in the truth, as I have served the strong hero Lukopyoro."[29]

Then Ivan, the peasant's son, saddled his good steed, gave him a tight bridle, laid on him the Chkassian saddle, and fastened to him twelve straps of Persian silk. He mounted the horse, urged him on in the flank, and the horse rose up. It climbed high, higher than the forest, just lower than the passing clouds. Mountains and valleys went past beneath its feet, and its tail swept across the great rivers. From his ears came thick smoke, from the nostrils blazed fire flames. Ivan, the peasant's son, came to strange, unknown land. He rode for thirty days and thirty nights and arrived in the Chinese Empire. Here he dismounted from his good steed and let it run out into the open field. He himself went into the city, got a hat[30], pulled it over his head and went to the royal court. People asked him from where he came, what kind of man he was and who his father and

---

29  The "yo" is Russian ё, pronounced like yo in "yolk" and always accented.
30  The Russian word for what he bought is пузырь (puzyr) which normally means a bubble or blister. Friedel Lenz translated it into German as *Blase*, which means a bladder or bubble. It is derived from пузо (puzo) meaning *belly* or *paunch*. Russian woodcuts show Ivan wearing an enormous, balloon-like headdress. But throughout the story, when wearing the пузырь Ivan wants to remain inconspicuous. Near the end, it emerges that he has golden hair and is wearing the пузырь to hide it. He clearly did not want to draw attention to his head. I conclude that he bought a simple hat perhaps made from the stomach of an animal but perhaps not. Accordingly, I have translated the пузырь simply as *hat*.

mother were. But he replied to all their questions only: "I do not know."

Then all thought him a fool and told the Chinese king. The king had him called to him and asked him who he was, what he called himself and where he came from. But he also answered the king: "I do not know." The king wanted to have him chased from the court, but the gardener asked that he give him the fool to help him in the garden. The gardener led him into the royal garden, told him to cleanse the garden, and when he had given the order, he went away. Ivan, the peasant's son, lay down under a tree and slept , In the night he awoke and broke all the trees in the garden. In the morning the gardener came, was startled, began scolding, and asked the peasant's son who had broken the trees. Ivan, the peasant's son, only answered again and again, "I do not know."

The gardener was afraid to report it to the king, but the princess looked out the window, wondering, and asked the gardener who had broken all the trees. The gardener replied, "The I-don't-know" broke off these precious trees."

He asked her not to say anything about it to her father and promised to repair the garden better than it had been in the shortest possible time The next night "I-don't-know" did not sleep at all but all night carried water from the well and watered the broken trees. In the morning they began to grow, and when the sun appeared, they grew out and became more beautiful than before. When the gardener came into the garden, he was astonished at the beauty, but he did not ask a question because he never got an answer. As soon as the princess had got up from her bed, she looked into the garden and saw how beautiful he was. She summoned the gardener and asked him how it had happened. The gardener replied that he could not understand it himself. But the king's daughter realized that great wisdom was in the fool. She began to love him, loved him more than herself, and sent him food from her table.

The Chinese king had three daughters of great beauty. The oldest was Duasa, the middle Siasa, the youngest, whom Ivan, the peasant's son, loved, was called Laota. The king called his daughters to him and said to them: "Dear daughters, beautiful royal daughters, the time has come for your wedding! I called you to tell you this. Choose princes for grooms who please you!"

The two older sisters chose two sons of kings, but the youngest began in tears to implore her father to give her "I don't know" for a bridegroom.

The king, when he heard this, was much astonished and said: "Are you out of your mind, my daughter, that you want to marry the fool I-don't-know who does not even know how to speak?"

"If he does not, then I'm a fool too, for I love him! "said the princess. "I beg you, Father, give me to him as a wife!"

"If you will have no one else," said the king sadly, "so be it. Go and take him."

Soon thereafter, the king sent messasges to the princes whom the elder daughters had chosen. As soon as they received the invitation, these princes hurriedly came to China and were married to the royal daughters. Likewise, the princess Laota was married to Ivan, the peasant's son. But her older sisters laughed that she had taken a fool for a husband.

After some time a large army invaded the Chinese empire. The mighty warrior Polkan spearheaded it. He demanded the king's dearest daughter, Laota, as his wife, and threatened to devastate the whole kingdom with fire, to slay the army with the sword, to throw the king and queen into prison, and to take the king's daughter by force. When the king heard such threats, he was alarmed and ordered to summon his whole army for defense. The assembled army confronted the mighty Polkan, and the royal sons led the way. Like two terrible storm clouds, the two armies began to fight.

Polkan defeated the Chinese army. So the king's daughter Laota went to her husband, Ivan, the peasant's son, and said to him: "My dear husband, I do not know what to do. Polkan, the infidel, invaded our kingdom, defeated our army with his stormy sword, and now wants to take me from you."

Ivan, the peasant's son, sent her away, jumped out of the window, ran into the open field, and shouted in a mighty voice:

Sivka burka, heh!
Come and stand without delay
We must charge into the fray!

Then his horse jumped, the earth trembled, the flames leaped out of his nostrils, and thick smoke rose from his ears. Ivan the peasant's son crept into his ear, ate and drank, and adorned himself, came out of the other ear, and was clad in a brightly colored coat, and became such a beautiful, brave youth that one can not describe it with the pen nor tell it in a folktale. He mounted his horse and rode towards the army of Polkan. With his sword he felled the whole army and drove it out of the realm. The Chinese king rode up, and because he did not know him, he invited him to the castle. Ivan, the peasant's son, replied, "I am not your servant, and I do not serve you." As he spoke these words, he rode off, letting his horse run into the open field, went back to the castle, and crept back in through the window. He pulled the hat over his head and went to sleep. But the king celebrated a great feast.

It was not long before Polkan again invaded the kingdom and demanded the king's youngest daughter, the beautiful Laota, as his wife. The king immediately ordered the army to be collected, and sent it out to fight against Polkan, but Polkan defeated the army. Then Laota rushed to her husband and said, "Polkan wants to steal me."

Ivan, the peasant's son, sent her away, jumped out of the window, hurried into the open field, calling his steed in a loud voice:

Sivka burka, heh!
Come and stand without delay
We must charge into the fray!

He mounted his steed, rode against the enemy, and struck him the sword and chased him out of the kingdom. The king came to thank and invite him to his castle. But Ivan the peasant's son rode away. He let his horse run into the field, returned home and went to sleep. Again the king celebrated the victory, not knowing who the hero was who had protected his kingdom.

After some time Polkan invaded the kingdom with his army for the third time, and demanded the king's daughter Laota to wife under dreadful threats. Again the king ordered an army to be collected and sent out against Polkan. When the battle broke out and Polkan began to beat the Chinese power, the king's daughter Laota hastened to her husband and told him in tears that Polkan wanted to take her from him. Ivan, the peasant's son, hurried away, jumped out the window, and ran into the open field. He called his horse in a powerful voice, mounted him and rode towards Polkan. Then the horse spoke in a human voice: "Ivan peasant's son, you and I are being asked a heavy duty today. Propel yourself with all your strength and stand firm before Polkan, otherwise you will perish with all the Chinese army!

Ivan, the peasant's son, spurred his horse, rode towards Polkan's army, and began to fight. When Polkan saw that his army had been defeated, he fell into terrible wrath and fell upon Ivan, the peasant's son, like a fierce lion. They fought and fought, the two mighty heroes, that the whole army was amazed. Finally, Polkan wounded Ivan, the peasant's son, on the left hand. Ivan, the peasant's son, became angry, seized his pointed lance, aimed at

Polkan, and pierced his heart. Then he cut off his head and drove the rest of the army out of China.

The Chinese king bowed to Ivan and invited him into his castle. The king's daughter Laota saw blood on his left hand, tied him with her cloth and also invited him to the castle. But Ivan, the peasant's son, did not listen to her and trotted off. He let his horse run out into the field, went home and went to sleep. The king again ordered a large festival. At the same time, on the orders of the father, the princess Laota went to her husband to wake him, but could not raise him by any means. Then suddenly she saw golden hair on his head, from which the hat had fallen off, and was very amazed. As she came closer she saw on his left hand the cloth with which she had bandaged the wound of the victor. And now she realized that it was he who had defeated Polkan three times and killed him at last. She ran quickly to her father, led him to her husband, and said, "See, Father, you said I had married a fool, but I see his golden hair, and I recognize the wound he sustained in the battle with Polkan!' The king then realized that it had been Ivan who had liberated his kingdom three times from the invasion of Polkan. and when Ivan, the peasant's son, awoke, the king took him by his hands, led him into his chambers, thanked him for his deliverance, and set his own crown upon his head. Ivan, the peasant's son, ascended the throne, now reigned in China and lived with his wife in love and peace. And they ended their lives in joy and happiness

Interpretation

This folktale was published already in 1831 by A. Dietrich in Leipzig in a collection of Russian folktales for which Jakob Grimm wrote the preface. The translator, who had been active in Russia as a jurist, had found it in one those printed sheets with illustrations then commonly sold in Russia. The pictures show Polkan as a centaur. The editor commented, "He was horse below and man above."

Just as the horse is the picture for the instinctive intellect so is the centaur an imagination for the condition before this instinct was mastered and bridled by the I but was itself the master. Man is still haunted by this dull instinct that hides within. The mother of the centaur race was a wolf. The centaurs represent a soul consciousness that was still mobile, fleeting, pictorial like the wolf itself. They represent a transitional stage between picture consciousness and intellectual consciousness. Originally, this consciousness still had nature wisdom, as shown by Chiron the wise centaur. But with the beginning of self-consciousness there was the danger that it would turn wildly passionate and egotistical. Man must grow beyond the half-horse, half-man stage to a become the all-man master and rider of the horse. The civilized peoples of southern, coastal Greece regarded the wild mountain people of the north as centaurs, something true, of course, only of their inner nature. The Greeks, who experienced the birth of the consciousness soul as the great event of their culture often represented themselves pictorially in conflict with the centaurs.[31] On the west pediment of the Olympia temple of Zeus the wedding of the Lapith king is depicted. The centaurs break in to carry off the bride. Behind the king stands protectively Theseus, the founder of Greek culture. The bride was Hippodameia (Horse Tamer). Here, at the site of the Olympic games, sounded the warning call to the Greek people: Be awake! Master and bridle your mind! Develop the intellectual soul!

In our folktale, the same struggle is depicted. When the young spiritual impulse is born, it cannot yet set out upon its life's journey (it cannot use its feet). In a hidden realm that one must first explore awaits in the depths a special intellect. Lukopyoro (the archer) – a

---

31  The best preserved of the metopes running around the outside of the Parthenon show men fighting centaurs. These have been reproduced and are easily seen in the full-scale reproduction of the Parthenon in Nashville. In the original, each metope was different, but because many of the originals have been lost, the reproduction repeats each metope several times.

force that gives aim and objective – has put it there. Only one who enters this realm – this realm that causes loud noise and violent shaking – and has Will stronger than iron can penetrate with thinking forces to this earth-shaking intellect (the horse) – but he needs as a handle the copper ring of devout feeling forces. Winning this intellect means at the same time to be "armed" with knightly virtue. He can, as if with spiritual wings, lift himself above the earthly.

The Johannine impulse must still long remain hidden, like the embryonic fruit in the ovary of the flower. Not yet knowing his own aim, he must, like Parzifal, go through the stage of the fool. But as a gardener, he can care for the life forces of inner growth. The consciousness soul recognizes his worth, loves him as he is, veiled and uncertain, and unites herself with him. He still sleeps a lot.

Called to battle, he goes through the window like a thief, for his time has not yet come. The great gray horse has now become reddish brown (Siva-burka). In his inner fire, Ivan is transformed into a hero. He is given food and drink and clothed with a new soul sheath. So can he conquer the centaur's might through the force of his understanding. When, after his third attack, Polkan is killed, Ivan has golden hair; his thinking is filled with radiant wisdom. He can throw off the hat and reveal his true identity. He becomes king in the inner realm and a kingly, leading spiritual impulse in the folk and mankind.

*Polkan as Centaur. Note Ivan in his "puzir" in the top panel. Illustration from the Nauka edition of Afanasyev.*

# 8. Sivka Burka and the Simpleton (A 182)[32]

Once upon a time there was an old man and an old woman. They had three sons. Two were clever and sensible, but the third was simple-minded. The time came for the father and mother to die, but before his death the father said to his sons: "My dear children, when I die, go and sit by my grave for three nights!"

When he had died, the sons cast lots to see who would first sit by the grave, and it fell on the simpleton to go to the grave. At midnight, his father came out and asked, "Who is there?"

"I, father, the simpleton."

"Sit, my son, the Lord be with you!"

On the second night, the eldest brother remembered to watch over the grave. But he begged the simpleton: "Go, simple-minded one, sit for me tonight over there, take for it what you want!"

"You can easily say that, but there the dead jump around."

"Just go, I'll buy you red boots!"

The simpleton could not refuse and spent the second night at the grave. As he sat, the earth opened, his father came out and asked, "Who is sitting there?"

"I, father, the simpleton."

"Sit, my son, the Lord be with you!"

On the third night the middle brother had to go to the grave. He too asked the simpleton: "Do me the favor and sit for me. Take for it what you want!"

---

32 The Russian titled translates as "The Gold-bristled Pig, the Gold-feathered Duck, and the Horse with the Golden Mane", but as these animals play a small role, I have used a more descriptive title.

"You can easily say go! The first night was terrible, the second even more terrible. The dead are shouting and screaming and a fever shakes me."

"Just go, I'll buy you a red cap!"

There was nothing to be done, the simpleton had to keep watch for the third night. Suddenly the earth opened and the father came out. "Who's there?"

"I, the simpleton."

"Sit, my son, the Lord be with you! Here you have my great blessing!" And he gave him three horsehairs.

The simpleton went to the green pasture, pressed the three hairs, and exclaimed in a ringing voice:

Sivka Burka, stallion dear,
Father's blessing, come now here.
Stand straight and tall as you are made,
Like on the grass stands the blade.

Sivka Burka, the gray stallion, arrived. Fire flamed from his mouth; from his ears rose a column of smoke. The horse stood silent in front of him tall and straight like the blade on the grass. The simpleton crawled into his left ear and ate and drank his fill. He crept into his right ear, adorned himself with a colorful garment, and became such a capable fellow as one cannot imagine, cannot guess, and cannot describe with the pen.

On the following day the Tsar made a pronouncement: "To whomever can fly with his horse to the third floor of my palace and kiss my daughter Milolika (fair-haired), I will give her as wife!"

The older brothers got ready to watch and called, "Come with us, simpleton!"

"No, I do not want to. I will go into the open field and fill a basket with crows for the dogs' food."

He went into the open field, pressing the three horsehairs and shouting:

Sivka Burka, stallion dear,
Father's blessing, come now here.
Stand straight and tall like you are made,
As on the grass stands the blade.

Sivka Burka, the dear gray stallion, arrived. Fire spurted from his mouth, a column of smoke rose from his ears. The horse stood in front of the simpleton tall and straight like the blade on the grass. The simpleton crawled into his left ear and ate and drank. Then he crawled into his right ear, adorned himself with a colorful garment and became more handsome than one can imagine or describe with the pen. The simpleton got on Siva Burka, waved his hand, kicked his foot and rode off.

The horse runs over hill and dale. When it rises, the earth trembles. His tail sweeps the mountains and valleys. In the court of the Tsar the horse jumped up to the first floor. Then it ran back to the fields.

When the brothers returned home, the simpleton was lying on the loft above the stove.[33] "Oh, you stupid fellow, why did not you go with us? A young man was there, so beautiful as you cannot imagine, cannot guess, and cannot describe with the pen."

"Was it not me, me, the simpleton?"

"You? How should you win such a horse? Wipe your dripping nose!"

The next morning the brothers got ready to watch the Tsar's court again. "Come with us, simple-minded one!" they called to

---

33  Russian homes, from the simplest to the most elegant, usually had a large ceramic stove. A small fire in the stove would warm the bricks of the stove which then radiated gentle warmth into the room. The best place to sleep was on the stove.

the youngest. "There was a handsome guy there yesterday; today an even more handsome one will come."

"No, I do not want to. I'll go to the field to kill crows to feed the dogs." He went to the open field, pressed the three horsehairs and called:

Sivka Burka, stallion dear,
Father's blessing, come now here.
Stand straight and tall lile you are made,
As on the grass stands the blade.

Sivka Burka, the big gray stallion, arrived. Fire spurted from his mouth, a column of smoke rose from his ears. The horse stopped in front of the simpleton, stood tall and straight like the blade on the grass. The simpleton crawled into his left ear and ate and drank his fill. Then he crawled into his right ear, adorned himself with a colorful garment and became as beautiful as you can not imagine, can not guess and can not describe with the pen. He got on horseback, waved his hand, kicked his foot, and dashed for the Tsar's court. There he flew over two floors, but not up to the third. Then he returned, leaving his horse in the green, protected pasture, went home and lay down on the stove. The brothers came in: "Oh, you stupid one, you should have gone with us! Yesterday came a nice guy, today he was even more beautiful. Where was such beauty born?"

"Well, was it not me, the simpleton?"

"The fool is talking foolishly! You stupid simpleton, from where would you get such beauty, from where win such a horse? Are you not always just lying on the stove?"

"Well, if it was not me, you might know tomorrow who it was."

On the third morning, the bright brothers got ready to go back to the tsar. "Simple-minded, come with us, today he will kiss her!"

"No, I do not want to, I will go to the field, kill crows and bring them home to the dogs for food." He went into the open field, pressed the three horsehairs and cried out in a ringing voice,

Sivka Burka, stallion dear,
Father's blessing, come now here.
Stand straight and tall like you are made,
As on the grass stands the blade.

He mounted the horse, waved his hand, kicked his foot, and flew up up to the third floor. He kissed the Tsar's daughter's mouth, and she slapped him on the forehead with her gold signet ring. Then he turned around, left his horse on the green fields and went home. He tied his head with a cloth and lay down on the loft.

The brothers came in: "Oh, you simpleton, those fellows yesterday were beautiful, but today was the most beautiful, where can such beauty be born?"

"Was not it me, me, the simpleton?"

"Ah, the foolish one screams foolishly! You stupid fool, from where should you get such beauty?" Then the simpleton untied the cloth, and the whole house shone.

"Where have you won this beauty?" cried the brothers.

"Wherever it was, I won it. You never believed me. But your fool was there."

The next day the Tsar gave a feast for the whole orthodox world. He commanded to invite the boyars and princes to court, old and young, high and low, husband and wife. The princess will choose her groom.

The wise brothers also made themselves ready for the banquet. The simpleton bandaged his head with a cloth and said:,"Today you do not need to call me, I will go by myself."

He came to the Tsar's palace and stood behind the stove. The Tsar's daughter served wine to all the guests to discover the bridegroom, and the Tsar walked behind her. When she had already served everyone else, she saw the simpleton behind the stove. His forehead was bandaged with a cloth, saliva drooled down from his mouth, and his nose dripped. Tsarevna Milolika brought him out, dried him with her cloth, kissed him, and said, "Lord, my father, here is my destined husband!"

The Tsar saw that the bridegroom had been found, and though he was a simple-minded one, he kept his word, for a tsar's word is law. He immediately had the two of them married, and since everyone knows that a tsar has plenty of beer and make wine on hand, they could quickly hold the wedding.

* * *

The Tsar already had two sons-in-law, so the simpleton became the third. Once the tsar called his wise sons-in-law and said: "My wise, my very wise sons-in-law, do me a service! In the steppe is a gold-feathered duckling. Can you give it to me?" And he ordered them to saddle up the good horses and ride out after the duckling. The simple-minded listened to this and began to ask, "Father, give me a horse, even if it is good only for hauling water!"

The Tsar gave him a miserable little horse. The simpleton climbed on it, sat down with his face to the rump, took the tail between his teeth and hit him with the flat hands on the flanks: "Hop, hop, hop, run, dog, in a canter!"

He rode into the open field, grabbed the nag by the tail, pulled off its skin and shouted: "Fly over here, you jackdaws, crows and magpies, father has sent you food!" The jackdaws, crows and magpies flew up and ate all the meat. Then the simpleton called Sivka Burka:

Sivka Burka, stallion dear,
Father's blessing, come now here.

Stand straight and tall like you are made,
As on the grass stands the blade.

Sivka Burka came up, fire spewed from his mouth, a column of smoke rose from his ears. The simpleton crept into the left ear and got a drink and food. He crawled into his right ear, adorned himself with a colorful robe and became a handsome fellow. Then he caught the gold-feathered duckling and pitched a tent. He himself sat in the tent, but the gold-feathered duckling ran around him.

Then the wise sons-in-law rode up and asked, "Who is in the tent? If he is an old man, he is our grandfather, if he is middle-aged, he is our father!"

Then the simpleton answered, "I am of your age, I am your brother."

"Well, brother! Will you sell that duckling to us? "

"No, it's not for sale, but I'll give it to you on one condition."

"Under what condition?"

"For the little finger of your right hand."

They cut off the little finger of the right hand and gave it to the simpleton. He put the fingers in his pocket. The sons-in-law rode home and went to sleep. Tsar and Tsarina came and heard what they said. "Still," said one to his wife, "my hand hurts." The other mumbled, "Oh, what a pain, my hand hurts!"

The next morning the Tsar called the wise sons-in-law and said: "My wise, my very wise sons-in-law, do me a service, I command you! In the steppe a golden-bristled pig walks around with twelve golden-bristled piglets. Get me the pig and the piglets!" He ordered them to saddle the best horses; but to the simpleton he gave a bad horse, which was good just for hauling water.

The simpleton rode into the open field, took the nag by the tail, pulled off her skin and shouted: "Fly over here, you jackdaws, crows and magpies, father has sent you food!"

The jackdaws, crows and magpies flew in and ate everything up. The simpleton called the Sivka Burka, the dear gray stallion. Then he caught the golden-bristled pig with the twelve golden-bristled piglets in the steppe and set up his tent. He sat in the tent, but the pig and piglets ran around outside.

Then came the wise sons-in-law: "Who, who is in this tent? If he's an old man, let him be our grandfather, if he's middle-aged, he's our father!"

"I am of your age, I am your brother," replied the simpleton.

"And is that your golden-haired pig?"

"It is."

"Well, brother, will you sell the golden-bristled pig?"

"No, it's not for sale. But I'll give it to you on one condition: for a toe frpm the foot! "

They each cut off a toe, gave them to the simpleton and took the golden-bristled pig with the twelve golden-bristled piglets.

The next morning the tsar called his wise sons-in-law to him and said: "My wise, my intelligent sons-in-law, do me a service! In the steppe a mare runs around with a golden mane, and she has twelve young foals. Can you give them to me?"

"Yes, Father."

The Tsar had the best horses saddled, but to the simpleton he again gave an old nag. which was hardly suitable for hauling water. The simpleton sat down on the horse, but facing backward, took the tail between his teeth and drove it with blows on the flanks. The clever sons-in-law laughed at him. But he rode into the open field, grabbed the nag by the tail, pulled off her skin and cried: "Fly over here, you jackdaws, crows and magpies, father has sent you food!" The jackdaws, crows and magpies flew up and ate everything. Then the simpleton called:

> Sivka Burka, stallion dear,
> Father's blessing, come now here.
> Stand straight and tall like you are made,
> As on the grass stands the blade.

Sivka Burka hurried up, fire spurted from his mouth, a column of smoke rose from his ears. The simpleton crept into the left ear and got a drink and food. He crawled into the right and became a handsome man. "I have to fetch the mare with the golden mane and her twelve foals!"

Sivka Burka, Good Gray, answered: "The first two tasks were child's play, but this is a difficult thing! Take three copper, three iron and three tin rods with you! The mare will run after me, chase me over mountains and valleys, but eventually she will tire and fall to the ground. Do not let up, sit down on her and beat her with all nine rods between the ears until the rods break into small pieces. Maybe then you will defeat the mare with the golden mane."

Said - done, the simpleton conquered the gold-maned mare with the twelve foals. Then he opened a tent. He sat in the tent, but the mare was tied to a pillar. The wise sons-in-law rode up and called, "Who is in the tent? If he is an old man, if he is our grandfather, he is middle-aged, be he our father!"

"I am of your age, I am your brother," replied the simpleton.

"Well, little brother, will you sell the mare with the golden mane?" "No, she is not for sale, but I'll give her to you on one condition: for a stip of skin from your back!"

The clever ones hesitated and hesitated, but then stooped and the simpleton cut a belt from their backs, put them in his pockets and gave them the mare and the twelve foals.

The next day the tsar made a great feast and all came. The simpleton took from his pocket the cut off fingers and toes and the two belts and said: "This is the gold-feathered duckling, this the gold-bristling pig and this the gold-mare with the twelve foals."

"You're talking like a lunatic," the tsar told him.

"My lord, my father, order the wise sons-in-law to take off their gloves!" They took off their gloves, and the little finger was missing on the right hand. "I took them off for the gold-feathered duckling," said the simpleton. He held his fingers in their place, then grew and revived.

"Father, have them take off their boots!" The brothers took off their boots and their feet lacked a toe. "I took them for the golden-bristled pig with the twelve piglets." He held the cut toes to their feet, and they instantly grew back again and revived.

"Father, have them take off their shirts!" They took off their shirts, and the sons-in-law had strips cut from their backs. "I took that for the mare with the golden mane with the twelve foals." He put the stripts in their old place, they grew and revived. "Now," said the simpleton, "let a carriage be brought!" The carriage was brought, and they sat down together and drove into the open field. There, the simpleton pressed the three horsehairs and shouted in a loud voice:

Sivka Burka, stallion dear,
Father's blessing, come now here.
Stand straight and tall like you are made,
As on the grass stands the blade.

From his mouth sprinkled fire, out of his ears rose a column of smoke. The horse stopped in front of the simpleton, stood straight and tall like on the grass stands the leaf. The simpleton crawled into his left ear and ate and drank. He crept into his right ear and adorned himself with a colorful garment and had become such a beautiful youth such as one cannot imagine, nor tell in a folktale, nor describe it with the pen. From that time on, he lived with his wife as tsar and tsarina, drove in a royal carriage, and gave rich feasts. I was at those feasts, drinking honey mead and wine. But however much I drank - I only wet my mustache.

## Interpretation

To practice Johannine Christianity means to continuously die and arise again. If the new being in us is to arise, the old must be laid in the grave. The German word *versenken* (sink) points to that. When we lay a body in the grave, we say that we *versenken* it. When we meditate inwardly on a truth, we say that we *versenken* ourselves into it. On the grave of the old being one attains a truth-bearing intelligence (the horse) capable of action that harmoniously unites the heavenly (white) and earthly (black).[34] This is the father's blessing, the great gray horse. To watch on the grave means to observe inwardly, to meditate. The son who devotes himself to such meditation (*Versenkung*) wins in the second night red boots – that is, the capacity to stand on the earth with a strong sense of one's I, for the blood is, more than any other organ, the organ of the I, the ego. On the third night, he receives the red hat, that is, the capacity to think with a strong sense of the I. He can now "take something on his cap" as the Germans say, that is, take responsibility.

Through "the father's blessing" (the horse) the inner life of "the simpleton" becomes richer and more diverse; his aural sheath is transformed. This is expressed in the picture language of the

---

34  The "unites black and white" part of this sentence is puzzling. There is no mention in the story of black and white. Sivka and Burka are said by some to mean chestnut-colored and gray.

folktale by the fine new bright-colored clothes he gets in the horse's ear. And the contact with the higher soul gives beauty – the spirit shines through the human being. His forehead, which bears the stamp of the tsarevna's ring, shines – for behind it new, spirit-rich thoughts are being thought. The tsarevna finds the simpleton behind the stove: hidden in the heart's sphere, he waits more humble than the poorest beggar. She recognizes him and acknowledges him. Her name is Milolika[35], that is Beautiful Face.

This folktale is a simpleton tale. In the age of development of thinking, the intellect counted as clever while the ability of the heart for knowing seemed dumb by comparison. Unused, held back forces work in the simpleton. The seeming foolishness of the simpleton third son is in reality Will stemming from the heart. It works also in the sphere of the soul, in the father of the bride. There the primitive, weak intellect that is suitable only for "hauling water"[36] must be sacrificed. After this sacrifice "in the open field" the simpleton can again call Sivka Burka, the great gray, wise stallion. With its help, the golden duck is won and also the wealth of the lower sense drives – the pig with gold bristles – and finally the mare with the golden mane.

The other sons-in-law must give up some use of their hands and feet, some *Handel und Wandel* as the German says. They must also sacrifice some lifting force. The sacrifices turn out to be temporary; once the tasks have been accomplished, the sacrifices are restored.

The total being of Man with all spiritual and soul forces can now experience the transformation of that originally so

---

35  Milolita = Милолика = Милое Лицо = dear, sweet, lovely, kind face.

36  This is one of the very few places that I differ from Lenz on the meaning of the Russian. The word is водовозница which I think is clearly a water carrier – a mare that carries water. So the horse is good only for carrying water – but Lenz translates into German as *Wasserfahren,* "good only for traveling by water", which makes no sense.

unprepossesing figure: the modest will force of the heart – once the simpleton, now the wise one – has attained its highest perfection.

# 9. Ivan from the Ashes - Ivan Popyalov (A 135)

Once there lived an old man and an old woman; they had three sons. Two were smart, one was stupid. The stupid one's name was Ivan, and he was called Ivan from the Ashes[37]. He lay on the ashes for twelve years, then got up, shook himself and shook out six poods of ash.

In the kingdom where Ivan from the Ashes lived there was never day but always night. The cause was a powerful dragon. Ivan from the Ashes offered to kill this dragon, and he said to his father, "Father, make me a very heavy cudgel, one which weighs five poods!"

With this cudgel Ivan went out of the ashes into the field, threw the cudgel up the mountain, and returned home. The next day he stood in the same field and held his forehead up. Suddenly the cudgel came down, struck him on the forehead and broke in half. Ivan from the Ashes went home and said to his father, "Father, make me another cudgel, one which weighs ten poods!"

With this cudgel he went into the field, hurled it up, and the cudgel flew for three days and three nights. On the fourth day Ivan came out of the ashes and held out a knee. The cudgel came back, hit the knee and broke into three pieces. Ivan from the Ashes again went to his father and urged him: "Father, make me a third cudgel, one who weighs fifteen poods!"

He took the new cudgel into the field, threw it up, and flew for six days and six nights. On the seventh day Ivan came to the same place, and the club flew with a mighty blow against his forehead, so that his head bent backwards. "This is the right cudgel," said Ivan from the Ashes, "that will withstand the dragon."

---

37 The tale is in a fairly easily understood dialect. The accent in Popyalov is on the first syllable: Пóпялов. *Ash* in standard Russian is пепел; *from ashes* is из пепла.

Ivan from the Ashes joined his brothers, and they went out to kill the dragon. They rode and rode and came to a little hut on chicken's feet, and in that little hut lived the dragon. There they stopped. Ivan hung his mittens on the wall and said to his brothers, "When the blood drips from my mittens, I need help immediately!" After saying that, he sat down under the floor of the hut. There came the dragon with the three heads. His horse stumbled in front of the hut, his dog howled, and his hawk bucked. Said the dragon, "Why are you stumbling, my horse? Why are you crying, my dog? And what are you struggling for, my hawk?"

"How could I not stumble," answered the steed, "since Ivan from the Ashes is sitting under the floor!"

"Come out, little Ivan," cried the dragon, "let us measure our strength!"

Ivan from the Ashes came out. They started beating each other, and Ivan from the Ashes killed the three-headed dragon. Then he sat down again under the floor.

Then came the dragon with the six heads, and he too was slain by Ivan. After that, the third appeared with the twelve heads. Ivan from the Ashes began measuring his powers with him. He knocked nine heads off, and the dragon's strength waned. Then he saw a raven flying who cried: "Crof, crof, blood, blood!"

The dragon said to the raven, "Fly to my wife, tell her to come and eat Ivan from the Ashes!"

Ivan from the Ashes cried, "Fly to my brothers, let them come, let us kill the dragon, and give you the flesh!"

The raven listened to Ivan from the Ashes, flew to the brothers and began to croak over their heads. The brothers awoke, heard the call of the raven and hurried to help Ivan. They killed the dragon, took one of the twelve heads, went to the dragon's hut and smashed the head, and the whole kingdom became light and bright.

After killing the dragon, Ivan from the Ashes started riding home with his brothers. But they forgot to take the mittens with them. Then Ivan called out to his brothers to wait for him and returned to fetch them. When he came to the hut and reached for the mittens, he saw that the dragon's wife and daughters were sitting around chatting inside. He quickly turned into a cat and started meowing at the door. The dragonwomen let him in, and Ivan from the Ashes heard everything they discussed among themselves. Then he took his mittens and ran away to the brothers. He quickly mounted his horse, and they rode on together. They rode and rode. Suddenly they came to a green meadow, and on this meadow lay silk pillows.

"Do we not want to graze our horses here and rest for a while?" cried the brothers.

Ivan from the Ashes said, "Wait, brothers!" He took his cudgel, and struck the silken pillows. Look, blood was flowing from the pillows! They rode on, rode and rode. Suddenly an apple tree stood before them with golden and silver apples.

"Do not we each want an apple!" cried the brothers.

"Wait, brothers, I will try first!" said Ivan. He took his cudgel and beat on the apple-tree, and out of the tree flowed blood!

They rode on, rode and rode. Suddenly a spring bubbled up in front of them. "Shall we not drink water?" exclaimed the brothers.

"Wait, brothers!" answered Ivan from the Ashes, took his cudgel and struck the spring. Lo, out of the water came blood! The green meadow with the silk pillows, the apple tree and the spring, these had all been the daughters of the dragon. After Ivan had slain the dragon daughters, he rode on with his brothers on their way home. Suddenly they heard the dragon's wife herself coming after them. She had her mouth open from the sky to the earth and wanted to devour Ivan from the Ashes. But Ivan and his brothers threw in their three poods of salt. The dragon swallowed the salt thinking it was Ivan from the Ashes. But when she tasted the salt and realized that it was not Ivan from the Ashes, she again began the attack. Ivan from the Ashes saw that he was in danger, spurred his horse, and jumped into the smithy of Cosmas and Damian behind the twelve doors. But the dragoness flew there too and said to Cosmas and Damian: "Give me Ivan from the Ashes!"

"Then you must lick away the twelve doors with your tongue!" answered Cosmas and Damian, "Then you can take him with you." The dragoness began to lick the doors, but Cosmas and Damian made the iron tongs glow red-hot, and when the dragoness had licked through the twelve doors and stuck her tongue into the smithy, they seized it with the tongs and slew her with the tongs and sledgehammer. When they killed her, they burned the body and scattered the ashes into the wind.

Then the three brothers rode home together. And they began to live together, to celebrate and to drink honey and wine. I was there too, and drank the wine, but it flowed over my beard and nothing came into my mouth.

## Interpretation

Ivan who lies on the ashes and then rises from them reminds us of the phoenix bird, who ever and again arises new born from the ashes. Ashes are what remains after burning, an indication that this Johannine impulse lives where there is continuous burning, purification and transformation. For twelve years Ivan lives in this realm of purification. In "The Witch and the Sister of the Sun (A 93)" (Number 17 in this book) it is also twelve years that Ivan does not speak.

Now, "in the kingdom where Ivan from the Ashes lived there was never day but always night. The cause was a powerful dragon." In the night, it is natural for Man to sleep, to dream and be passive. If this becomes a continual state, then the cause must be found and overcome. The cudgel is the picture of the inner "weapon" needed for the task. It must go through a threefold development, for it comprises day-wakeful thinking, I-conscious feeling, and self-aware willing, for these are the properties of Day. He who has won these forces has become free in his inner being and can defeat the forces of darkness.

But when the dragon has been defeated as a spiritual power, there still threatens the soul danger pictured by the dragon women. Silken cushions beckon to rest, but this rest would be a sleeping of the Will, for blood is in the cushions; egotism fills them. Gold and silver apples on the tree of knowledge can still an inner hunger, but these fruits grow from the self-seeking blood-nature of Man. And also the spring of living feeling, from which the brothers want to drink, is filled with egotism.

The capacity of salt to purify and defend against laziness is proverbial. To form a life of crystal clear thoughts that work against inner laziness is to throw salt in the mouth of the dragon.

But still other forces must come to the rescue. We bear within us an invisible smith. Where the iron processes of the blood work, there is this smith. Iron deficiency makes one dull, de-spirited, weak-willled. We cannot be wide-awake, stong-willed and I-conscious without the forces of iron in our blood.

Cosmas and Damian were two early Christian arab physicians, reputedly twin brothers, who practiced their profession in the seaport of Aegeae, then in the Roman province of Syria. They did not charge for their services and thereby won many converts to Christianity. They died as martyrs in the persecutions of Diocletian about AD 287. They are the patrons of physicians and pharmacists. The picture in the folktale says: where true I-forces are combined with healing forces, there can Evil be seized (the tongs) and through the impulse force of the heart (the smith's hammer) be beaten down.

# 10. Vasilisa of the Golden Braids and Ivan from the Pea (A 560)

Once upon a time there lived a tsar named Svietozar who had two sons and a beautiful daughter. For twenty years she lived in a magnificent tower, lovingly guarded by the tsar and tsarina and her maids and attendants. She was so beautiful that nobody could ever see enough of her. Never had a prince or a royal son seen her face.

The splendid princess never left her tower, she had never breathed open air. She had precious, multi-colored robes and beautiful jewelery. But time was heavy on her hand, and the seclusion weighed on her. Her silken hair was thick and gold-like; plaited into long braids, it hung down to her heels, her head was uncovered. The people called her Vasilisa of the Golden Braids and Uncovered Head, or Vasilisa the Magnificent. Her fame spread far and wide, and many kings sent messengers to Tsar Svietozar seeking her hand.

Tsar Svietozar took his time. When he thought the time had come for her to wed, he sent messengers to all countries to invite kings and sons of kings to a feast so that Vasilisa might choose a husband. He himself went to the high tower to announce it his daughter.

The princess was happy to hear this news. She looked out of the gold-barred little window into the green garden, into the colorful, flowery meadows and wanted to stroll down there. "Dear Father," she said, "I have never seen God's world, never have I walked across the grass and flowers, never seen your splendid court. Let me walk with my maids and maidens outdoors!"

The Tsar granted it, and Vasilisa the Magnificent descended from the high tower into the wide courtyard, the wooden doors opened, and she stood on a green meadow before a high mountain. Gorgeous trees grew on this mountain, many-colored flowers on the meadow. The princess was picking blue flowers, guilelessly she withdrew a little from her companions, for a young heart knows no caution. Her face was open; her beauty, unveiled.

A storm blew up such as even the oldest people had ever known. No one had ever seen or heard of such a thing. Everything was whirled around and broken. All at once the Whirlwind seized the Tsar's daughter and carried her away through the air, carrying her across vast lands and deep streams, through three kingdoms to the fourth kingdom, into the realm of the cruel dragon.

The maids shouted, ran everywhere and searched everywhere, but it was all for naught. Then they hurried back to the castle, threw themselves crying at the Tsar's feet, and cried, "Mighty Tsar, we are innocent of the misfortune, though we appear guilty before you. Say a word of mercy and do not punish us! The Whirlwind carried away our sun, our Vasilisa with the golden braids, the incomparably beautiful, and we do not know where to go." And they told how it all happened. The tsar was sad and angry, but he pardoned the poor souls.

The next morning princes and royal sons appeared at the castle. When they saw the sadness and melancholy of the tsar, they asked what had happened.

"Woe is me," said the Tsar, "the Whirlwind carried off my dear child, Vasilisa with the Golden Braids, and no one knows where she is," and he told all that had happened. There arose a murmur among the guests as to whether the Tsar might be using an excuse so that he would not have to give his daughter away. Princes and royal sons rushed into the tower, but they did not find the princess. The tsar gave them of his treasures and gave them an honorable escort. They mounted horses and retired back to their lands.

The two sons of the tsar, Vasilisa's courageous brothers, saw the tears of their father and mother and asked, "Let us go, great

Father; bless us, gracious Mother. We will seek your daughter, our sister!"

"Children of my heart, dear sons," said the Tsar sadly, "where do you want to go?"

"Father, we will ride everywhere - wherever the road may lead, wherever the bird may fly, wherever the eyes may look."

The tsar blessed them, their mother clothed them with festive robes, and in tears they departed.

The princes rode over mountain and valley. Whether it was short or long, whether it was near or far – neither knew. They rode a year and a second year and came through three great empires. At last distant mountains gleamed, and between the mountains sandy steppes, the land of the cruel dragon. The sons of the tsar asked all whom they passed about Vasilisa with the Golden Braids. "Did not you hear, did you not see where Vasilisa with the Golden Braids is?" But the people said, "We never knew her, we have never heard of her," and went on.

At last the sons of the tsar came to a great city. At the gate stood a frail old man, crooked and lame, with crutch and satchel, begging. The sons of the tsar stopped, gave him silver money, and asked him about their sister, Vasilisa with the Golden Braids and the Bare Head.

"Ah, my friends, I know that you are from a foreign land. Our master, the cruel dragon, has strictly forbidden us to talk to strangers. No one here is allowed to speak for fear of punishment of how the storm wind carried the beautiful princess past the city."

The brothers then suspected that their sister was near. They drove their fiery horses and rode to the castle of the dragon. The castle was made of gold and stood on a silver pillar. The shielding roof was made of precious stone, the stairs were made of mother-of-pearl and spread out like wings. Vasilisa was looking sadly out of her gold-barred little window.

Suddenly she screamed with joy; she had seen the two princes from afar, and her heart told her that they were the brothers. Secretly she sent a messenger to meet them and lead them into the castle. The dragon was not at home. Vasilisa was afraid that he would see the brothers. But no sooner had they entered than the silver pillar groaned, the mother-of-pearl stairs fell apart like wings, all the precious-stone roofs flashed, and the whole castle turned and moved.

The tsar's daughter was startled: "The castle is staggering, the dragon is flying. Hide, my brothers!"

As soon as she had said it, the cruel dragon flew up, whistled, and shouted in a loud voice, "Is there here a living man?"

"It is we, cruel dragon!" answered the tsasrevichs unflinchingly. "We come from home and seek our sister."

"Oh, so it's you, boys," shouted the dragon, flapping its wings. "Yes, you have found your sister, and you are also brave heroes, but only small ones. I will quickly conquer you!" And with his wing he took one brother and with him killed the other. Then he whistled and shouted. The castle guard came running, seized the two dead brothers and threw them into a deep pit. Vasilisa of the Golden Braids wept bitter tears. She did not eat or drink and hid herself from the light of heaven with her grief. Two days passed, three days passed - she would have loved to die - but because of her beauty she decided to live. And on the third day she ate. Then she wondered how she could rid herself of the dragon herself, and tried it with clever flattery: "Cruel dragon, your strength is great, your flight mighty. Is not there a match for you? "

"The time has not yet come. At my birth I was told that my adversary was Ivan from the Pea, and that he was born of the pea."

The dragon said it as a joke, thinking of no opponent. Thus, the strong relies on his strength, and yet joking is often dead serious.

The mother of the beautiful Vasilisa mourned. The sons were gone after the tsar's daughter. Once the tsarina walked with the wives of boyars in the garden. The day was hot and she wanted to drink. A spring bubbled from the hillside and the water was caught in a basin of white marble. She scooped up the bright water clear as a tear with a golden dipper and drank. And as she drank hastily, she swallowed a pea.

The pea began to swell, and the queen felt strange. The pea grew and grew, and it became clear that the queen was carrying a child. When the time came, the queen gave birth to a son, who was named Ivan from the Pea. The boy did not grow by years, but by hours, beautifully smooth and round. He looked around and laughed, hopped and jumped, rolled across the sand and was so full of strength that at the age of ten he was already a real hero. Once he asked his father and mother if he had any siblings, and then he learned that the sister had been carried away by the whirlwind and the two brothers had gone to look for her.

"Father, Mother, give me your blessing, let me go to look for my sister and the brothers!"

"But child," cried father and mother in one voice, "you are still so young and green, your brothers went out and came not back. You will not fare better!"

"Nothing bad will happen to me," said Ivan from the Pea, "I want to find my brothers and sister!"

Father and mother wanted to hold back their dear son, but he shed tears until they equipped him for the journey. Ivan from the Pea was now free to go and rode into the open country. He rode away, rode one day and another day, and came at night into a dark forest. In the woods stood a little hut on chicken feet, which swayed in the wind and turned on its own. According to ancient custom, as his mother had taught, the tsasrevich blew on the little hut and said: "Little hut, little hut, turn to me and turn your back on the forest!"

And immediately the little hut turned to Ivan. From the little window a gray-haired old woman looked out and asked, "Whom has God brought here?"

Ivan bowed and asked, "Granny, did you see the whirlwind fly past? Do you know where he was carrying the beautiful virgin?"

"Oh, brave young man," answered the old woman, coughing and looking at him, "the whirlwind frightened me also. For a hundred and twenty years, I'm sitting in this little hut and do not dare to go outside, because he could come and kidnap me. It's not a whirlwind, it's the cruel dragon!"

"How can I get to him?" asked Ivan.

"What do you want there, my dear? He'll devour you quickly."

"Well, maybe he will not devour me."

"Oh, brave hero," pleaded the old woman, "you cannot save your head! But if you do conquer the dragon, give me your word that you will bring me some rejuvenating water from the dragon's palace. Anyone who sprinkles with it will be young again," she added, speaking with difficulty.

"My word upon it, old mother. I'll bring you the rejuvenating water!"

"I gladly believe it. Always go straight ahead in the direction the sun is going[38]. In a year you will come to the Fox Mountain; there ask again the way to the Dragon Kingdom!"

"Thank you, Granny! "

"Nothing to thank, brave youth."

---

38  That is, to the west.

So Ivan from the Pea followed the direction of the sun's movement. Quick is a tale told - not so quick is the deed done[39] - he moved through three kingdoms until he came to the kingdom of the dragon. Outside the gates of the city he saw a beggar standing, a lame, blind poor man with a crutch. He gave him alms and asked if perhaps Vasilisa with the Golden Braids, the incomparably beautiful, was trapped inside. "Yes, she is here, but it is forbidden to say it." Then Ivan from the Pea knew that his sister was near.

The brave youth rode to the dragon's castle. Vasilisa, the glorious one, looked out the window to see if the dragon had flown, and saw the young hero coming from afar. She would have liked to know who it was. She secretly sent a messenger to meet him, to ask from which country, from which tribe he was, and whether he was not sent by her father and mother. When she heard that Ivan had come, the youngest brother, she ran to him with tears in her eyes: "Fly, fly, my brother, the dragon will soon come, and when he sees you, he will kill you!"

"Dear sister, you did not say that, and I did not hear it. I do not fear the power of the dragon!"

"Are you perhaps from the pea? "asked Vasilisa, "then you could defeat him."

"Just wait, sister. First, give me a drink, I wandered far through the blazing sun. I'm tired of the road and thirsty!"

"What do you want to drink, brother?"

"A bucket full of sweet honeymead, dear little sister." Vasilisa brought him a bucket of sweet honeymead. Ivan from the Pea drank it straight down and asked for a second. The Tsar's daughter was astonished and ordered another bucket. "Brother, I did not know you, but now I think you're Ivan from the Pea."

---

39  A favorite alliterative phrase of the teller of tales: Сказка скоро сказывается, а дело долго делается.

"Bring me a chair so I can rest a little!" Vasilisa had a sturdy chair brought down, but the chair collapsed under him , They brought another, covered in iron, but it too bent and collapsed. "Ah, brother," cried the princess, "that was the dragon's seat!"

"Oh, I weigh more than he does," said Ivan from the Pea, laughed and went to the blacksmith shop. From the wise old court smith he ordered a staff weighing, five hundred pood.. The blacksmiths immediately set to work and forged the iron staff. Day and night the hammers boomed and the sparks flew. In forty hours the staff was forged. Fifty people dragged it out. Ivan from the Pea took it with one hand and threw it into the air. The bar flew with a thundering roar over the clouds and soared out of sight. All the people ran away in fear. If the staff fell on the ground, it could shatter walls and kill people, but if it fell into the sea, the waves would wash over the bank and flood the city. Ivan from the Pea commanded to report when the staff could be seen flying. Then he quietly went back to the castle. The people ran away and looked out the windows and doors for the staff. They waited an hour, a second and third. Then they trembled, shouted and shouted that the staff could be seen flying. Ivan from the Pea jumped out onto the square, opened his hand and caught it in in mid air. He did not give way as he caught it, but the staff bent in his hand and became crooked. He took the staff, straightened it over his knee, and returned with it to the castle.

Suddenly a terrible whistling noise arose – the cruel dragon rode up. His horse flew like an arrow, and flames leaped out of his nostrils. The dragon had the body of a hero the head of a dragon. Normally, when he had flown to within ten versts, the castle began to waver and spin. But today it remained calm and did not move. Apparently a guest more weighty than the dragon was in the house. The dragon hesitated, whistled and screamed. The hurricane horse shook its black mane, flapped its big wings, roared and whinnied. It flew to the castle, but the castle did not move. "Oho," the dragon roared, "my adversary is here! Pea, are you my guest?" Ivan Bogatir quickly came.

"I'll put you on the palm of one hand, beat you the other, and no one will ever find your bones!" sneered the dragon.

"We'll see," said Ivan from the Pea and strode toward him with his staff.

"Little pea, don't try to roll away!" said the dragon sneeringly from the hurricane horse.

"Come on, cruel dragon!" cried Ivan from the Pea and raised his staff. The dragon came charging and thrust his lance at Ivan, but Ivan jumped to one side without stumbling and the lance struck beside him.

"Now I'll finish you," shouted Ivan, hurling his staff at the dragon. The dragon was smashed and torn to bits, and Ivan scattered the pieces. The staff penetrated the earth and went through two kingdoms to the third.

The people threw their hats into the air and called Ivan to be their tsar. But Ivan pointed to the wise blacksmith who had forged the staff so fast, and said to the assembled people, "He is your head; obey him for good as well as you once obeyed the dragon for evil!"

Then Ivan brought the water of life and death and with it sprinkled the dead brothers. Then the youths stood up, wiped their eyes and said, "We slept for a long time, God knows what has happened in the meantime."

"You would have slept forever without me, dear brothers," said Ivan from the Pea and pressed them to his brave heart.

He did not forget to take the dragon's rejuvenating water with him. Then he prepared a ship and took Vasilisa with the Golden Braids and his brothers with him. They moved along the Swan

River to their homeland; through three kingdoms to the fourth empire. Ivan from the Pea did not forget the old woman in the hut and brought her the promised water for washing. She washed herself with it, changed and became young again. Singing and dancing, she ran after Ivan and accompanied him along the way.

Father and mother were full of joy, saluted the tsarevich with great honors and sent messengers all over the world with the news that Vasilisa with the Golden Braids had returned. The guns' thunder roared, the trumpets blew, and the bells of the city rang. Vasilisa's constant patience was rewarded, she found the perfect bridegroom, and a lovely bride was found for Ivan of the Pea. Four bridal crowns were ordered; two weddings held. That was a joyous feast with mountains of food, and honey-mead flowed in torrents. The grandfathers of the fathers were there and drank honey-mead. I was there and the honey-mead flowed up to me. It ran over my beard, but did not come into my mouth. Of course Ivan received the royal crown after the death of his father. He reigned gloriously, and many generations celebrated the Tsar from the Pea.

Interpretation

From the golden hair of the incomparably beautiful Vasilisa streams the light of wisdom. Her name comes from Basileus, the kingly; and her father is Svietozar (Светозар) and *Sviet* (Свет) means both *light* and *world*. The Light-maiden in Man, the Enlightened One is intended. Her hair is not covered. Just as the uncovered head is subject to the air and to the sun, so was once the inner consciousness in the head of Man not covered, that is, it was open to all the forces streaming in from the cosmos. Man was still not closed off, had not yet become self-conscious. As he began to build his self-awareness, he more and more dclosed himself off from cosmic consciousness. His self-awareness was formed in his head through thinking. The brain became the seat of responsibility an of knowledge based on thinking. Man experienced it as a sort of cap that had been acquired, and in German we have the expression, "I'll take it on my cap" meaning "I'll take responsibility for it."

In this tale is shown how the consciousness still open to the cosmos and not yet closed off in itself falls prey to the dragon of unconstrained egotistical sense nature.

Hidden in Man – hidden also in the outer world behind the historic events – matures the Johannine force, the third brother, which alone can deal with the dragon. He wins and masters the iron staff. The relation to the Apocalypse of John becomes obvious here. "And he shall rule them with a rod of iron." (Rev. 19. 15) In the age when the great lawgivers ruled the peoples, they gave them commandments which supported and guided them. Man had to learn to find this support more and more within himself. The iron processes in the blood gave inner support for this development when they were forged by an unselfish I that is connected to the Christ. Ivan throws the staff heavenward. Having come back to the earth, it was ready to fight the dragon. When Ivan hurls it against the dragon, it not only rips the dragon to bits, it "penetrates the earth and goes through two kingdoms to the third." The whole earth shares in the deed of Ivan of the Pea.[40]

---

40 The author makes no comment on the significance of Ivan's birth from the pea. It is surely a good topic for thought and discussion.

# 11. The Two Ivans, Soldier Sons (A 155)

In a kingdom, in a realm, once lived a peasant who was compelled to be a soldier. His wife was expecting a child, and when he said goodbye to her, he said: "My dear, preserve our house, live in peace with the neighbors and wait for me. Perhaps God will tell them to release me soon. Here are fifty rubles for the child. If it is a daughter, she has a dowry; if it is a son, it will be of great help to him."

With that he took leave and went to war as he was commanded.

After three months, the wife gave birth to twin boys, and she called them both Ivan Soldier Son. The boys grew and rose like yeast dough, as if they were being inflated. At age ten, their mother sent them to school to study. They learned quickly and soon overtook merchant and boyar sons; no one could read, write or answer better than they could. The boyar and merchant children envied them and pushed and pinched them every day.

"Must we let them go on pushing and pinching us?" they asked. "Mother, sew us clothes and hats that will fall apart when they push and pinch us! Then we will repay them in our own way."

When the other children again began to pester them, the soldier sons no longer tolerated it and beat them up. They gave one a black eye, broke the hand of another, and beat up still others.

Then the police came and put them both in jail. The king heard of it and brought the boys before him. He questioned them and then ordered them released.

"They are innocent," he said, "They just defended themselves. May God punish the attackers."

The two Ivans Soldiersons grew up and asked: "Mother, give us money, we want to buy good horses at the market."

The mother gave them the fifty rubles and told them: "Listen, sons, on the way to the city, kindly greet everyone who meets you!"

"Yes, dear mother."

The brothers went into town to the horse market. There were many horses there, but none they liked. Then one said to the other: "Let's go to the other end of the square and see why there is such a crowd there!"

They went and saw that two fillets were tied to two oak posts with iron chains, one with six, the other with twelve chains. The animals tugged at the chains, gnashed their teeth and ripped up the earth with their hooves. Nobody could approach them.

"What do the horses cost?" asked Ivan Soldierson.

"They are not for you; you do not need to stick your nose everywhere and ask!"

"Why do you say things you do not know? Maybe we'll buy them, we just have to look at their teeth."

The horse trader laughed: "Look, if you do not feel sorry for your head!"

One brother went to the foal which was tied to six chains, the other to the one held by twelve chains. They tried to see the teeth, but the horses stood on their hind feet and snorted. The brothers pushed their knees into the chests of the horses so that the chains tore and the horses flew five fathoms and fell on their backs.

"Oh, how did you boast! We cannot use such miserable nags!"

The people marveled and admired the heroes. The horse dealer almost cried. The foals raced out of the city and across the open field. No one dared to approach and try to capture them. Then the two brothers took pity on the horse dealer, went out of the city and called the animals in a powerful voice. The horses came and stood still and silent before them. The brothers put the iron chains back on them, led them into the city and fastened them to the oak posts. Then they went home again.

On the way, the met an old man, but they forgot what their mother had commanded, and passed him by without saying hello. But then they remembered: "Brother, what did we do? We forgot to greet this old man. Let's hurry after him!"

They hurried after the old man, pulled off their caps and bowed to him: "Grandfather, forgive us for passing by without greeting. Our mother ordered to greet everyone we meet on our way."

"Thank you, brave lads, where are you coming from?"

"From the city horse market. We wanted to buy good horses, but they were not good for us."

"Should I give each of you a horse?"

"Oh, Grandfather, if you do that, we always pray to God for you."

"Oh, then come with me!"

The old man led them to a large mountain, opened an iron door and led out two steeds fit for bogatirs. "Here you have horses, good boys. May you go forth with God and be in good health!"

They thanked him, mounted and rode home. There they tied the horses to a post and entered the house. Their mother asked, "My sons, did you buy horses?"

"We did not buy them, but we were given two."

"Where are they?"

"In front of the hut."

"Oh, children, what if someone were to steal them!"

"Mother, nobody will lead them away, for no one dares to approach them."

The mother stepped out to look at the horses. Then she burst into tears, "Oh, you sons, you no longer need my protection!"

The next day the sons asked their mother, "Let's go to town to buy sharp sabers!"

"Go, my dears !" They went to the blacksmith and said," Forge us sharp sabers!"

"Why forge? Many are already made. Choose what you want!"

"No, we need sabers weighing three hundred poods."

"What are you asking! Who can swing such a saber? You can not find any forge in the world large enough to make such a saber."

There was nothing to be done, the brothers hung their heads and started home. Towards them came the old man.

"Good day, brave fellows!"

"Good day, grandfather!"

"Where are you coming from? "

"From the blacksmith in the city. We wanted to buy sabers, but there are no such sabers as we need!"

"That is too bad. Shall I give each of you a saber? "

"Oh, Grandfather, if you do that, we will always pray to God for you!" The old man led them to the great mountain, opened the iron door, and brought out a mighty saber for each of them. They took the sabers, thanked the old man, and were happy at heart.

At home the mother asked, "Well, dear boys, did you buy sabers?"

"We did not buy them, but we got them for free."

"Where do you have them? "

"They lean against the hut."

"What if someone carries them away?"

"No, mother, no one will steal them; they're too heavy!"

The mother went out and saw the sabers. They were long and sharp. The mother burst into tears, "You will not, God knows, be my breadwinner!"

The next morning the two Ivans Soldiersons saddled their horses, took their sabers, and bid farewell to their mother.

"Mother, give us your blessing for the long journey!"

"May there be upon you, my sons, my eternal maternal blessing! Ride forth with God. Show your true selves and observe others carefully! Injure no one needlessly, and never yield to an evil foe!"[41]

"Fear not, mother, we have a motto: "When I ride, I don' whistle; when the enemy comes, I don't yield."[42]

The brave youths mounted their horses and rode away. Whether the ride was short or long, whether it was near or far, we do not know. The tale is quickly told; the deed is long in doing. They finally came to a crossroads where there were two signs. On the one sign was written: "He who rides to the right becomes king." On the other, "He who rides on the left is killed." The brothers stopped, read the inscriptions, and considered where to go. If both rode to the right, it was not glorious for their knightly strength and daring, but neither of them wanted to ride on the left and die. But they had to decide. Then one said: "Brother, I am stronger than you, I will ride to the left and see what death is like. You ride to

---

41 This is a formulaic, rhyming blessing: "себя покажите, людей посмотрите; напрасно никого не обижайте, а злым ворогам не уступайте"

42 еду — не свищу, а наеду — не спущу!

the right and may God make you a king!" They took leave of each other. Each one gave the other a cloth and vowed to make signs everywhere on his way. Every morning each should rub his face with the cloth. If there was blood in it, it meant the death of the other. Then the survivor was to look for the other. So off they rode to different sides.

He who let his horse go to the right side came into a glorious kingdom. There lived a king and a queen with their daughter, Anastasia the Beautiful. The king saw Ivan, the son of a soldier, liked him because he was so bold, and gave him without hesitation his daughter to wife. He called him Ivan Tsarevich and gave the administration of the kingdom into his hands. Ivan Tsarevich King lived in joy and glory; he loved his wife, kept the kingdom in order, and went hunting. Once, when he set out to go hunting and bridled his horse, he found two vials in the saddlebags, one with healing water, the other with water of life. He looked at them, put them back in their place, and said, "I will keep them until the hour comes when I need her."

His brother who had taken the path to the left rode without rest day and night for a month, two months, three months. Finally, he came to the capital of a foreign land. There was great sadness there. The houses were covered with black cloth, and people went about as if in a dream. He went to an inn and asked an old woman, "Tell me, little mother, why are all the people mourning? Why are the houses covered with black cloth?"

"Oh, good young man, great misfortune has struck us! Every day, out of the blue sea, behind the gray stone, a twelve-headed dragon emerges and devours one of our people. Today is the king's turn. He has three beautiful daughters. and the oldest one has just gone to the sea to feed the dragon."

Ivan Son ot the Soldier mounted his horse and rode to the sea and to the gray stone. There stood the beautiful princess chained to the stone. When she saw the knight, she called to him: "Get away from here, brave hero, the dragon will soon come to devour me; he should not kill you also!"

"Fear not, beautiful maiden, maybe he will swallow me!" He took the chains with a strong hand broke them as if they were sewing thread. Then he put his head in her lap and said, "Now look at my head, but look to the sea as often as to my head. And when a cloud arises, the storm rages, and the sea shakes, then wake me up, beautiful maiden!" She obeyed him and looked at the sea as often as at his head. Suddenly a cloud rose, the wind stormed, the water roared, and the dragon rose from the blue sea. The maiden woke the knight, he jumped up and mounted his horse.

Then the dragon flew up and shouted, "Hey, Ivanushka, why did you come here? This is my place! Take leave of the wide world and climb into my maw – you will find it better there!"

"You lie, you damned dragon, you will not swallow me, you would choke on me!" Ivan drew his sharp saber, swung it and cut off the twelve heads off the monster. Then he picked up the gray stone, put the dragon's heads under it and threw the corpse into the sea. He went home, ate and drank, went to sleep, and slept for three days and three nights.

In the meantime the king called to him a water carrier and said: "Take your cart, go to the sea and collect the bones of my daughter!" The water-carrier drove to the blue sea and found the king's daughter alive. No harm had happened to her. He put her on his cart, took her deep into a dense, dark forest, and began to sharpen his knife.

"What are you doing?" asked the princess.

"I am sharpening my knife to stab you!" Then she wept and said, "Do not stab me, I did you no harm!"

"If you will tell the king that I have freed you from the dragon, I will have mercy on you."

She could not help but agree. When she returned to the castle and the king saw her, he rejoiced and made the water-carrier captain. When Ivan, the son of a soldier, awoke, he gave the old woman money and said, "Old woman, go to the market, buy what is needed and hear what people are talking about. Perhaps there will be something new."

The old woman went to the market, bought supplies, heard what people were talking about, ran back home, and said,"There is a rumor among the people that the king was giving a big banquet. Kings' sons, boyars, and many other great men were sitting at the great table when a glowing arrow flew through the window into the middle of the room. On it hung the letter of a twelve-headed dragon. The dragon wrote: "If you do not give me your second daughter, I will devastate your kingdom with fire and scatter the ashes in the wind. And today they lead the maiden to the blue sea and the gray stone."

Ivan, the soldier's son, immediately mounted his good steed and dashed to the sea. Then the king's daughter cried: "Why are you coming, brave hero? The turn to suffer death is mine. My warm blood will flow. Why do you want to die? "

"Fear not, beautiful maiden, perhaps God will save you!" No sooner had he arrived than the dragon flew in. Fire-breathing, he threatened death. But the knight swung his saber and struck off all twelve heads with one stroke. He hid his heads under the stone, threw the body into the sea and rode home. He ate and drank and slept for three days and three nights.

Again the water-carrier came and found the king's daughter alive and well. He put her on his cart, drove into the dark woods and whetted his knife."Why are you grinding your knife?"

"I'm sharpening my knife to stab you, but if you swear to tell your father what I ask, then I'll spare you!" The king's daughter swore it. The water carrier took her to the court.

After three days, Ivan the soldier's son awoke and sent the old woman to the market to hear news. The old woman went away and soon returned: "Now a third dragon has sent word that the king must deliver the third and youngest daughter." Ivan, the soldier's son, saddled his good steed and dashed to the blue sea. On the shore stood the maiden bound to the stone with iron chains. The hero seized the chains and snapped them like sewing thread. Then he laid his head on her knees: "Guard my head, but look at the sea as often as at my head, and when a cloud rises, the storm rages, and the sea shakes, then wake me up!" The princess guarded his head. Then a cloud rose, the storm roared, the sea shook, and out of the water the dragon rose and began to climb the hill.

The princess tried to wake Ivan, the soldier's son, but no matter how much she shook him, she could not wake him. Then she wept bitterly, and her hot tears fell on his cheeks, so that he finally awoke. He ran quickly to his horse, which had already churned the earth two cubits deep. The twelve-headed dragon came flying, and the fire blazed from his throat: "You are handsome, young knight, and certainly useful, but you have lived long enough! I'll eat you up to the last bit!"

"You're lying, damned dragon, you would choke on me!" A deadly fight began. Ivan swung his saber so often and so fast that the iron glowed, and he barely managed to hold it.

"Save me, beautiful maiden!" He begged the king's daughter, "take off your precious handkerchief, dip it into the blue sea, and wrap it around my saber." The princess took her handkerchief, dipped it into the blue sea, and gave it to the hero. He wrapped it around the handle of his saber, swung it with all his might, and cut off the dragon's twelve heads. He laid the heads under the gray stone and threw the corpse into the sea. Then he hurried home, ate and drank, and slept for three days and three nights.

The king again sent the water-carrier to the sea. He took the princess, led her into the dark forest, and began to sharpen his knife."What are you doing?" she asked.

"I am sharpening my knife to stab you. But if you say to your father that I have freed you from the dragon, then I will show mercy." The beautiful maiden was afraid and swore obedience to him.

The youngest king's daughter was the king's favorite, and when he saw her alive and unharmed, he rejoiced even more than the other times. He wanted to reward the water carrier in particular and promised him the youngest daughter to be his wife. The rumor went through the whole empire. Ivan the soldier's son also learned that the princess was to be married and went to the castle. The meal was in progress, the guests ate and drank and enjoyed themselves. Then the king's youngest daughter saw Ivan, the soldier's son, and recognized her handkerchief on his saber.

She jumped up and took him by the hand, shouting: "Royal Father, this is he who freed me from the dragon and saved me from death. The water carrier only sharpen his knife to stab me."

The king was angry and ordered the water carrier to be hung. The king's daughter, however, he gave to Ivan, the son of a soldier, as his wife. The newlyweds began to live together, and they lived and lived and prospered.

\*\*\*

While all this happened, the other brother's life was different. Once he rode hunting and came across a fast-footed stag. Ivan gave his horse a stroke, rode and rode and pursued the deer to a large meadow. There the deer vanished, and Ivan did not know where to go. Through the meadow flowed a stream, on it swam two gray ducks. He aimed at them, shot them, picked them up, put them in his knapsack and rode on. He rode and rode and finally came to a white stone castle. He dismounted, tied his horse to a post, and went inside. Everything was dead silent, not a single person was in the rooms, but in one room there was a fire in a stove. A pan stood in front of it, and on the table lay a place setting, plate, fork, and knife. Ivan Tsarevich took the ducks out of the satchel, plucked and cleaned them, put them in the pan and pushed them into the oven. When they were done, he took them out and started to eat. Suddenly there was a maiden by his side, so beautiful that no pen can describe it, no tale can tell it."Do not you want to dine with me, beautiful maiden?"

"I would like, but I do not dare, you have a magic horse."

"No, beautiful maiden, my magic horse is at home, I came riding on a common horse."

When the beautiful maiden heard that, she began to swell, became bigger and bigger and turned into a terrible lioness. The lioness opened her throat and devoured Ivan Tsarevich; for she was not a maiden; she was the sister of the three dragons whom the other Ivan, the son of a soldier, had slain.

At that moment Ivan, the son of a soldier, remembered his distant brother. He took his little cloth, wiped himself, and behold, the whole cloth was full of blood. He became sad and thought in his heart, "What a fate! My brother rode on the good side and should be king, and yet death overtook him." He took leave of his wife and his father-in-law and rode to seek the brother.

Whether it was short or long, whether it was near or far – he came into the realm of his brother. Then he inquired and learned that his brother had gone hunting and had not returned. Ivan's soldier's son rode the same way his brother had ridden, and he too came upon the fast-footed stag. He pursued him to a large meadow and lost him there out of sight. A stream flowed through the meadow, and two ducks were swimming on the water. He shot the ducks and rode to the white castle, went into the chambers and found everything empty. Only in one room burned the stove, and a pan was ready. Ivan soldier-son roasted the two ducklings, carried them into the yard, sat down on the stairs, cut them apart and began to eat. Again the beautiful maiden appeared and said, "May it taste good to you, brave hero! Why do you eat outside in the yard?" "I had no desire to eat in there. It is more cheerful outside. Sit down, beautiful maiden!" "I would gladly do what you desire, but I fear your magic horse."

"Do not worry, beautiful maiden, I rode an ordinary horse today."

She was stupid, believed him , began to inflate, became a terrible lioness and wanted to devour Ivan. His magic horse came running and kicked her down with strong feet. Ivan the son of a soldier drew his saber and shouted in a ringing voice: "You devoured my brother, Ivan Tsarevich, give him to me again, or I will cut you to pieces!"

The lioness choked and spit out Ivan Tsarevich. He was dead and half decayed, and his head was bald. Ivan the soldier's son took from his saddlebag the two vials containing the healing water and the water of life and sprinkled his brother. The flesh grew together and became firm and healthy. Then he sprinkled him with the water of life, and Ivan Tsarevich son stood up and said, "Oh, how I slept so long!"

"You would have slept forever if I had not been," answered Ivan the soldier's son. He took the lioness and wanted to cut off her head. But she turned back into a lovely maiden and was so beautiful, so beautiful, that one can not tell it. And she bitterly cried and begged for forgiveness. Seeing her indescribable beauty, Ivan the soldier's son took pity on her and gave her her freedom. The brothers rode home to the royal castle and gave a feast that lasted three days. After that, they took leave of each other. Ivan the King remained to his kingdom; the other Ivan returned home to his wife and continued to live with her in love and harmony.

***

When some time had passed, Ivan the soldier's son went out in the open field. Then a small child met him and asked for a gift. Ivan felt pity, took a piece of gold out of his pocket and handed it to him. The child took it, began to swell, turned into a lion, and tore Ivan to pieces. Some time later, Ivan Tsasrevich did the same; he went into his garden where an old man came to meet him, bowed low to him and begged for alms. Ivan Tsarevich gave him a gold piece. The old man took it, began to swell up and turned into a lion, seized Ivan Tsarevich and tore him to pieces.

## Interpretation

When the I of Man becomes a fighter it is like the soldier. The twin sons of the soldier represent the two sides of the I, one turned to heaven, the other, to earth. Both brothers are equipped with splendid gifts. One wins quickly royal status and lives in wealth and splendor of inner kingship. The other wants to know "what Death is like." He wants to contend with death and grasp earthly knowledge.

This contrast is found also in mankind: eastern mankind is more turned to the other worldly, while western mankind must learn to master forcefully this world. (In the Grimm story "Two Brothers" one goes to the east and one to the west.)[43]

The second brother must win his kingdom. In persistent struggle he conquers the power of lower egoism that lurks in all the senses and drives and the soul's whole lower reaches. He saves his soul from these temptations.

---

43 The author assumes that the brothers were riding northwards. So the one who went to the left went west and encountered dragons; the one who went to right went east and was soon made king. I have checked the original carefully, and the east-west identification is not in the folktale itself, nor is it in the author's own translation. It is more a feeling on her part. But if you are thinking you missed something, you didn't.

Other experiences await the brother who has not been through these trials. He hunts the deer and is swallowed by the lion. Just as the innocent desires for wandering in the sense world appear in the picture of the deer, so the stag with his magnificent antlers represents the most beautiful, positive side of wandering and hunting. From his head sprout the living, yearly renewed antlers. In their branching form the antlers resemble the blood circulatory system and appear like two trees branching upward. Thus the deer became the symbol of the pure desire in Man to reach upward and grasp the heavenly world. (Thus we have the deer in Psalm 42, in medieval art, and in the legend of St. Hubertus, who – about to shoot the stag he has chased all day – sees a glowing cross between his antlers and hears a warning voice. The experience changes the life of Hubertus, who in due course becomes a bishop.)

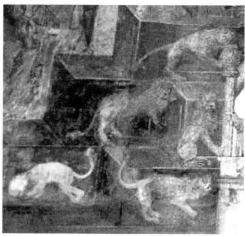

The reader of this folktale is almost certain to have been shocked by the epilogue, where both brothers are – seemingly for a good deed – devoured by the dragon sister in the form of a lion. Let us try to understand it.

The lion as a symbol of courage is well known. But lion courage is a special kind of courage.

*The five best preserved of the Lübeck lions (Source: German Wikipedia)*

Look at him; he is all head and chest. Combine that with his majestic expression, his imposing peacefulness, his mighty roar and powerful spring and we have the perfect symbol for courage of the heart. Power, fortitude, energy and and readiness for action are all expressed in his visage. The English saw these qualities in their king Richard I and called him Richard the Lionhearted. Wherever we detect traces of Johannine Christianity we find the image of the lion. In a fresco in the chapel of the Holy Spirit hospital in Lübeck[44] twelve lions surround the throne of Solomon. Above Solomon on his throne are the thrones of Christ and Mary. The lions are shown in various natural positions, but held in sway by the presence of the Christ above.

Johannine Christianity, correctly practiced, leads to an initiation of the heart. In it, wisdom comes not only from the head but also from the force of love. All the forces of courage must be summoned up – the lions must be in place. But they must be controlled. In his devotion to the spirit, Man can also fall prey to his impulses, to his his natural compassion. Indeed, he can become so dedicated to the heavenly that he neglects the earth and its tasks. Then courage and spiritual excitement ignite fires of love that become little fires of self satisfaction. One turns from the world and revels in one's own goodness and compassion. The whole inner life becomes self-centered and stuffy. In this inner atmosphere lives and thrives one and only one inspiring genius: the dragon sister, puffed-up pride, the Luciferic soul.

Inside the dragon sister, the one-sided, heavenly-oriented consciousness begins to decompose. His head becomes bald: he loses all forces of inspiration. The wide-awake and battle-proven I must come to the rescue. This soldier son never parts from his magic horse; the other had ventured forth with only his ordinary understanding. In the former, heart and intellect work together. But he has not attained full knowledge: he should have cut off the head of the lion.

When the twin figure of the I seeks to live and act out of inner freedom, one more temptation is encountered. To one of the brothers it appears as a child, innocent, and in need of help. To the other it takes thee form of a poor old man. Both brothers

---

44  The Heiliggeist (Holy Spirit) Hospital in Lübeck, completed in 1286, is one of the oldest existing social institutions in the world. (German Wikipedia)

incautiously give of their treasure of wisdom (gold) without verifying to whom they are giving. But the Johannine virtues of compassion, courage and capacity for love must be paired by wide-awake knowledge, for in their greatness lies also their danger. Like the great Greek tragedies, this folktale shows the fate of the kingly ruler and of the heroic fighter who nevertheless lack this full knowledge.

In the Grimm Brothers' folktale "The Two Brothers" (Number 60) the brother from the east saves the one from the west: an old motif, that the brother serving the spirit saves the one indulging in earthly pleasures (*ex oriente lux*). In our story, it is the other way around. The earthly I that has won knowledge and wakefulness helps the other brother in both inner life and humanity (*ex occidente lux*).

# 12. Ivan Cowson (A 137)[45]

In a kingdom, in a realm, once there lived a tsar and tsarina who had no child. And they asked God every day to give them a son. They wanted to rejoice in him as long as they were young, and he should take care of them in their old age. They prayed and slept and fell into a deep, deep sleep. In a dream they saw a quiet pond, not far from their castle and in it a ruffe[46] with golden fins. If the tsarina eats this golden-finned ruffe, she would soon be with child.

When the tsar and the tsarina awoke, they immediately called the maids and attendants and told them the dream. "What happened in the dream can happen in real life," the women answered.

Then the tsar called his fishermen to him and ordered them to catch the golden fish. In the dawn the fishermen went to the still pond and threw out their nets. Luck was with them, and on the first draw they caught the golden fish. They took it to the palace; the Tsarina rushed to meet them, took them by the hand and rewarded them with rich treasures. Then she called her personal cook and gave her the ruffe. "Prepare it for the midday meal, but see that no one touches it!"

The cook cleaned the fish, washed and cooked it. But she put the water in which the fish had been washed out in the yard. A cow came and drank the wash water.

The tsarina ate the fish, but the cook licked the dishes. After a while, all three became pregnant, the tsarina, the maid and the cow, and at the same time they each had a son. The tsarina gave

---

45 The Russian title is *Иван Быкович*, Ivan Bullson, but there is no bull in the story, only a cow; and Cowson seems to be the usual title in English.
46 The Eurasian ruffe (*Gymnocephalus cernua*), also known as pope, is a freshwater fish found in temperate regions of Europe and northern Asia. The Russian name is *ёрш (yorsh)*.

birth to Ivan Tsarevich, the cook to Ivan Cookson, and the cow to Ivan Cowson. The infants grew not by the day but by the hour. As good yeast dough rises in the warmth, so too did they grow. All three boys had the same face, and it was not possible to know who was the child of the tsarina, who belonged to the maid and who to the cow. They differed only in one thing: when they returned home from a walk, Ivan Tsarevich wanted to change clothes, Ivan Cookson asked for food, and Ivan Cowson lay down to sleep.

In the tenth year the three boys went to the Tsar and said: "Dear Father, let us forge an iron rod of fifty pood weight!"

The tsar immediately ordered his blacksmiths to make a staff of fifty pood. The blacksmiths began to forge and forged for a whole week. Neither of them could lift the staff. But Ivan Tsarevich, Ivan Cookson, and Ivan Cowson twirled it between their fingers like a goose quill. They stepped out onto the wide yard. "Well, my brothers, let's see who is the strongest of us," said Ivan Tsarevich.

"Good," replied Ivan Cowson, "take the staff and whack us on the shoulder!"

Ivan Tsarevich took the iron rod and struck Ivan Cookson and Ivan Cowson on the shoulder, and drove them into the ground up to their knees. Ivan Cookson drove both brothers into the ground up to the chest, but Ivan Cowson drove the other two up to the neck into the ground.

"Let's try our strength again!" said Ivan Tsarevich. "Let's throw the iron rod up into the air. Whoever throws it the highest will be the strongest."

"Well, so you throw first!"

Ivan Tsarevitch threw, and the staff fell down after fifteen minutes. Ivan Cookson threw it, and it came back after half an hour. But when Ivan Cowson threw it, it came to earth only after an hour.

"Well, Ivan Cowson, be the strongest of us brothers!"

Then they went into the garden and found a huge stone. "What a stone!" said Ivan Tsarevich. "Can we roll it from the spot?" He braced himself, pushed and shoved, but the stone did not budge. Ivan Cookson tried, but the stone barely moved. "You swim only in shallow water," shouted Ivan Cowson, "let me try!"

He went to the stone, and when he only touched it with his foot, the stone came loose and rolled to the other end of the garden knocking down many trees. Under the stone a cave opened. Inside were three horses fit for bogatirs and on the walls hung all the armor.

Immediately the brave lads hurried to the tsar: "Lord, our father, give us your blessing! We want to ride to foreign countries, we want to see other people and let ourselves be seen!"

The tsar blessed them and gave them goods and money from the treasury. They took their leave, sat on their horses and rode away. They rode over mountains and valleys and over green meadows and came into a deep forest. In the forest stood a little hut on chicken legs and ram's horns. If necessary, it turned around. "Little hut, little hut, turn your face 'round to us and with your back to the forest. We want to go in and eat bread with salt in it!"

The hut turned, and the boys went inside. On the stove the Baba Yaga was lying with her bony body reaching from corner to corner, her nose reaching up to the ceiling.

"Fu, fu, fu, until today I have never seen a Russian soul with my eyes nor heard it with my ears. Now the Russian soul sits on my spoon and even rolls into my mouth!"

"Do not chastise us, old woman, climb down from the stove and sit on the bench! Ask us where we are going and we will gladly say!"

The Baba Yaga climbed down from the stove, approached Ivan Cowson, and bowed deeply, and said, "Greetings, Ivan Cowson, where are you going? Where does your road lead "

"Mother, we ride to the Currant River, to the Viburnam Bridge. I heard that terrible monsters live there."

" Yes, Ivanushka! There you have a nice good deed. Yes, the evil ones have struck and torn down everything and razed the neighboring kingdoms to the ground."

The brothers stayed with the Baba Yaga, got up early in the morning and set out on their way. They came to the Currant River. The banks were full of human bones piled knee-high. Towards evening they came to a hut. They entered, it was empty, and they thought to stay. When the evening came, Ivan Cowson said: "Brothers, we have come to a distant, foreign area, we must be careful. Let us go step by step!" They drew lots: Ivan Tsarevich was to watch the first night, Ivan Cookson the second, Ivan Cowson the third. Ivan Tsarevich went to the guard, crept into a bush, and went sound asleep. Ivan Cowson did not trust him. When it was midnight, he took sword and shield, went out and stood under the Viburnum Bridge. Suddenly the waters of the river rose, the eagles screamed on the oak trees, and a six-headed monster, Chudo Yudo, came over. The horse stumbled under him, the black raven on his shoulder jumped, the fur of the dog behind stood on end. Said the six-headed Chudo Yudo: "What's with you, you dog-meat nag? Why are you trembling, fearful raven, and you mutt, why does your fur bristle? Or do you think that Ivan Cowson is there? He, the brave one, is not born yet, and if he is, he is not yet fit to fight. I could put him on one hand, slap him up with the other – and he would be just a damp spot."

Ivan Cowson jumped out: "Do not boast, you unclean spirit! A hawk cannot be plucked before it is caught, and a good man can not be belittled before he is tried. Let us test our stregnth; may whoever wins be praised!"

They went at each other, they measured their strength and beat each other so hard that the earth shook. The Chudo Yudo lost, Ivan Cowson struck off three heads with one blow. "Stop, Ivan Cowson, let me breathe!"

"What do you mean breathe, you unclean spirit? You still have have three heads left and I only one. When you have only one left, we can catch our breath." Again they charged each other, again they hit each other. Ivan Cowson cut off the last three heads of the Cudo Yudo. Then he sawed the body into small pieces and threw them into the Currant River. But he put the six heads under the Viburnum Bridge. He returned to the hut himself.

Ivan Tsarevich woke up in the morning. "Well, how was it, did you see anything?" asked Ivan Cowson.

"Nothing, nothing, not even a fly flew past me."

On the second night Ivan Cookson went to watch. He crawled into the bushes and fell asleep. Ivan Cowson did not trust him. As it approached midnight, he prepared himself, took his shield and sword, went out and stood at the Viburnum Bridge. Suddenly the waters of the river rose, the eagles screamed on the oak trees. A nine-headed monster came. The horse stumbled, the black raven on its shoulders flapped its wings, the fur of the big dog behind bristled. The monster struck the horse in the flanks, tore a feather from the raven, cuffed the dog's ears: "Why are you stumbling, you nag? Why are you flapping your wings, raven? And you mutt, why is you fur on end? Do you think that Ivan Cowson would be here? He is not yet born, and if he is, he is not fit to fight yet. I would beat him with one finger."

Ivan Cowson jumped out: "Do not blab, just wait! Pray to God, wash your hands and get to work. Who will win is still not known!"

The hero swung his sword once, twice, and knocked six heads off the evil power. But the Chudo Yudo hit him and drove him him down to his knees into the damp earth. Ivan Cowson took a handful of earth and threw it into his opponent's face. While the Chudo Yudo was wiping his eyes, Ivan cut off his remaining heads. He sawed the body into small pieces and threw them into the Currant River. But he put the nine heads under the Viburnum Bridge.

In the morning Ivan Cookson arrived. "Well, brother, did you not see anything during the night?" "No, not a fly flew by, not a mosquito hummed."

Ivan Cowson then led the brothers under the Viburnum Bridge, showing them the severed heads and shaming them. "Oh, sleepers, how could you fight, you'd better lie on the stove at home!"

On the third night, Ivan Cowson got up to watch. He took a white towel, hung it against the wall and put a bowl underneath it on the floor. Then he said to his brothers, "I'm going into a terrible fight, you brothers, watch and look around! If the blood flows out of the towel when the bowl is half full, things are fine. Even if the bowl is completely full, it does not matter. But if the blood overflows the bowl, then release my bogatir's horse from the chain and you yourselves hurry to help me!"

Then Ivan Cowson stood under the Viburnum Bridge. Time passed until midnight. Then the waters rose in the river, the eagles screamed on the oak trees, a twelve-headed monster came out. His horse had twelve wings, his coat was of silver, but his tail and mane were of gold. The Chudo Yudo starts to ride but the horse stumbled, the black raven on his shoulder flapped his wings, the big dog behind bristled. Chudo Yudo kicked the horse in its flanks, tore a feather from the raven, boxed the dog's ears, and shouted: "Why are you stumbling, dog meat? What are you doing with your wings, raven? And you mutt, what is bothering you? Do you think Ivan Cowson is here? He is not born yet. And if he is, he is not fit to fight yet. I would just just need to blow, and not a pebble would remain of him."

Then Ivan Cowson jumped out: "Do not praise yourself, rather pray to God!"

" Oh, you are here. Why did you come here?"

"To look on you, you unclean power. To test your strength!"

"Why do you want to test my strength? You're like a fly before me."

Ivan Cowson replied, "I did not come here to tell fairy tales with you, but to fight with you to the death."

Ivan Cowson swung his sharp sword and knocked three heads from the monster. The dragon grabbed the heads, touched them with his fiery finger, and immediately they grew on again, as if they had never come off their shoulders.

It looked bad for Ivan Cowson; the monster was about to overcome him. It drove him up to his knees into the damp earth.

"Stop, unclean spirit, when tsars and kings fight, they sometimes hold a truce. Do we want to fight without catching our breathe? Just let me breathe three times!"

Chudo Yudo agreed. Ivan Cowson took off his right mitt and threw it at the hut. The mitt knocked on all windows, but the brothers slept and heard nothing. Ivan Cowson brandished his sword a second time, stronger than first, and cut off six heads from the monster. But the dragon grabbed them, touched it with his fiery finger, and they grew bacl again. Then he drove the hero into the earth up to the waist. Ivan Cowson again asked for an truce, took off his left mitten, and threw it at the hut. The glove broke through the roof, but the brothers slept and heard nothing. For the third time, Ivan Cowson brandished his sword even more than the other times, and cut off nine heads from Chudo Yudo. But the dragon touched them and they all grew up again, and Ivan Cowson was pushed down to his shoulders into the damp earth. Once again the hero asked for truce, took his helmet and threw it at the hut. From this blow the roof collapsed, the hut fell apart in splinters, and finally the brothers awakened. They looked at the bowl - look, the blood flowed over the edge! In the stable, the stallions whinnied and tore at the chains. Then the brothers ran out, untied them, and rushed to the rescue. "Ah," shouted Chudo Judo, "you are cheating on me, you have help!"

The hero-horse struck him with his hoofs, and bogatir Cowson rose from the ground and cut off the fiery finger of the monster. Then he cut off every last head of the monster, tore the body apart and tossed the pieces into the Currant River.

Now the brothers came. "Ah, sleepers!" shouted Ivan Cowson, "I almost had to pay for your sleep."

In the early morning Ivan Cowson went into the open field, sat down on the ground, and changed into a sparrow. He flew to the palace, to the white-stone chambers, and sat down in the open window. An old witch lived in the palace. Suddenly she saw him, scattered grains and lured:

"Sparrow, Sparrow! You flew here grain to eat, but listen to my grief. Ivan Cowson laughed at me, took away all my sons-in-law."

"Do not worry, mother," said the daughters, the wives of those three monsters, "we'll pay him back!"

"Look," said the youngest, "I'll make them hungry as they walk on the path and turn myself into an apple tree with golden and silver apples. He who eats a little apple will burst at once."

"And I," said the middle daughter, "will make them thirst and turn myself into a fountain. Two goblets will float on the water, one golden and one silver. Whomever reaches for the goblets I will drown."

"And I," said the eldest, "will cast a deep sleep on them and turn myself into a golden bed. He who lies down on the bed is consumed by fire."

Ivan Cowson heard all these speeches, flew back, landed, and again became the young bogatir. The three brothers got ready and started home. When they were on the way, hunger tormented them, but there was nothing to eat anywhere. But lo! there stands an apple tree with golden and silver apples! Ivan Tsarevich and Ivan Cookson wanted to pick the apples, but Ivan Cowson jumped ahead and split the tree crosswise with his sword. Blood spurted out on all sides. The same thing happened with the fountain and the golden bed. Thus the wives of the three monsters perished.

The old witch learned this, dressed herself as a beggar, and made her way with her knapsack. When Ivan Cowson came with the brothers, she reached out and asked for alms. Then Ivan Tsarevich said to Ivan Cowson: "Brother, does not our father have rich treasures? Give pious alms to the poor." Ivan Cowson took out a piece of gold and handed it to the old woman. But she did not reach for the money, but for his hand, and instantly disappeared with him.

The brothers looked around, and when they could not find him, they rushed home in terror. They had all lost courage. The witch dragged Ivan Cowson into the underground world and led him to her husband: "Here you have our enemy!"

The old man lay on an iron bed and saw nothing. Long eyelashes and thick eyebrows closed his eyes. Then he summoned twelve mighty men and ordered them: "Take an iron pitchfork and raise my eyebrows and black eyelashes! I want to see what that bird is that killed my sons." The men raised his eyebrows and black eyelashes with the iron pitchfork. And the old man saw: "Ah, you are Vanyushka, the brave fellow! You were so bold to fight my children, what should I do with you?"

"It's up to you, do whatever you want with me, I'm ready for anything."

"Well, there's a lot to talk about, since my children can no longer wake up. But you can do me a better service! Go to the never-seen empire, to the non-existing state and bring me the Tsarina with the Golden Hair. I want to marry her."

"That might be a woman for me," thought Ivan Cowson to himself, "What are you thinking, you old devil, marrying her!"

But the old woman became furious, tied a rock around her neck and drowned herself.

"Here you have a club," said the old man to Ivan Cowson, "go to that oak, hit the trunk three times with the club and shout: Come out, ship, come out! And when the ship has come out to you, command three times the oak to close again. But be careful and do not forget it, otherwise you'll insult me badly!"

Ivan Cowson went to the oak tree. He beat on it and shouted, "All that is in there, come out!" Then came the first little ship. Ivan Cowson stepped inside and shouted, "Everyone else come behind me!" And he sailed off. When he had gone a little way, he looked back: As far as the eye could see stretched a row of ships and boats behind him. Everyone on board was praising and thanking him.

An old man approached in a boat and called, "Cowson bogatir, long may you live! Take me as a companion!"

"And what can you do?"

"I can eat bread."

"Bah, I can do that myself," said Ivan Cowson, "but climb into the ship, I am glad to have a brave companion!"

In another boat, a second old man rode up. "Greetings, Ivan Cowson, take me with you!"

"And what can you do?"

"Oh man! I can drink wine and beer."

"That is not a learned science, but get into the ship!"

A third approached, "Greetings, Ivan Cowson, take me with you!"

"And what can you do?"

" I can bathe in any bath."

"The devil take you! Is that wisdom?" But he also took this one into the ship.

As he sailed, a fourth old man approached, "Long may you live! Take me among your companions!"

"And what kind of guy are you?"

"Ah, kind sir, I count stars," he said.

"Well, the companions are not too many yet, come with us!" Then a fifth old man asked for admission. "What shall I do with you all, what can you do?"

"I, my father, can swim like a ruffe."

"Well, come on!"

So they sailed for the land of the Tsarina with the Golden Hair. They came to the unseen empire, to the non-existing state. It was known there for a long time that Ivan Cowson would come. They had baked bread for a full three months, made wine and brewed beer. Ivan Cowson saw countless loaves of bread, countless barrels of wine and beer. He wondered and asked what that all meant. "That's all set for you."

"Shucks, I can't eat and drink that much in a year." But he remembered his companions and shouted, "Hey there, you old youths, who of you can eat and drink?"

The eater and the drinker answered,

"It's nothing for us."

"Well, get to work!" First came the old man who ate bread. He ate it a loaf at a time. "That was a nice snack. Give me more!" The other old man hurried over and began to drink wine and beer. He drank it all down. "That was a nice nip," he said, "give me more!" The servants rushed anxiously to the Tsarina and reported that neither wine nor bread had been enough.

Now the Tsarina, with the Golden Hair told Ivan Cowson to go into the bathhouse. The bathhouse had been heated for three months and was so hot that you could not approach within five versts. They brought Ivan Cowson to bathe. He saw that the bathroom was glowing fire and exclaimed, "Have you gone mad? I would burn alive in there!"

But he remembered his companions." Hey, you old ones, who of you can bathe in this bathhouse?" Then that old man came up and shouted: "I, Father, for me it is child's play. "He jumped into the bathhouse, blew in one corner and spit in the other. Then the hot bath turned cold, and there was snow in the corners. "Oh, I freeze," cried the old man, "heat the bath for another three years." The servants rushed to the Tsarina with the message that the bath was completely frozen.

Now, however, Ivan Cowson demanded the Tsarina with the Golden Hair. The maiden came over and gave him her hand. They sat down in the ship and sailed off. They sailed one day, two days. Then the Tsarina became sad, even melancholy, beat her breast, changed into a star, and flew up to the sky. "Oh, now she is lost to me!" exclaimed Ivan Cowson, but then he remembered his companions:

"Hey, where are you, star counter?"

"It's child's play for me," answered that old man. He stamped his foot and turned into a star, flew up to the sky and began to count the stars. Soon he detected the extra star, and nudged it. The star broke free from its place, rolled across the sky, fell down onto the ship and turned back into the Tsarina with the Golden Hair.

They sailed on, one day, two days. Then the tsarina was once again beset by deep grief. She slapped her breast, changed into a pike and swam out into the sea. "Oh, now she's lost to me!" cried Ivan Cowson. But then he remembered his last companion and asked, "Can you swim as well as a ruffe can swim?" "Yes, Father, this child's play." He sat down on the floor, transformed himself into a ruffe, swam up to the pike and began to prick him in the side. Then the pike jumped onto the ship and became the Tsarina with the Golden Hair again.

Then the old men took leave of Ivan Cowson returned to their homes. Ivan Cowson went with the golden-haired Tsarina to the father of the Chudo-Yudo. He summoned the twelve most powerful heroes, ordered them to bring the iron pitchforks and prop up the black eyelashes and eyebrows of the old man. He looked at the Tsarina with the Golden Hair and, thinking that she would now be his, said: "Vanyushka, dear fellow, I forgive you, and now you may return to the bright world!"

"Oh no," replied Ivan Cowson, "not quitw so fast!"

"Oh? What then?"

"I have prepared a deep pit, and above this pit lies a thin pole. He who can cross the pit on this pole wins the Tsarina with Golden Hair."

"Good, Vanyushka, you go first!"

Ivan Cowson went to the pit. Softly whispered the golden-haired maiden to herself, "Go over, lighter than a swan's down!" Ivan Cowson walked across the pole, and ite did not even bend under his feet. But when the old man stepped on it, he got only to the middle and fell into the pit.

Ivan Cowson then took the Tsarina with the Golden Hair and returned to his home. They were married and gave a banquet for the whole world. Ivan Cowson was sitting at a table with his brothers, and could not help boasting, "It's true I had to fight a long time, but in the end I won a beautiful wife, while you are still lying on the stove alone, gnawing on the firebricks!"

> And I was at this feast;
> Mead and wine I took,
> Down my beard it flowed,
> But came not in my mouth.
> Bread into milk they dipped
> And offered me to eat.
> I did not eat nor drink.
> My mouth alone I wiped.
> I tried in vain to leave,
> They would not let me out
> Till they had beat me up.
> A sleeping cap they gave to me
> And threw me in the street. [47]

---

47 A free and somewhat bowdlerized translation. The Russian is evasive at one point but probably says "They took the scrotum of a bull, made a pouch, poured milk into it, dipped bread into the milk, and gave to me to eat."

Interpretation

If one observes a cow – best in a meadow – how she is so totally devoted to her seven-fold[48] digestion, one comes to experience her as the very image of metabolism. She seems to be dreamily devoted to digestion. When you stop to think about it, metabolism is amazing, full of mighty processes. The ancient Germanic peoples saw in it the action of creative cosmic forces without which no life on earth can sustain and renew itself – the holy cow Audumla. In the Hindu religion, the cow is holy symbol of life forces.

The tale depicts the three forces of the soul – feeling, thinking, and willing – as the three bogatirs. In man these soul forces are each mainly connected with a bodily zone. Thinking is connected to the head; feeling with the heart and lung area; and willing sleeps secretly and mostly unconsciously in the metabolic and limb system. Through both our limbs and our metabolism, we act directly on external material world. (English has the expression "It takes guts," meaning "it takes strong will power". As for the limb system, the way one walks often reveals what kind of Will one has.) The cow, as we have noted, is strongly connected with the digestive, metabolic system, and thus Ivan Cowson will naturally represent the Will. (The other two Ivans – Tsarevich and Cookson – are not clearly delineated, but they are clearly lacking in Will power and cannot stay awake.) The Will has a double aspect: the forceful, driving Will is represented by the bull; and the patiently maintaining, nourishing and creating Will is represented by the cow.

The the third and most dangerous Chudo-Yudo is also carefully pictured as reflected in his horse. (Remember that in

---

[48] A cow has a four-part stomach, to which one can add mouth, small intestine, and large intestine to get the seven-fold system. Because of "chewing the cud" the cow's mouth – and thus her consciousness – is much more involved in digestion than is the mouth of most other mammals.

describing the horse, the tale is describing the kind of thinking represented by the Chudo-Yudo.) A purely intellectual understanding instinct which can only – moon-like – reflect wisdom is shown in the image of the silver horse. The horse has twelve wings; that is, like Pegasus, it represents an intellect of unreal fantasy. But where unreal thinking that cannot penetrate to wisdom presumes to rise to world supremacy – soaring on twelve wings and flaunting golden mane and tail – there lies great danger for mankind. Especially when this kind of thinking serves the whole lower sense nature – the twelve-headed dragon.[49]

As we move to the second part of the story, we encounter new pictures and in particular those of the oak tree and of the boat. Our brain floats in cerebrospinal fluid like a boat in water. The thought life of our brain is a ship; the navigator who steers it is our spirit. It requires strong will forces to extract from the life forces connected with the tree-like nervous system (the oak tree) a strong life of thought. If the hero succeeds in doing so – and sets out in the boat – then old forces that were locked in become free and cooperate in the thought life – they get in the boat.

The ship lands: the logical thinking practiced in the sense world carries the heroes into the realm of the spirit. His helpers, the brave old graybeards digest all the already prepared knowledge, cope with the hottest and most painful purification, and drink any amount of beer and wine. The cheering wine is especially a product of the sun. In the past it had the great mission to strengthen the I-consciousness of Man as this began to be formed. (The drunkenness of Noah and the cult of Bacchus of Dionysus relate to this mission.) In the picture language, wine drinking represents taking in forces that lstrengthen the I and lead to individualization.

Beer drinking points to something else. Beer is a fermented slurry of cracked barley kernels, and – like wine – was in former

---

49  Anthroposophic physiology and medicine recognize twelve senses.

times brought as an offering. (Hops – a member of the Cannabaceae (marijuana) family – was first added in the Middle Ages.) Moon forces are at work in all seed-forming processes, so we have a hint of the meaning of this picture.

    The spiritually enlightened soul yields to the comprehensive spiritual will force of Ivan Kuhson. The ship sails in the water: that is, the life of thought moves in the soul world. Pictures, imaginations arise. Here in the soul world must the inspired soul be recognized as a being belonging to the highest worlds – as a star. As a stellar being she must be won anew. Then she becomes a fish – to a being of the soul world. She manifests herself in the soul world and so must be caught in brain thinking and "brought to land." Here is clearly a path of knowledge depicted. Finally, the powers of Underworld try to take possession of the enlightened soul, but are defeated by Ivan Cowson who returns triumphant to the upper world.

## 13. The Chrystal Mountain (A 162)

In a country, in a kingdom once lived a king, who had three sons. One day the sons said to him, "Gracious Lord and Father, bless us, we want to go out hunting!" The Father blessed them, and they rode away, each in a different direction..

The youngest son rode and rode and got lost. Finally he came to a meadow. On this meadow lay a fallen horse, and all sorts of wild beasts had gathered around the horse, including birds and reptiles. A falcon got up, flew to the king's son, sat down on his shoulder, and said, "Ivan Tsarevich, divide this horse for us! It's been here for thirty-three years, and we're still arguing over it, but we do not know how to distribute it." The king's son dismounted from his good steed and distributed the dead horse. He gave his bones to the wild beasts, his flesh to the birds, his skin to the worms, and his head to the ants. "Thank you, Ivan Tsarevich!" said the falcon. For this service, you can turn yourself into a fine falcon or a small ant as often as you like."

Then the Ivan Tsarevich struck the damp earth, became a fine falcon, soared up and flew into the thirtieth kingdom. More than half of this kingdom was in the crystal mountain. He flew straight to the castle, turned back into a youth and asked the guards, "Will your master take me into his service?"

"Why should he not take such a stately youth?" Ivan Tsarevich entered the service of that king and lived with him for a week, a second, and a third. Then the king's daughter began to ask, "Lord, my father, allow me to ride with Ivan Tsarevich on the crystal mountain."

The king allowed it, they mounted their good horses and rode away. When they came to the crystal mountain, a golden goat sprang out suddenly - no one knew whence. The king's son chased after her, rode and rode, but he could not catch her. When he returned, the princess was gone. What was to be done? How could he look the king in the eye? He disguised himself as an old man, so that he could not be recognized, returned to the castle and said to the king, "Lord King, take me as a herdsman!"

"All right, be my herdsman! If the dragon with the three heads comes, give him three cows. If the six-headed one comes, give him six cows. But if the twelve-headed one approaches, let him have twelve cows!"

Ivan Tsarevich drove the herd out over mountain and valley. Suddenly the dragon with the three heads rose out of the lake. "Oh, tsarevich, what kind of work do you do here? A brave lad should rather fight than keep cows. But now give me my three cows!"

"Is not that going to be too big a bite?" asked the tsarevich. "A duckling is enough for me for twenty-four hours, and you want to have three cows? You get none!"

The dragon became angry and lunged at the cows; but Ivan Tsarevich quickly turned into a mighty falcon and tore off his three heads. Then he drove the herd home.

"Well, grandfather," asked the king, "did the three-headed dragon come? And did you give him the three cows? "

"No, King, I did not give any."

The next day the king's son again drove the herd over mountain and valley. Out of the lake the dragon with the six heads rose and demanded six cows.

"Oh chudo-yudo, what a fantastic glutton you are! A duckling is enough for me for twenty-four hours, and you want six cows? Not one will I give you!"

The dragon became angry and grabbed twelve cows instead of six. But Ivan Tsarevich turned into a mighty falcon, threw himself on the dragon and tore off his six heads. Then he drove the herd home.

"Well, grandfather," asked the king, "did the six-headed dragon fly up and diminish my flock?"

"If he was there, he did not get anything!"

In the late evening, the king's son turned into an ant and crawled through a tiny cleft into the crystalline mountain. Inside, in the Crystal Mountain, sat the princess.

"Hail," said Ivan Tsarevich, "How did you get here?"

"I was abducted by the dragon with the twelve heads. He lives in my father's lake. In that dragon a box is hidden, in the box a rabbit, in the rabbit a duck, in the duck an egg, in the egg a seed. If you kill the dragon and gain that seed, you can destroy the Crystal Mountain and free me."

Ivan Tsarevich crawled out of the hole as an ant, became a herdsman again and grazed his flock. Suddenly the dragon with the twelve heads rose out of the lake.

"Oh, you brave young man, what are you doing here? Instead of fighting, you are guarding a herd! Well, count twelve cows for me!"

"That meal would be too much for you! A duckling is enough for me for twenty-four hours, and you want so much?"

They began to fight, and Ivan defeated the twelve-headed dragon. He cut his body in half and found the box on the right side. In the box was a rabbit, in the rabbit a duck, in the duck an egg and in the egg the seed. He took the seed, lit it, and carried it to the Crystal Mountain. The mountain melted away, and Ivan Tsarevich led the king's daughter out and brought her to her father. The king was full of joy and said to him, "Thou shalt be my son!" Then the

Ivan Tsarevich was wedded to the king's daughter, and the wedding feast was held.

## Interpretation

When we say "to crystallize" we have in mind a hardening. A kingdom that is more than half a crystal mountain means a spiritual realm that has become very rigidified. It is no wonder that in this realm the cows are prey to dragons. Such a realm can only be rescued by a Johannine spiritual power so encompassing that it unites within itself thoughts like the soaring flight of the falcon and down-to-earth work like the diligent labor of the ant.

# 14. Ivan Tsarevich and Byely Polyanin[50] (A 161)

In a land, in an empire once lived a tsar who had three daughters and a son, Ivan Tsarevich. The tsar became old and died, and Ivan Tsarevich took the crown. When the neighboring kings heard this, they immediately gathered countless armies and went to war against him. Ivan Tsarevich did not know what would happen to him and went to his sisters and asked: "Dear sisters, what should I do? All kings go to war against me!"

"Oh, you brave warrior, what are you afraid of? Byely Polyanin has been waging war against the Baba Yaga with the Golden Leg for thirty years. He never gets off his horse and knows no rest or peace. And you are afraid even before you have seen anything?"

Immediately Ivan Tsarevich saddled his good horse, put on his armor, seized his mighty sword, long lance and silk whip, prayed to God and rode against the enemy. He killed many with the sword, trod down many more and broke up the hostile army. Then he returned to his city, lay down and slept. For three days and three nights, he slept soundly and was unable to wake up. On the fourth day he awoke, stepped out onto the balcony, and looked out into the open field. The enemy kings had gathered an even larger army and stood close to the city walls. The Tsarevich became sad and went to his sisters: "Sisters, what shall I do? I have destroyed one force, but a second is already more powerful than the first."

What kind of hero are you? One day you fought and slept without ceasing for three days, look at Byely Polyanin, who fights the Baba Yaga with the Golden Leg - for thirty years he does not get off his horse and knows no rest."

---

50. Белый Полянин

Ivan Tsarevich ran to the white-stone stable and saddled his hero's horse. He put on the armor, girded the sword, took the long lance in one hand, the silk whip in the other, prayed to God and rode against the enemy. The mighty falcon tears not into swans, geese, or gray ducks like Ivan Tsarevich tore into that hostile army. He slew many, even more were crushed by his horse, and so he destroyed the power of the enemy. Then he returned home and lay down. For six days and six nights, he slept deeply and was unable to wake up.

On the seventh day he awoke, stepped on the balcony, and looked into the field. Lo, the kings had set up an army larger than before, and surrounded the city. Ivan Tsarevich went to his sisters and asked, "My dear sisters, what should I do? I have destroyed two armies, but a third is standing in front of the walls even more threatening."

"Oh, you brave hero! One day you fought and slept incessantly for six days. Byely Polyanin fights the Baba Yaga with the Golden Leg - for thirty years he does not get off his horse and does not know rest or peace."

It seemed a bitter fate to Ivan Tsarevich. He ran into the white-stone stable and saddled his good horse. He put on the armor, girded on his mighty sword, took the long lance in one hand, the silk whip in the other, prayed to God and rode against the enemy. The bold falcon does not join the flock of swans, geese and ducks, and Ivan Tsarevich flew against the hostile army! Many he slew, even more were crushed by his horse. And so he destroyed the great power of the enemy. Then he returned home and lay down. For nine days and nine nights he slept and was not to be awakened.

On the tenth day he awoke, gathered together the senators and ministers of his, and said, "I intend to go to foreign lands to see Byely Poiyanin. I ask you to judge, order and handle all matters properly and truthfully while I am away."

Then he took leave of his sisters, got on horseback and rode off. Whether much time passed or only a little - finally he came into a dark forest. Inside stood a hut and in the hut lived an old man. Ivan Tsarevich approached him: "Greetings, grandfather!"

"Greetings, Russian Tsarevich! Where is God leading you?"

"I'm looking for Byely Polyanin; maybe you know where he is?"

"I do not know myself. But wait, I will call my faithful servants and ask them." The old man stepped to the threshold and blew on a silver horn. Then the birds flew together from all sides, and there were so many of them that the sky was darkened by a black cloud. The old man cried aloud and whistled like a youth: "You birds of passage, my faithful servants, have you seen or heard of Byely Polyanin?"

"No, we never saw him with our eyes, we never heard of him."

"Go on, Ivan Tsarevich, to my older brother, maybe he'll tell you. Here you have a ball - where it rolls, there steer your horse."

Ivan Tsarevich mounted his faithful horse, let the ball roll and rode behind it. The forest became darker and darker. Finally he came to a hut and entered. Inside sat an old man with hair silver like the moon.

"Greetings, grandfather!"

"Greetings, Russian Tsarevich, where are you going?"

"I'm looking for Byely Polyanin. Do you know where to find him?"

"Wait, I will call all my loyal servants and ask them." The old man stepped out onto the threshold, blew on a silver horn, and suddenly all sorts of animals gathered around him. And he called to them loudly and whistled like a young man:

"You leaping beasts, my faithful servants, have you seen Byely Polyanin, have you heard of him?"

"No," answered the animals, "we have never seen him, we have never heard of him."

"Count, whether you are complete, perhaps not all came!" The animals counted and behold, the one-eyed she-wolf was missing. The old man sent messengers to look for her. Immediately the runners brought her.

"Tell me, one-eyed she-wolf, do you know where Byely Polyanin is?"

"How could I not know? I'm always with him. He defeats armies, and I eat the bodies."

"And where is he now? "

"He sleeps in his tent in the open field. He waged war on the Baba Yaga with the Golden Leg. And after the fight he lay down to sleep, and he sleeps for twelve days and twelve nights, and is not to be awakened."

"Lead Ivan Tsarevich to him!" The wolf ran ahead, and the Tsarevich followed her trail. They came to the big hill and he entered the tent. Byely Polyanin lay sound asleep.

"My sisters said that Byely Polyanin was always fighting, but here he is, sound asleep for twelve days. Should not I just sleep until he awakens?" Thus thought Ivan Tsarevich and lay down next to him.

Then a little bird flew into the tent, flew to their heads and called, "Get up, wake up, Byely Polyanin, and deal my brother Ivan Tsarevich a bad death; otherwise he will kill you!"

Ivan Tsarevich jumped up, caught it Bird, ripped off his right leg out and threw it out of the tent. Then he lay down next to Byely Polyanin. But before he had fallen asleep, another bird flew in, flew to their heads, and said, "Arise, wake up, Byely Polyanin, and deal a bad death to my brother Ivan Tsarevich, or he will kill you!" Ivan Tsarevich jumped up, caught the bird, tore off his right wing and threw it out of the tent. Then he lay down in the same place.

Then the third little bird flew in, flew to their heads and said: "Get up, wake up, Byely Polyanin, and deal my brother Ivan Tsarevich a bad death, otherwise he will kill you!" Ivan Tsarevitch jumped up, seized the little bird and tore take off his beak. He threw out the little bird and laid himself down and was soon fast asleep.

When the time was up, Belyan Polyanin awoke and saw a strange man lying beside him. He grabbed his sharp sword and started to kill him. But then he quickly stopped. No, he thinks, he came to me while I slept and did not want to stain his sword with blood. It would be inglorious and dishonorable for me to kill a brave young man in his sleep. A sleeping man is like a dead man. I want to wake him up.

He woke Ivan Tsarevich and asked, "Are you a good man or a bad man? Tell me what you call yourself and why you came." "My name is Ivan Tsarevich and I came to see you and to test your strength."

"You are very daring, tsarevich. You entered my tent without permission and slept in it without asking. I could kill you for that alone."

"Eh, Byely Polyanin, you're not over the precipice yet, and you're already bragging! Just wait, maybe you'll stumble! You have two hands, but even my mother did not give birth to me with only one hand."

They climbed their steeds, charged against one another, and clashed so hard that the lances splintered and their horses fell to their knees. Ivan Tsarevich threw Byely Polyanin from the saddle and drew his sharp sword.

"Do not kill me," pleaded Byely Polyanin, "let me live and call me your younger brother! I want to honor you as a father." Ivan Tsarevich took him by the hand, picked him up from the ground, kissed him, and called him his younger brother.

"Brother, I heard that you were fighting the warlike Baba Yaga with the Golden Leg for thirty years. Why are you fighting?"

"She has a beautiful daughter whom I want to win and take to wife."

"One friend must help another," said Ivan Tsarevich. "Let us go together against the Baba Yaga!" They mounted their horses and rode into the field. But the Baba Yaga threw an immense force against them.

The bold falcon does not join the flock of doves, and the powerful heroes charged the hostile army. They knocked many enemies to the ground, even more their horses trampled. Many thousands they killed.

The Baba Yagas fled, and Ivan Tsarevich pursued her. As he closed in, she suddenly ran down into a deep ravine, picked up an iron trapdoor and disappeared under the ground.

Ivan Tsarevich and Byely Polyanin caught and killed many bulls, killed them and cut their skin into long strips. From them they formed a rope so long that when they held one end the other reached down to the other world. Ivan Tsarevich said to Belyan Poljanin: "Let me down quickly into the gorge and do not pull up the rope, but wait." Byely Polyanin lowered him to the bottom. Ivsan Tsarevich looked around went to search for the Baba Yaga. He walked and walked. He saw tailors sitting behind a lattice. He asked, "What are you doing?"

"We are sewing an army for the Baba Yaga with the Golden Leg."

"How do you do that?"

"Oh, everybody knows that. Every time we prick with a needle, a Cossack with lance mounts his horse and lines up to fight against Byely Polyanin."

"Eh, brothers, you work fast, but not well. Stand in line, I want to teach you to sew better!" The tailors immediately lined up in a row. Ivan Tsarevich swung his sword - and their heads flew.

After defeating the tailors, he moved on. He walked and walked. Then he saw cobblers sitting behind a railing and asked: "What are you doing?"

"We are creating an army for the Baba Yaga with the Golden Leg."

"How do you do that?"

"Eh, it's simple. Every time we prick with an awl, an armed soldier on horseback gets in line to do battle with Byely Polyanin."

"Well, lads, you work fast, but not well. Stand in line, I will teach you to do better!" They lined up. Ivan Tsarevich swung his sword - and off flew their heads.

Ivan Tsarevich walked on. After a long time – or maybe a short time – he came to a big beautiful city. In it was a royal palace, and in it sat a maiden of indescribable beauty. From the window she saw Ivan Tsarevich, and took a liking to him, to his black curls, to his eyes like a falcon, to his beautiful dark brows, and his stride of a bogatir. She called the Tsarevich to her and asked him where he was going.

"I'm looking for Baba Yaga with the Golden Leg."

"Oh, Ivan Tsarevich, I'm her daughter. She lay down to rest for twelve days and nights, she sleeps a sleep from which she can not be awakened."

The maiden led Ivan Tsarevich out of the city and showed him the way. Ivan Tsarevich went to Baba Yaga with the Golden Leg. He found her sleeping and cut off her head with his sword.

The head rolled and prayed, "Strike again, Ivan Tsarevich!"

"One blow is enough for a bogatir," the Tsarevich replied. He returned to the palace to the beautiful maiden and sat down with her at the oak tables with the patterned cloths. He ate and drank, and said to her, "Is there anyone in the world who is stronger than me or prettier than you?"

"Oh, Ivan Tsarevich, what am I for a beauty? Behind the thrice-ninth land, in the thrice tenth kingdom lives a tsar's daughter with the king of the dragons. She is truly an unspeakable beauty. I am only worthy to bathe in the water in which she washed her feet."

Ivan Tsarevich took the beautiful maiden by the hand, led her to the place where the rope hung, and signaled to Byely Polyanin. Byely Polyanin grabbed the rope and began to pull, pulled and pulled – and pulled Ivan Tsarevich up with the beautiful maiden.

"Greetings, Byely Polyanin," said Ivan Tsarevich, "here is your bride! Live happily with her and worry about nothing, I'm off to the dragon kingdom!"

He mounted his horse, bid farewell to Byely Polyanin and his bride, and rode off past the thrice ninth land, into the kingdom of the dragon. Whether it was a long ride or a short ride, whether it was deep or high - a tale is quickly told, a deed not so quickly done!

Ivan Tsarevich came to the kingdom of the dragon and slew the dragon king. Then he released the beautiful princess from captivity and took her to wife. He then returned home to his kingdom and began to live with her. And long they lived and prospered.

Note
Byely means white; Polyanin means man from the field.

(There is no further interpretation of this story. Maybe as math books say when a theorem is stated but no proof given, the interpretation "is left as an exercise.")

# 15. Alyonushka and Ivanushka (A 261)

Two orphans, little sister Alyonuschka and little brother Ivanushka, were walking along a long road across a wide field. The heat oppressed them and the little brother became thirsty.

"Sister Aljonushka, I want to drink!"

"Wait, brother. we will come to a well."

They walked on and on. The sun stood high in sky, the well was far and the heat was oppressive. They were dripping wet with sweat. Suddenly they saw a cow's hoof, full of water.

"Sister Aljonusdika, I want to drink from this hoof!"

"Do not drink, brother, or you'll turn into a calf!"

The little brother listened to her, and they went on. The sun was high, the well was far, the heat oppressive and sweat pouring.

Suddenly there was a horse's hoof, full of water. "Sister Aljonusdika, I drink from this hoof!"

"Do not drink, brother, or you'll be a foal!"

Ivanushka sighed and kept going. The sun was high, the well was far, the heat oppressive, and sweat pouring.

Suddenly there was a sheep's hoof full of water. The little brother saw it and, without asking, drank it all.

Alyonushka calls Ivanushka, but instead of Ivanushka, behind her ran a white lamb, and she guessed what had happened and burst into tears. She sat down next to a haystack and cried, and the lamb frolicked on the grass beside her.

A nobleman drove past, stopped and asked: "Why are you crying, beautiful girl?" Then she told her misfortune.

"Come with me," said the nobleman, "marry me, I will give you beautiful clothes and silver, and I will not forget the ram; where you are, there will it be also!"

Alyonuschka agreed. They married and lived so that good people rejoiced when they saw them, and bad ones envied them.

Once when the nobleman was away and Alyonushka was alone, a witch came, tied a stone around her neck and threw her into deep water. The witch then dressed herself in Alyonushka's clothes and settled into the mansion. No one recognized her, not even the husband. Only the ram knew what had happened. It was sad, hung my head, took no food, and every morning and evening it ran beside the water where Alyonushka had been thrown and said "Baa, baa!"

The witch noticed it and was uncomfortable. She ordered fires to be built, cast iron cauldrons to be heated, butcher knives to be sharpen, and said: "The ram must be slaughtered!" And she sent a servant to catch the ram.

But the husband wondered: "How can this be? She loved the goat like her own brother, and almost pestered me with caring for it: "water it, feed it," – and now she commands it to be slaughtered! "

The ram figured out what they were doing, went to the edge of the water and said,

Alyonushka, sister dear,
They want to slaughter me.
They've built a fire so very high,
So very hot the water heat.
Their knives they whet to make them sharp.

Alyonushka answered:

Oh Ivanushka, brother dear,
The heavy stone has frayed my neck!

The silken twine has tied my hands,
And yellow sand has fallen on my breast!

O wonder of wonders! A human heard it! He told the nobleman, and they went together to watch. The ram came and began again to call Alyonuschka and grieve beside the water:

Alyonushka, sister dear,
They want to slaughter me.
They've built a fire so very high,
So very hot the water heat.
Their knives they whet to make them sharp.

Alyonushka answered:

Oh Ivanushka, brother dear,
The heavy stone has frayed my neck!
The silken twine has tied my hands,
And yellow sand has fallen on my breast!

"Men, men," cried the lord, "come! Servants of the court, come! Let down nets, let down the silk nets!"

Then the servants of the court came running, cast out silken nets, and Aljonushka was caught. They pulled her up to shore and cut the stone from her neck. She was dipped, washed with pure water, and wrapped in white linen. And she became even more beautiful than she had ever been and hugged her husband. And the goat became her brother Ivanushka again. And they lived again in the old way, and all was well.

Only the witch got what was coming to her. But she deserved it, so you need not feel too sorry for her.

## Interpretation

The human being has become an orphan. Motherly-sheltering soul forces, fatherly-creative spiritual forces no longer work. The time for day-wakeful thinking has come. "The sun stands high in the sky" and the thirst for existence awakens. Naive young beings are described here: active, willful and more spiritual as the little brother; full of feeling, more soulful as the little sister.

"Do not drink, or you will become calf." = "The cow in you will get the upper hand; you will live in your metabolism; you will vegetate and dream."

"Do not drink, or you will become a foal." = "You will become a one-sided intellectual, lost in thought and oblivious of life around you." This is the other extreme.

From these two temptations the protecting soul can warn and protect, but not from the third: to become a lamb. (In a Russian variant: a goat; and in the Grimms' "Little brother, little sister" a roe deer.) The innocent desire for the sense world that like a little ram hops around, roams about, and nibbles a little on everything can tear the Will-being out of the purely human sphere down into the animal sphere of drives. Then the Will works just as instinct.

But where the young sentient soul in pain remembers herself, the I-being can step in: the nobleman appears and invites her to unite with him.

But the witch gets in. Evil moves into the house of the body. It lives is the sheaths of the soul, in the clothes. The I is deceived and does not notice. The instinctive will being (the ram) notices but cannot help; doom threatens him also. Materialism, with which the soul must deal, becomes a heavy stone that drags her down; she can no longer breathe the air of the spirit; her hands are tied; she has lost all buoyancy.

It was true humanity that heard the voices, but true humanity is weak. (In old Russia the guardian of the court was called "man" человек (chelovek),[51]) Forces of transformation must come to help. Silk nets are cast down. Wherever in folktales silk appears it points to light transformative forces, for it requires an extraordinary metamorphosis to form the shimmering silk filaments. Now the I can help the soul. Deep into the ground of the soul the transformative forces reach down. The soul "catches itself." It is purified and unfolds a new thinking: the white linen. And the soul is better than it every was, for having withstood the trial of evil, it is more mature than the untried soul. And thereby can also be redeemed the will forces that had fallen to the state of animal-like drives.

---

51  The text says that человек heard the voices of the ram and the true wife. Perhaps it means the guardian of the court, perhaps any human. Russian has no articles, so it is impossible to say *the* человек or *a*  человек.

# 16. The Witch (A 108)

Once upon a time there was an old man and an old woman. They had a son, Ivashesko, whom they loved more than can say in words. One day Ivashesko asked, "Father, mother, let me catch a little fish!"

"Where are you going, child, you're so small, you could drown. What's that good for?"

"Oh, no, I'll not drown, I want to catch a little fish for you. Let me go!"

Then the woman put on him a white shirt, girded it with a red belt and let him out.

Sail, little boat, sail away!

And the little boat sailed far, far, and Ivashesko began to catch fish.

After a while, the mother came to the bank and called to her son: "Ivashesko, Ivashesko, my little son, sail, sail to the shore. I brought you food and drink!"

And Ivashesko said, "Sail, little boat, sail to the shore; my mother calls me!"

And the little boat sailed swiftly to the shore.

The woman took the fish, gave her little boy food and drink, put a fresh shirt and a new belt and let him go catch fish again.

Ivashesko sat down in the boat and said:

Sail, little boat, sail away!

And the little boat sailed far, far, and Ivashesko again began to catch fish.

After a while, the father came to the bank and shouted to his son: "Ivashesko, Ivashesko, my little son, sail, sail to the shore, I brought you food and drink!"

And Ivashesko said: "Sail, little boat, sail to the shore; my father calls me!"

The boat came back to shore, the father took the fish, gave his little son food and drink, put a fresh shirt and a new belt on him and let him go to catch fish again.

A witch heard how father and mother called Ivashesko and wanted to take control of the boy. She came to the shore and shouted in a hoarse voice: "Ivashesko, Ivashesko, my little son, sail, sail to the shore, I brought you food and drink!"

But Ivashesko heard that it was not the mother's voice, but the voice of the witch. And he sang:

Little boat, my little boat, sail as far as you can!
That is not my mother who calls me, that's the witch."

Then the witch realized that she had to call Ivashesko with his mother's voice. Quickly she ran to the blacksmith: "Blacksmith, blacksmith, make me little voice as fine as Ivashesko's mother has! And if you do not, I'll devour you. "

Then the blacksmith forged the same fine little voice that Ivashesko's mother had.

At night, the witch came to the shore and sang:

"Ivashesko, Ivashesko, my little son,
Sail, sail, sail to the shore,
I brought you food and drink!"

Then Ivashesko sailed to shore. The witch quickly took all the fish, then grabbed Ivashesko and brought him to her house. At home she said to her daughter Alyonka: "Stoke up the stove, and bake Ivashesko brown and crisp. I want to run around and invite my friends to a treat."

Alyonka stoked the stove and shouted: "Ivashesko, come here and sit down on the oven peel![52]"

"Oh, I'm so small and so stupid," answered Ivashesko, "I do not understand at all. First teach me how to sit on the oven peel!"

"All right," Alyonka said, "teaching does not take long," and sat down on the oven peel. Ivsasheshko quickly put her in the oven, closed the door and ran out of the house. He locked the house and climbed a tall, tall oak.

The witch came home with the guests, knocked on the door, but nobody opened it. "That miserrable Alyonka, off playing somewhere again!"

She stepped through the window, unlocked the door, and let her guests in. Everyone sat down at the table. The witch opened the oven door, pulled out the roasted Alyonka and set it on the table. They ate and ate, they drank and drank, went out into the yard and began to roll on the lawn. "I turn, I roll, full of Ivan meat. I turn, I roll, full of Ivan meat," cried the witch.

And Ivashesko called from above: "Turn, roll, full of Alyonka meat!"

"Oh," murmured the witch, "I hear something, maybe the leaves rustle?" And again she says: "I turn, I roll, full of Ivan meat!"

And Ivashesko called: "Turn, roll, full of Alyonka meat!"

The witch looked up and saw Ivashesko. Quickly she rushed to the oak and began to gnaw the trunk. She gnawed and gnawed and broke two front teeth. Then she ran to the blacksmith and said,

---

52 An oven peel is a long-handled, flat, spade-like tool used to put food into an oven or take it out.

"Blacksmith, blacksmith, make wrought iron teeth for me, or I'll eat you alive!" And the blacksmith forged two iron teeth.

She returned, began again to gnaw at the oak, gnawed and gnawed. Just when she had nearly gnawed through the tree, Ivashesko jumped over to another oak, and the one she had gnawed through crashed to the ground. The witch saw Ivashesko sitting on the other oak tree. Gritting her teeth with rage, she started to gnaw again. She gnawed, gnawed and gnawed and broke two lower teeth.

Again she ran to the blacksmith and said: "Blacksmith, blacsmith, make me iron teeth or I will devour you!" And the blacksmith forged once again two iron teeth. She returned and continued to gnaw the oak on which Ivashesko sat.

Ivashesko did not know what to do. Then suddenly he saw a flock of geese and swans fly past.

"My dear geese, and my dear swans,
Take me on your wings!
Bring me to my parents' house.
There is food and there is drink.
You are welcome there to eat!"

"The next flight should take you!" cried the birds, and flew past, and Ivashesko waited. Then a second flock flew by and Ivashesko asked,

"My dear geese, and my dear swans,
Take me on your wings!
Bring me to my parents' house.
There is food and there is drink.
You are welcome there to eat!"

"The last flight will take you!" And Ivashesko waited. Finally the third flock came past and he called again. The geese and swans took him on their wing, carried him home and set him up in the attic.

The next morning, very early, the mother began to make blini, began to cook, and thought of her little son,

"Where oh where is my Ivashesko? If only I could dream of him!"

Then the father said, "I dreamed that geese and swans had brought our Ivashesko home on their wings."

The mother finished the cooking and said, "Well, old man, let's divide the blini. This one, Pa, for you – this one for me; this one Pa, for you – this one for me."

"And is there none for me?" exclaimed Ivashesko. "This one for you, that one for me, but none for Ivashesko?"

"Oh," said the mother, "what's that I hear! Father, go look!"

The old man went up to the attic, brought down Ivashesko; and they were full of joy. They asked Ivasheshko about everything that had happened. From then on, they lived happily together and prospered all their days.

Interpretation

To shove off from land and sail out to sea always means to leave behind the sense world with its hard and fast objects, facts and concepts and to venture forth in the boundless etheric-soul world. To bring up forces from the depths in this world is called in the picture language "to catch fish".

Fatherly spiritual consciousness and motherly soul consciousness accept what the young human spirit brings them. But evil, magical soul forces that would destroy the inner being of Man grasp for this young spirit. But where the witch's daughter, the undeveloped sentient soul – Alyonka – is, there innocent orientation to the sense world becomes the lower fire of sensuality. Ivan turns the soul devoted to sense pleasure over to the destroying fire which she herself has stoked. He flees to the top of the oak tree. One could say that his whole being grows like a tree[53] in an effort to save himself, and the pure growth forces, the innocent life forces hold him aloft. Thrice called, geese and swans bear homeward the pure being forces of his higher nature.

---

53  More or less untranslatable German: *das ganze Wesen bäumt sich aus.*

## 17. The Witch and the Sister of the Sun (A 93)

In a land, in a far-off kingdom, once lived a king and a queen who had a son, Ivan, who was mute from his birth. When he was twelve, one day he went to the stable to see his favorite servant who always told him folktales. He went to hear folktales, but he heard something very different.

"Ivan Tsarevich," said the stable hand to him, "your mother will soon have a daughter and you will have a sister. But she will be a terrible witch. She will devour your father and mother and all subjects. Go, pretend you want to go for a ride, and ask your father for his best horse. Mount it and ride away, ride wherever your eyes turn, so you can escape misfortune!"

Ivan Tsarevich went to his father, and for the first time in his life he could address him. The king was so glad that he did not ask why Ivan needed the horse. And he immediately ordered that the very best horse from his paddocks be saddled.

Ivan Tsarevich mounted the horse and rode away. He rode wherever his eyes turned: he rode for a long, long time. Finally he came to two old seamstresses, and asked if he could stay with them. "We would like to welcome you here, Ivan Tsarevich," replied the two old ladies, "but we do not have much longer to live, for we will open one more box of needles, sew another box of thread, and then death will come to us."

Ivan Tsarevich began to cry, rode on and rode for a long, long time. Then he came to the Giant Oak Puller: "Take me up with you!" "I would gladly receive you with me, Ivan Tsarevich, but I have not much longer to live. When I have torn all these oaks out by the roots, then death comes immediately."

Ivan Tsarevich wept even more and rode on and on. Finally he came to the giant Mountain Mover and asked him for admission. "I would like to receive you, Ivan Tsarevich, but I have not much longer to live. You see, I am put here to move these mountains, and when I have relocated the last one, death comes at once."

Ivan Tsarevich shed bitter tears and rode on, rode long, long. Finally he came up to the Sun's sister. She took him in, gave him food and drink, and looked after him like her own son. There the tsarevich had a nice life. But he always grieved, for he was homesick, wanted to know what was happening in his father's house. Again and again he climbed a high mountain and looked for the royal castle. But everything was devoured, and only the walls were left. He began to sigh and cry. When he once again came down from the mountain, the sister of the sun met him and asked, "Ivan Tsarevich, why did you weep?"

"The wind blew in my eye" - and another time he answered the same. Then the sister of the sun forbade the wind to blow. So when Ivan Tsarevich came down from the mountain for the third time, there was nothing to do; he had to confess everything. And he began to ask the sun's sister to let him go home so he could see his homeland again. She did not want to let the brave lad go, but he begged and asked until she finally let him go home.

When he left, she gave him a precious brush. a comb and two fresh apples. No matter how old a person was, if he ate one of these apples, he immediately became young again.

Ivan Tsarevich rode away and came to the giant Mountainmover. Only a single mountain remained. The tsarevich took his brush and threw it into the open field. All at once high, high mountains grew out of the earth. Their peaks rose to the sky, and there were so many of them that one could not count them. Mountainmover was happy and got down to work joyfully.

Sooner or later, Ivan Tsarevich came to the Giant Treepuller. There were only three oaks left. He took the comb and threw it into the open field, and suddenly a dense oak forest arose, thicker than the firstt. Treepuller rejoiced, thanked the tsarevich, and happily set about clearing the centenary oaks.

After a long time, or maybe not so long, Ivan Tsarevich came to the two elderly ladies. He gave each a little apple, they ate it and became young on the spot again. Then they gave him a handkerchief: "If you swing it, a whole lake will emerge behind you."

When Ivan Tsarevich came home, his sister ran to him and caressed him tenderly: "Sit down, brother, take the Gusli and play, but I go and prepare the noon meal!"

Ivan Tsarevich sat down and played the Gusli. Then a little mouse crawled out of a hole and spoke to him in a human voice: "Save yourself, tsarevich; You must hurry away! Your sister left to sharpen her teeth for you."

Ivan Tsarevich hurried out, mounted his horse and dashed back. But the little mouse ran over the strings of the Gusli and they began to sound, so the sister did not notice that the brother had fled. When she had sharpened her teeth, she stormed back into the room, but there was no soul left, only the mouse who slipped into the hole. Then the witch became angry, gritted her teeth, and took off in pursuit of her brother. Ivan Tsarevich heard the noise, turned and saw that his sister had almost overtaken him. Quickly he waved his handkerchief, and behind him a deep lake arose. The witch swam through it, but Ivan Tsarevich was already far away. She chased after him even faster, and again she came very close to him. Then Tree Puller guessed that the tsarevich was trying to save himself from his sister, and began to rip the oaks out, and threw them in her way. A whole mountain he piled up; there was no way through for the witch! She began to gnaw her way and finally gnawed through, But Ivan was already far away. Again she stormed after him, she raced and raced and she almost caught him. But Mountain Mover saw it, seized the highest mountain, set it in her way, and piled others over it. The witch crawled and climbed. But Ivan Tsarevich rode and rode, and was already far ahead.

When the witch was over the mountain, she pursued her brother again, and when she saw him she shouted: "Now you will not escape me!"

But he charged up to the towers of the the castle of the sister of the sun shouting: "Sun, sun, open your window!" And the sister of the sun opened the window and Ivan Tsarevich jumped in with his horse.

The witch began to ask the sister of the sun to give her the brother. But the sister of the sun did not listen to her and did not give him to her.

"Ivan Tsarevich shall go to the scales with me," demanded the wicked sister, "we want to see who outweighs. If he weighs more, I'll eat him; if I weigh more, he'll kill me!"

So they went to the scales with each other. First the tsarevich sat down on the scales, then the witch crept up. No sooner had she set her foot on it than Ivan was thrown so high in the air that he flew straight into the towers of the Sun's sister. But the witch-dragon remained on the earth.

Interpretation

Afanasyev writes: "This folktale is especially noteworthy and is puzzling in many ways. The sister of the sun mentioned here is dawn. Ivan Tsarevich, who is pursued by the all devouring witch-dragon, reaches the castle of the Sister of the Sun and calls, "Sun, Sun, open your little window!" The Serbs call the sunrise 'God looks' or the 'Light of God's eyes', The same word, *procor*, to the Bulgarians means *window*. Compare this word with the words *dawn, look, window,* and *eye*."[54]

---

54  I have not been able to locate the Russian original of this quotation. The point seems to be a connection between the words for *window* and *sunrise*.

The folktale itself is like the dawn. Just as it precedes the sun, so this tale points to a time yet to come but drawing near, a Man-devouring age. The Johannine spirit experiences how in individuals and in mankind old forces are coming to an end.

One who has grasped the image of spinning and weaving will also be able to understand the image of sewing: to combine meaningfully what is available as individual pieces of fabric of thought. And such a own will also feel why, for these seamstresses, the needles of active work must break and why their thread is about to give out.

The gnarled oak with its iron-hard wood points to life forces that are related to the will. When the relation between the planets and the plant world was still understood, the oak was associated with Mars. These strong life forces are coming to an end, and it will no longer be possible to uproot them. Likewise, inner heights will no longer be found, nor faith to move mountains.[55]

Out of strongest connection with the spirit, with the sun of enlightenment, out of the force of love won in this sphere, the Johannine spirit can work lovingly and helpfully. Ivan enlivens the withering soul and spiritual forces, so that they can, out of freedom, work anew. But evil has initially the greater weight, for on the way to freedom mankind must experience evil. While Johannine spiritual work lives through the strength of the inner sun, the witch temporarily rules on earth.

---

The last sentence makes no sense to me in German nor in English. The Russian word for window, окно (okno) is related to the old Russian око, eye, which is related to the word for eye in most Indo-European languages such as: Latin oculus, German Auge, English eye.

55  The tale does not say why Oak-puller is pulling up oaks or why Mountain-mover is moving mountains, but perhaps Oak-puller represents exploitation of forest and other living resources, while Mountain-mover represents exploitation of mineral resources, including the atmosphere. If so, the old tale is truly prophetic of our time.

# 18. The Bear Tsar (A 201)

Once there lived a tsar and a tsarina, but they had no child. Once the tsar went hunting to shoot deer and birds of passage. It got hot, he thirsted, and he wanted water. Then he saw a well away from the road, came to it and leaned down to drink water. But no sooner had he drunk than the Bear Tsar appeared and grabbed his beard.

"Let me go!" said the tsar.

"Give me what you have at home and do not know of, then I'll let you go!"

"What do I not know of in my house?" thought the tsar. "It seems to me, I know everything."

"I would rather give you a herd of cows," he said to the Bear Tsar.

"No, I wouldn't take two herds."

"I'll give you a paddock of horses."

"No, I do not want two paddocks either; give me that in your house, of which you know nothing!"

Finally the Tsar consented, the bear released his beard, and the Tsar rode home.

He entered the castle, and behold, his wife had borne him twins, Ivan Tsarevich and Maria Tsarevna. That was what he did not know. He clenched his hands in despair and wept bitterly.

"What are you so tearful?" asked the tsarina.

"How should I not cry? I promised my own children to the Bear Tsar."

"How did that happen?" asked the tsarina, and the tsar told her.

"We will not give them to him," said the tsarina.

"Oh, that's not possible, he'll destroy our empire to the last and still take them."

They thought and thought what to do, and finally hit on a plan. They dug a deep pit, decorated it like a room, brought in all sorts of supplies, food and drink. Then they put their children in this pit, made a roof over it, threw earth on it, and covered it over. Soon after, the tsar and tsarina died. The children, however, grew and grew.

Finally the Bear Tsar came to fetch the children. He looked here and there, but no one was there, the castle was empty. He went through the whole castle and thought to himself, "Who will tell me where I can find the royal children?" Then he saw a chisel stuck in the wall.

"Chisel, chisel," the Bear-Tsar asked, "tell me where the royal children are!"

"Carry me into the yard and throw me into the air; where I land, there dig!"

The Bear Tsar took the chisel and threw it into the air. The iron circled, turned, and struck the ground at the spot where Ivan Tsarevich and Maria Tsarevna were. The Bear Tsar dug up the earth with his paws, smashed the roof and shouted, "There you are, Ivan Tsarevich and Maria Tsarevna. You wanted to hide from me; your father and your mother tried to cheat me. I'll eat you for that."

"Oh, Bear Tsar, do not eat us, our father has left many chickens and geese and all sorts of other good things; there is still plenty for you to eat."

"Well, I'm fine. Sit on my back; I'll take you into my service."

The royal children sat on his back, and the Bear Tsar brought them to high, steep mountains that rose to the sky. Everything was empty, nobody lived there.

"We want to eat and drink," said the Ivan Tsarevich and Maria Tsarevna.

"I'll run and get you food and drink," the bear answered. "Meanwhile, stay here and rest!"

The bear ran off to get food, and the children stood there crying bitterly. Suddenly a bright falcon appeared, folded his wings, landed and said: "Ivan Tsarevich and Maria Tsarevna, what fate has brought you here?"

They told him.

"Why did the bear take you?"

"To perform all sorts of services."

"If you like, I will carry you away. Sit on my wings!"

They sat down on the bird, the bright falcon rose, higher than the towering tree, lower than the floating clouds, and flew into distant wide lands.

Just then, the Bear Tsar came back, spotted the falcon in the sky, struck the damp earth with his head. Fire leaped up and singed the wings of the falcon. The falcon had to bring the tsar's children back to the earth.

"So," said the Bear Tsar, "you would flee from me! For that I will eat you to the last bone."

"Do not eat us, Bear Tsar, we will serve you faithfully!"

The Bear Tsar forgave them and brought them into his tsardom. The mountains were even higher and steeper than before. When it had passed a while, Ivan Tsarevich said: "I want to eat!" "Me too," said the Maria Tsarevna. The Bear Tsar went running for food and sternly told them not to move. And while he was running away, they sat on the grass and cried.

Then an eagle appeared and let himself down from the clouds and asked, "Oh, Ivan Tsarevich and Maria Tsarevna, what fate has brought you here?" They told him.

"If you want, I'll take you away."

"How can you do that? The bright falcon wanted to carry us away, but he could not, and you too will not be able to do it."

"The falcon is a small bird, I will fly higher. Sit on my wings!"

The tsasrevich and the tsar's daughter sat down, the eagle flapped its wings and rose into the air, higher than the falcon. The bear came back, saw the eagle under the sky, struck its head on the damp earth, and seared the wings of the eagle. The eagle put down the royal children on the earth.

"Oh, you wanted to flee again," said the bear, "but now I will eat you."

"Be so good and do not eat us, the eagle has seduced us, we will serve you faithfully and honestly!"

The Bear Tsar forgave them for the last time. Gave them food and drink and brought them on. But sooner or later Ivan Tsarevich became hungry again and said, "I want to eat!" "Me too," said Maria Tsarevna. The Bear Tsar left them, ran away to fetch food. But they sat on the grass and wept.

Suddenly a bull appeared. shook his head and asked, "Ivan Tsarevich and Tsar Daughter, what fate has brought you here?" They told him everything.

"If you wish, I will take you away."

"Oh, how are you going to do that? The falcon has borne us and the eagle, and they have not been able to do it, you will certainly not be able to do it." They were melting into tears, unable to say a word without crying.

"The birds could not carry you, but I carry you. Sit on my back!" They sat down, the bull started to run but did not run so fast. The bear-Tsar saw that the Tsar's son and the Tsar's daughter were fleeing, and rushed off to pursue them.

"Oh, bull, bull, the bear is after us!"

"Is he still far?"

"No, near!"

The bear jumped and tried to grab the children. The bull, however, lifted his tail and shot dung into both eyes of the bear. The bear ran off to the blue sea to wash his eyes. The bull, however, trudged on and on. When the Bear Tsar had washed his eyes, he returned to the pursuit.

"Oh, Bull, Taurus, the bear is after us!"

"Is he still far?"

"Oh no, close!" The bear leaped, but again the bull lifted his tail and splattered the bear's eyes. As the bear ran off to wash his eyes, the bull kept going. And when for the third time the bear tried to grab the children, his eyes were again splattered and he had to run to the sea to wash them.

Then the bull gave Ivan Tsarevich a small comb and a towel and said: "When the Bear Tsar is near, first throw the little comb, and if he comes again, wave the towel! "

The bull went steadily on and on. Ivan Tsarevich looked around, and again the Bear Tsar is after them and will soon reach them. Then Ivan took the comb and threw it behind them. And a forest grew so dense, so dark - no bird could fly in it, no animal crawl through, no man could walk, no rider ride through it. The bear gnawed and gnawed, with difficulty he gnawed a narrow path, came through the forest and rushed after them. But the bull and the children were already far away.

Again the bear was getting close to them. Ivan Tsarevich looked around and waved the towel behind him. Suddenly a lake of fire arose, so large, so wide, the tide billowed from bank to bank. Then the Bear Tsar stood on the bank, could not go on, stood and stood, and finally returned home.

The bull, however, came with the royal children to a field. On this field stood a beautiful, large house.

"There you have a house," said the bull, "live there and do not grieve! Light a brushwood fire in the yard, cut me to pieces and burn me in the fire! "

"Oh," cried the royal children," why should we cut you? Live with us, we will nurture and care for you, feed you with fresh grass and quench your thirst with fresh spring water."

"No, children, cut me to pieces, burn my body and sprinkle the ashes on three beds! Out of one bed a horse will jump, out of the second a dog will spring, and out of the third an apple-tree will grow. You, Ivan Tsarevich, ride the horse and go hunting with the dog! "

And so all was done.

One day Ivan Tsarevich decided to go hunting. He took leave of his sister, mounted his horse and rode into the forest. He shot a goose, a duck, caught a little wolf alive and brought all this home. The tsarevich saw that he was able to hunt. He rode out again, shot many birds and caught a small bear. For a third time he went hunting, but this time he forgot to take the dog with him

Soon Maria Tsarevna went to the lake to do the laundry. But a six-headed dragon flew to the other shore of the fiery lake. He transformed himself into a beautiful youth, saw the princess, and exclaimed in a flattering voice, "Greetings, beautiful maiden!"

"Greetings, good youth!"

"I have heard from old people that in days past this lake did not exist. If a high bridge could be thrown across it, I'd come to the other side and marry you!"

"Wait, the bridge will be ready soon," Maria Tsarevna answered. She threw the towel; it formed itself in an arch and soon swung into a high, beautiful bridge over the lake. The youth came over the bridge, resumed his dragon form, locked up the tsarevich's dog, and threw the key into the lake. Then he seized the Tsarevna Maria and carried her away.

Ivan Tsarevich came back from the hunt. His sister was gone, and the dog howled in the locked cage! Then he saw the bridge over the lake, and said, "Surely the dragon has abducted my sister." And he went in search of the Tsarevna Maria.

The Tsarevich walked and walked. In an open field stood a little hut on chicken feet and dog paws. "Litle hut, little hut, turn your back to the forest and your front to me!" The hut turned, and Ivan Tsarevich entered. In the little hut Baba Yaga lay with her with her bonny body stretching from corner to corner and her nose reaching the roof.

"Fu, fu, until today I have heard nothing of the Russian spirit, but now the Russian spirit is rising before my eyes, and he throws himself into my nose too! Why did you come, Ivan Tsarevich?"

"Oh, if you could but help me in my suffering!"

"What sorrow do you have?" Ivan told her everything.

"Now, Ivan Tsarevich, go home, in your court is growing an apple tree! Break off three green shoots, tie them together and where the dog is trapped, hit the castle! Immediately the castle will burst into small pieces. Then fearlessly attack the dragon; he cannot resist you."

Ivan Tsarevich returned home and freed the dog. It jumped out, took the little wolf and the little bear and together they threw themselves angrily on the dragon and tore it to pieces. Ivan Tsarevich, however, took Maria Tsarevna back to himself, and they began to live together, and they lived and lived and prospered all their days.[56]

## Interpretation

If one observes the heavy, clumsy bear, how he tries to stand up – and indeed can learn to stand up and dance on two feet – but always falls like a lump back to earth, then one sees in the bear the living picture of the dull carnal nature in us that strives to be spiritually awake but is ever and again dragged down by its own weight. The spiritual consciousness in Man (the king), in search of existence and experience, falls prey to this dullness and weight and must sacrifice the fruits of its own being – even before it is aware of them – namely the newborn understanding soul Maria and her brotherly I-conscious spiritual counterpart Ivan. In vain the old forces seek to protect the young being; their time is past. The dull, bear-like forces – working with the iron forces of the blood (the chisel) – find their goal and become master of the young soul and spirit. Now this young double being is indeed carried to a high place, but in the high places to which the carnal nature can carry it, the young soul and spirit nature must hunger and thirst. While the bear is gone, the human being experiences an uplift; thinking forces stir. Falcon and eagle forces take it on their wings. But even winged thinking cannot save Man from the ever and again upward flaming fire in the blood.

---

56 Afanasyev's source seems to have forgotten about the shoots from the apple tree and striking the palace. Presumably these details belong in the story and the teller would be justified in restoring them. Surely the palace also comes back together. And does not the death of the dragon break the enchantment on the little wolf and the little bear who become a prince and princess and marry Ivan and Maria?

In crying, Man draws back into his inner self; he pulls himself together in pain and remembers himself. But when through pain one pulls oneself together, other bearing forces awaken: the bull nature in the Will. It can hold back the blood-based forces that repeatedly attack. Three times it can do so from itself; then it needs the help of the developing I through the comb and the towel. The modern German word for "to comb" is much like the English, *kämmen,* but formerly we had a much more graphic word: *strählen,* kin to the word *strahlen,* to radiate. So to comb was to make the flow radiantly. With the comb we order and care for the hair that surrounds our head. Translated to inner processes, "to comb" means means to control those forces that order and promote thinking. Where such forces are thrown against the dull desires of the "bear" nature, upward-striving life forces arise in such abundance that the bear is held up. One who can throw this forest against the bear can also wave the linen towel. In the hands of the prince, it creates a sea of fiery will forces. This holy fire of the Will lets the royal children finally attain safety, peace and security. "There you have a house," said the bull. Now the double being of soul and spirit can move into the house of the body, of which it has so long dreamed: it has now "come into its own."

Beginning in about the first century, the Mithras mystery religion became widespread. It originated in Persia[57] but was carried throughout the Roman Empire by the legionnaires. This was the age of development of the intellectual soul. In the center of this religion was a bull-related mystic ceremony. We know about it mainly from countless meeting places of adherents, many with statues of Mythras slaying the bull. Mythras kneels with one knee on the kneeling bull and plunges his sword into the side of the bull. The picture was intended stimulate the participant in the ceremony. The bull is the picture of the powerful will forces that live in lower

---

57 This was the opinion of Franz Cumont, the first and for many years the main modern scholar. Current scholarship favors a Roman origin with reference to Persia.

Man. Man must master these forces. He must kill them them as lower drives in order to win them in the spirit.

Our folktale describes the development of the intellectual soul. From the ashes of the cleansing transformation arise new forces: the horse (which we already know), the dog that finds the track and the way, and the apple tree of knowledge. The Will of the bull inspires Man to "Use your understanding, find the right path, and know good and evil". Ivan now wins the wolf and the bear; the bear instinct that previously mastered and persecuted him now serves him.

But progress in the spirit must often be bought with a failure on the other side: Ivan forgets the dog, the guardian of the way. While the I is seeking knowledge the soul is busy with itself; Maria Tsarevna does her washing, that is, the soul cleans its sheaths and is without their protection. This is often a good opportunity for the dragon, for never does he find easier access than when the soul is alone and occupied with reviewing its own inner life. For such activity, the testing, verifying I should always be present. On the other side of the sea – where waves of feelings and sensations rise and fall – the dragon appears as a human being, as a being permeated with spirit. But once on this side, he is the dragon of the lower sense nature. On the other side, he is the magnificent Lucifer; on this side, the old serpent. The intellectual soul has learned to live and weave in thoughts, but with her thoughts she builds the bridge for the dragon and delivers herself to him. The I that has fought its way to freedom consults old soul wisdom (the Baba-Yaga) finds guidance, and realizes that at last forces have develop;ed with which the dog can be freed. In combination with all of the instinctive forces which the spiritual seeker now has in his service, the soul is redeemed.

# 19. Legs of Silver, Arms of Gold (A 285)

Tsar Dodon had three daughters. Then the Ivan Tsarevich came to court his daughters. His legs were silver up to his knees, his arms were gold up to his elbows, he had a beautiful sun in the middle of his forehead, and the bright moon on the back of his head.

And he began to woo the daughters of Tsar Dodon: "I will take the one who gives me seven splendid boys in three pregnancies, all of them the way I am: with legs of silver up to the knees, with arms of gold up to the elbows, with a beautiful sun in the middle of the forehead and a bright moon on the back of the head."

Then the youngest jumped up, Maria, Dodon's daughter: "In three pregnancies I will give you seven magnificent boys, and better and more beautiful than you are!"

This pleased the Ivan Tsarevich, and he took the princess Maria to wife. A short time passed, and she became pregnant. But the Tsar's son had to leave to attend to his duties.

"What, you are leaving me?" asked Maria, the princess.

"I will send for your sister to be with you!"

The sister came, and Ivan Tsarevich went about his duties.

When the time came, Maria the Princess gave birth to three magnificent boys. All three had legs of silver up up to the knees, arms of gold up to the elbows, on the forehead a beautiful sun and on the back of the head abright moon. To her misfortune, at the same time a dog gave birth to her pups. The sister took the three sons away from the Maria Tsarevna and sent them to an island. When the Ivan Tsarevich came back, the sister brought him three puppies and said, "Look, your boaster has given birth to three pups!"

"Well," said Tsar Ivan, "let's wait for the next birth!"

Maria, Dodon's daughter, became pregnant a second time. And again Ivan's Tsasrevich had to leave to attend to his duties. Again Maria gave birth to three magnificent boys just like their father. Unfortunately for her, the mother dog again gave birth . The sister took the little ones away, did not show them to their mother and put them out on the same island.

When the Ivan Tsarevich came home, she showed him three young dogs and said: "Again, your boaster has given birth to three young dogs!"

"Well," said the son of Ivan, "let us wait until the third birth!" For the third time, Dodon's daughter, Maria, became pregnant, and Ivan Tsarevich had be away to attend to his duties.

She gave birth to a boy just like his father, but to her misfortune the mother dog again gave birth to a pup. Maria, Dodon's daughter, did not show the child to anyone and hid him on her breast. But the sister did not let up, "If you do not show me the child, I will strangle you!" But no, Maria, Dodon's daughter, did not show her child.

When the Ivan Tsarevich came back, the sister brought him the puppy and said: "Look, your boaster has again given birth again to a dog!"

Then Ivan Tsarevich put Maria, Dodon's daughter, into a barrel and let the barrel down into the blue sea. But Maria had the baby with her.

Maria and the baby floated and floated in the blue sea. The Infant grew and grew and began to speak: "Mother, may I stretch?" "No, my dear, the barrel is not yet scraping the bottom; there is still a great depth below us, we would perish!"

The barrel floated on and on, and the waves carried it nearer and nearer the shore, and suddenly it was on the sand. "Now, mother, now we are sitting on the sand, may I stretch now?"

"Yes, now stretch, my darling!"

He stretched, and the iron hoops of the barrel broke. Mother and son got out of the barrel and came onto the island. They went back and forth looking for a path. Where should they go? They walked and walked and found a narrow path and followed it and came to a house. They entered and looked around; shirts were everywhere in the chairs, worn and unwashed. Maria, Dodon's daughter, immediately took the shirts, washed and rinsed them, dried and ironed them and put them folded in the right front corner (the sacred corner). And she looked around again: all the dishes had been used, eaten from and left unwashed. She washed and dried the dishes, swept the floor, and cleaned everywhere.

Then Maria said to her son: "I hear someone coming; let's quickly hide behind the stove!"

They hid behind the stove, and soon six young men entered the house. They came in and were glad that everything was so clean and tidy. "Who was here, who washed and cleaned up? Show yourself! If you are a beautiful maiden, you shall be our sister, but if you are half a century young, you will be our mother!"

Then Maria, Dodon's daughter, came out from behind the stove. The six youths threw themselves on her neck and shouted, "Well, so be our dear little mother!" And they began to live together. And they asked her, "Where did you come from, dear mother?"

And Maria told them, "Ivan Tsarevich was my husband. In my first pregnancy I gave birth to three boys, each with legs of silver up to the knees, arms of gold up to the elbows, on the forehead a beautiful sun,and on the back of the head a bright moon. But my sister stole them away and said to my husband: 'Look what your boasting wife gave birth to: three young dogs!' Ivan did not harm me. In my second pregnancy I again gave birth to three boys with legs of silver up to the knees and arms of gold up to the elbow, on the forehead a beautiful sun, and on the back of the head a bright moon. Once again my sister stole the boys and showed my husband three puppies, Again Ivan Tsarevich did not harm me until the third childbirth. The third time I gave birth to one boy and hid him by my bosom. Again my sister ran to Ivan Tsarevich, showed him a dog and said, 'Look what your boaster has given birth to!' Then the Tsarevich had me put me into a barrel and lowered me into the blue sea. For a long time we floated around, my little son grew, and when the barrel scraped the bottom he stretched, and the barrel broke in half. We came onto this island and here to your house.

And you, young men, where were you born, where have you been raised? "

"Where we were born we do not know, we grew up on this island, and here a lioness nursed us with her milk."

The youths removed their caps, and Maria, Dodon's daughter, saw that they all had the beautiful sun on their foreheads and the bright moon on the back of their heads. "Oh, my dear children, you were born of me!" And she fell with joy dead to the earth. But the sons lifted her up, wiped her, and she came to life again.

Then they said to her, "Dear mother, bless us for the long journey, we will go and seek our father!" "God bless you!" And they all went away. At last they came into the land where Ivan Tsarevich lived. They asked for him and were immediately allowed into the castle. All seven had pulled their caps low over the forehead. "Tsar Ivan, do you want to hear a story?"

"Yes, I like to hear stories." And the young men told how the wicked sister had exposed them on an island, how they grew up and found their mother. And then they took off their caps, and Tsar Ivan recognized that they were his children. All had legs up to the knees in silver, arms up to the elbows in gold, on the forehead a beautiful sun and on the back of the head a bright moon.

Ivan Tsarevich hugged his sons and, without hesitation, sent messengers for his wife. But the wicked sister was tied behind a horse. The horse was chased over a field, and she was torn to bits.

Maria, Dodon's daughter, returned to her husband, and they lived and prospered all their days.

Interpretation

To the inner sight everything connected with the moon appears silver. Our dream life is subject to the the influence of the moon. It has its seat mostly in the cerebellum, which is in the lower back part of the brain. The cerebrum (in the front of the brain) serves for the development of thinking and understanding, and its development has reduced consciousness of what is going on in the cerebellum. Clairvoyance is connected also connected to the cerebellum. (The Spanish conquistador Hernan Cortes reports that among the royal children in the Aztec court, the development of the cerebrum was artificially retarded to the benefit of the cerebellum by strapping the front of the head between boards. In the royal line, clairvoyance should be preserved.)

Similarly, to the inner sight everything related to the sun appears as gold. Our waking thought life is under the influence of the sun. Every morning we awaken out of the dream realm of the night. The sun brings us to conscious existence.[58] It was a long, continuous development as mankind awoke to thought. Novalis described this development in his *Hymnen an die Nacht* (*Hymns to the Night*). The Man of the Night must become the Man of the Day. Man should bear on his forehead the golden sun. But also the forces of the back brain, the cerebellum, should not fade. They

---

58 Untranslatable word play: "die Sonne lässt us "da" sein." Literally, "the sun lets us be there"; but *Dasein* means *existence*.

should work together harmoniously with the sun forces: on the back of the head should be bright moon.

Seven spiritual forces are begotten and released. They should be cosmic forces, but the evil drives six of them away into isolation. Just as we have learned to recognize in the dog the finder and protector of the ways, so here we see the other, more negative aspect. When the instinct – that should guide us in the right direction – fails, and in us there is nothing more than tired resignation, then have we "gone to the dogs." "*Cave canem* – Beware the dog!" was sometimes found written on the threshold of Roman houses,[59] but it is not so much of the outer as of the inner dog that we must beware if it has a sniffer only for lower things, if it only finds what serves the lower sub-human and not what serves the human and superhuman. Deep within us threatens the she-hound when creative forces are released in the soul. [60]

The barrel depicts the greatest possible isolation and constriction of the human soul. Only when the soul is put entirely on its own and in inner iron concentration (the hoops around the barrel) protects and nourishes the fruit of the spirit (the boy) does a force mature that can redeem the six brothers from isolation. Thereby is Man restored to the totality of his being.

---

59 For example, in mosaic on the floor to the entrance to the "House of the Tragic Poet" in Pompeii. A similar mosaic is found in the Naples Archaeological Museum.

60 This is a rather veiled reference to the mother dog in the tale who gives birth at the same time that the two sets of teriplets are born.

## 20. Golden Legs, Silver Arms (A 284)

In a kingdom, in an empire once lived a king and a queen who had three daughters, three sisters. The eldest daughter said to her sisters, "Sisters, shall we go to the grandmother's house at dusk? Shall we talk to her and let her advise us?" They agreed and left.

"Greetings, grandmother! We want to talk to you and let you advise us."

"Welcome, my girls!"

Then the eldest tsarevna said, "If Ivan Tsarevich wanted to marry me, I would embroider a flying carpet for him, so he can fly wherever he wishes."

But Ivan Tsarevich was standing outside the window, listened to her and thought to himself: Bah, what an act! I can get the flying carpet myself.

The second tsarevna said, "If Ivan Tsarevich, chose me, I would give him my cat, who can tell folktales, and these tales can be heard for three versts."

Ivan Tsarevich, thought to himself: Bah, what is that!, A cat that tells folktales I can procure for myself.

But the youngest tsarevna said, "If Ivan Tsarevich chose me, I would give him nine sons with legs of gold up to the knees and arms of silver up to the elbows and temples thick with stars!"

Ivan Tsarevich heard these words, went home to his father and mother, and said, "Father, mother, I will marry. I take the youngest king's daughter from the thrice-tenth empire." Father and mother blessed him, and he went to fetch his bride.

He came to the far lands, bowed to the king and asked, "Give me your youngest daughter!"

The king prepared the wedding and set up the oak tables. He put the tsarevich and his bride in the best place. They ate and drank and had a joyful wedding.

Ivan Tsarevich lived for a year or two with his father-in-law. Then he got a letter that his father and mother had died, and that the time had come for him to take over his kingdom. He went with Martha, his young wife, into his country and began to rule there.

Whether much time passed or only little, the queen became pregnant. Tsar Ivan[61], however, rode hunting geese and swans, and he stayed away for a long time. While he was gone, Martha gave birth to three little sons. Their legs were gold up to the knees; their arms were silver up to the elbows and their temples thick with stars. They were so beautiful you could not see enough of them. The queen immediately sent a messenger to the wise woman.

On the way the messenger met Baba Yaga who asked, "Where are you going?"

The messenger answered, "Not far, just near."

"Tell me where you are going! If you don't I'll devour you!"

"I'm going to see the wise woman. Tsarina Martha has given birth to three little sons just as she promised."

"Take me as a midwife!" said the Baba Yaga.

"No, Baba Yaga, I dare not take you. Tsar Ivan would have my head cut off."

"Good, then I'll devour you!"

"Well, what can I do? Come along!"

---

61  When Ivan Tsarevich assumes the rulership, he becomes Tsar Ivan. Though the Russian text does not make this distinction, it bothered me to call the tsar "Tsarevich".

The Baba Yaga came into the castle and started her evil work. She took away Martha's little sons and gave her three ugly dogs. Then she ran into the woods and hid the little ones beneath an old oak tree.

When Tsar Ivan, came home, he was immediately informed that his wife had only given him three dogs. He became very angry, ordered the dogs thrown into the sea and wanted to cut off Martha's head. But then he reconsidered. "Well," he said, "I can forgive a first mistake. Let's wait until the second birth!"

Much time passed or only a little - his wife became pregnant a second time. Tsar Ivan went hunting again. Martha the Beautiful, did not want to let him go and wept bitterly. But he did not listen to her, mounted his horse, and rode into the open field.

When the time came, Martha the Beautiful gave birth to six little sons. their legs were gold up to the knees, their arms were silver up to the elbows and the temples full of radiant stars. You could not see enough of them. She sent the messenger to the wise woman. "Do not call Baba Yaga!" she ordered with tears in her eyes.

The messenger left, but met the Baba Yaga on the way and she asked, "Where are you going?"

"Not so far."

"Say where, if you do not say, I'll devour you!"

"Oh, Baba Yaga, I'm going to the midwife. Martha the Beautiful has given birth to six little sons: their legs up to the knees in gold, their arms up to their elbows in silver and their temples thick with little stars."

"Take me as a midwife!"

"No, I will not take you, I am afraid of Tsar Ivan. He will cut off my head."

"If you do not take me," threatened the Baba Yaga, "I'll devour you right down to the last bone!"

"Well, let's go."

The Baba Yaga came to the castle and brought six ugly dogs. When Martha the Beautiful saw her, she took one of her little sons and hid him in her sleeve. The Baba Yaga put the ugly dogs in the bed and took the five children with her. She searched for the sixth, searched and searched, but she did not find him. The others she took with her into the dark forest.

When Tsar Ivan came home, he was immediately informed that his wife had given birth to dogs again. Terrible wrath overcame him. He ordered Martha to be put into a barrel, to put iron bands around the barrel, to close it tight, cover it with pitch and throw it into the sea.

All this was instantly done, The tsar's daughter and her little son were put into a barrel, the barrel sealed, covered with pitch and let down into the wide sea. For a long time the barrel floated on the sea. Finally it drifted to a shore and sat firmly on the sand. The son of Tsarina Martha grew not daily, but hourly. When he grew up he said, "Mother, I must stretch!"

"Go ahead, my child!" He stretched, and the barrel burst. Mother and son came out and came to a high, high mountain. The son of Martha looked to all sides and said: "Mother, if there was a house here with a green garden around it, then this would be a beautiful life!"

And the mother said, "May God grant it!"

And at once an empire was created around them. There were white-stone palaces surrounded by green and cool gardens, and a wide, smooth, paved path led to these palaces. Along this path came poor beggars, holy people who asked for pious charity. Martha the Beautiful called them all together into the white-stone palaces, gave them food and drink, and accompanied them to the gate.

Then beggars went to Tsar Ivan and told him, "In a place where once there were only high mountains, impenetrable forests and deep streams, now a vast empire has arisen. There lives a widow with her son. And this son is of such great beauty that no one has ever seen or heard of such a thing. His legs are of gold to the knees; his arms are of silver up to the elbows; his temples, thick with little stars. You cannot see enough of him. And mother and son have given food and drink to us, bread for the way and a place of honor."

Tsar Ivan said, "Shall I go and see for myself what kingdom is there?"

But the Baba Yaga who now dwelt with Tsar Ivan heard him and said, "What is so special about that? I have eight such youths sitting in the woods by an old oak tree, and all have legs up to the knees in gold, arms up to the elbows in silver, and temples thick with stars." So Tsar Ivan remained at home and did not go into the new kingdom.

Again the beggars and the poor people went on pilgrimage to ask for pious alms. Martha the Beautiful called them all together into the white-stone palaces, gave them food and drink and shelter for the night. The next day she asked them all, "You cripples, you who must beg, where have you been, where have you been, what have you heard?"

And the cripples answered: "When we left you, we went straight to the Tsar Ivan, and he sat down and asked us, 'What have you seen? What have you heard?' We have told him all that we have seen in your new realm, that you live here as a widow and have a son such as there is none more beautiful in the whole wide world. Ivan Tsarevich wanted to come and see everything, but the Baba Yaga did not let him go. 'Well," she said, "what a miracle! I have eight such magnificent young men living in the woods near the old oak tree, and all have legs up to the knees in gold, their arms up to the elbows in silver and the temples full of little stars."

When the beggars, the poor people, left, Martha the Beautiful, said to her son: 'These are my children, your brothers, who are in the woods by the old oak."

"Mother," replied the son, "give me some bread, I'll go and get my brothers and bring them home."

"Go with God, my child," said the mother, and taking milk from her own breast, baked eight loaves of bread. She gave them to him and blessed him for the way.

Whether much time passed or only a little - the brave youth strode to where his brothers were. Quickly is told the tale, not so quickly is done the deed. He came to the old oak. By this oak lay a huge stone. The youth rolled the stone aside and saw his brothers; down in the earth they sat around a table. He dropped each of them a loaf of bread. The brothers ate the bread and began to shout, "This bread is baked with our mother's milk!" Then the youth lowered his straps and pulled them all up into the free world. They greeted each other, kissed, and went home to their mother.

Martha the Beautiful ran out of her castle and went to meet them. She caressed and kissed them and pressed them to her heart. And from then on they all lived together.

Again the beggars, the poor people, came to beg pious alms. Martha the Beautiful called them into the white stone palace, gave them food and drink and a place to sleep. The next day she gave them bread and honored them.

The beggars came to Tsar Ivan and he began to ask them, "You cripples, you beggars, where have you been, what have you seen? "

"We were in the new kingdom and spent the night in it. The young widow gave us food and drink and bread for the way. And she has nine sons, there are no more beautiful ones in the whole world - all have their legs up to their knees in gold, their arms up to their elbows in silver and their temples thickly full of stars."

Ivan Tsarevich immediately gave the order to prepare the horses. The Baba Yaga no longer had anything to boast about; she just sat and said nothing. Ivan Tsarevich drove off to the new kingdom. After a long time – or maybe a short time – all at once he saw a great city and stopped in front of the white-stone palaces. Martha the Beautiful and the nine sons came to meet him. They fell into each other's arms, kissed each other, shed many sweet tears, and gave a feast for all Christendom.

And I have also been to this feast, drinking beer and wine. It flowed over my beard, but nothing came into my mouth.

## Interpretation

The eldest daughter offers the flying carpet, such a rich life of feeling, so vivid that one can soar body free into a higher world. The second promises a cat that can tell folktales, an instinctive life that is still inspired by ancient wisdom. But the bridegroom of the soul can get both of them by himself. Martha promises him nine sons whose actions will be shaped by cosmic forces and who will bear star wisdom in their heads. All nine members of Man – three bodily components, three soul components, and three spiritual components – should bear these cosmic forces.

In the early Christian community – so says the legend – it was Martha, the sister of Lazarus who cared for the ill and saw to it that the poor had food and clothing. She was the founder of Christian social engagement, and legend shows her in this role. That is why in the last picture in our tale there appear the white-stone palaces, the image of enlightened social community. But when the human spirit "rides into the open field" and on the hard-won ground of freedom hunts for knowledge but forgets the soul, then the spiritual fruit (the sons) falls prey to retarded forces (the Baba Yaga), for forces opposing advance are always present. The Baba Yaga wishes to hold back in the earthly realm the more cosmic forces released in the soul. That is, if the Baba Yaga has her way, the soul will not connect with the world as a thinking, free, I-conscious being of intellectual soul but instead as a sentient soul being, full of felling but left behind in the Middle Ages.

The spirit child, protected by the soul, matures in isolation and stillness. The solar son treads the earth with golden feet, and in the heights – "a high, high mountain" – a new realm arises. Matter itself brightens – white-stone palaces arise – where this mother and son appear. And the way is opened for those who, having had only the old wisdom, have become poor in spirit and beg for the bread of new knowledge. They are, as the Beatitudes say, the beggars for the spirit. Our story assures us that "they shall be filled."

A drama of the Intellectual soul is shown in this and the previous folktale. It must grow out of its Medieval habits of thought and stretch forth to develop and hold cosmic, world-encompassing thoughts.

# 21. Marya Morevna (A 159)

Translated by Irina Zheleznova

In a certain kingdom, in a certain realm there once lived a king and a queen with their son, Prince Ivan, and their three daughters, Princess Marya, Princess Olga and Princess Anna. The time came for the mother and father to die, and as they lay on their death-bed they told their son not to keep his sisters long unwed but to marry them off to whoever came to woo them first. The king and queen died, Prince Ivan laid them to rest, and, his heart filled with sorrow, went for a walk in their green garden with his three sisters.

All of a sudden a black cloud came over the sky: a terrible storm was about to break. "Come, sisters, let us go home!" said Prince Ivan. No sooner were they back in the palace than the thunder crashed, the ceiling was rent in two, and a falcon flew into the chamber. He struck the floor, turned into a tall and handsome youth, and said: "Good morrow to you, Prince Ivan. Many a time did I come to your house as a guest, but now I come as a wooer. For I wish to ask for the hand of your sister, Princess Marya." "If my sister likes you, I'll not say nay; she can marry you, and may God bless you both!" said Prince Ivan. And Princess Marya being willing, Falcon married her and carried her off to his kingdom.

Day followed day, and hour followed hour, and a whole year went by before ever they knew it. Prince Ivan went for a walk in the green garden with his two sisters, and again a black cloud covered the sky, the lightning flared, and a fierce wind began to blow. "Come, sisters, let us go home!" said Prince Ivan. No sooner were they back in the palace than the thunder crashed, the ceiling was rent in two, and an eagle came flying in. He struck the floor and turned into a tall and handsome youth. "Good morrow to you, Prince Ivan," said he. "Many a time did I come here as a guest, but now I come as a wooer." And he asked for the hand of Princess

Olga. "If Princess Olga likes you, you can have her," said Prince Ivan. "She is free to do as she chooses." And Princess Olga being willing, Eagle married her and carried her off to his kingdom.

Another year passed, and Prince Ivan said to his youngest sister: "Come, Sister, let us take a walk in the green garden." They had a little walk, and again a black cloud covered the sky, the lightning flared, and a fierce wind began to blow. "Let us go home, Sister!" said Prince Ivan. They came home, and before they had time to sit down, the thunder crashed, the ceiling was rent in two, and a raven came flying in. He struck the floor and turned into a tall and handsome youth, more handsome even than the other two. "Many a time did I come here as a guest, but now I come as a wooer," said he. "Let me have Princess Anna in marriage." "My sister is free to do as she chooses," said Prince Ivan. "If she likes you, she can marry you." And Princess Anna being willing, Raven married her and carried her off to his kingdom.
Prince Ivan was left all by himself. He lived alone for a whole year, and he missed his sisters very much. "I think I'll go and look up my sisters," said he.

Off he set from home, he rode and he rode, and by and by he came to a field where a whole host of warriors lay routed and dead. "If there is a man left alive among you, let him answer me!" Prince Ivan called out. "For I wish to know who it was that vanquished this whole mighty host." And the only living man there replied: "This whole mighty host was vanquished by Marya Morevna, the fairest of queens."

Prince Ivan rode on. He came upon a number of white tents set up in a field, and there, coming out to meet him, was Marya Morevna, the fairest of queens. "Good morrow, Prince," said she, "Whither are you bound? Do you come of your own free will or at another's bidding?"

Said Prince Ivan in reply: "Men who are bold of spirit never go anywhere but of their own free will." "Well, if you are in no great haste, then be my guest and bide in my tent awhile." This Prince Ivan was pleased to do. For two days and two nights he was Marya Morevna's guest, and so well did they like one another that they became man and wife, and Marya Morevna, the fairest of queens, took Prince Ivan with her to her kingdom.

They lived together for a time, but then came a day when Marya Morevna bethought her of setting out again for the wars. She left her palace and everything in it in Prince Ivan's care, and, showing him a room the door to which was locked and bolted, said: "You must look after everything and are free to enter any room in this palace save this one!" But Prince Ivan's curiosity got the better of him, and no sooner had Marya Morevna left than he hurried to the room and unlocked the door. He looked in, and whom should he see hanging there, chained to the wall with twelve chains, but Koshchei the Deathless. Said Koshchei the Deathless in pleading tones: "Take pity on me, Prince Ivan, give me some water to drink. For ten years have I been held here and great have been my torments. I have had no food and nothing to drink, and my throat is all dry and parched." Prince Ivan gave him a whole pailful of water to drink, and Koshchei drank it and began pleading for more. "One pail is not enough, do let me have another," he begged. Prince Ivan gave him a second pail of water, and Koshchei gulped it down and asked for a third. But when he had finished his third pailful he got back all of his strength, and, shaking his chains,
broke all twelve of them. "Thank you, Prince Ivan," said he. "Now you will never see Marya Morevna, no more than you can see your own ears."

He flew out of the window like a whirlwind, caught up Marya Morevna, the fairest of queens, and carried her off with him. Prince Ivan wept long and bitterly, and then he made ready and set off in search of Marya Morevna. "Come what may, I shall find her!" said he.

A day passed, and another, and at dawn on the third day Prince Ivan saw a beautiful palace before him. Beside the palace there grew an oak and on its bough there sat a falcon. The falcon flew off the oak, struck the ground and turned into a handsome youth. "Ah, my own dear brother-in-law, I am indeed glad to see you!" he cried. "How have you been?" And now Princess Marya came hurrying out of the palace. She welcomed Prince Ivan joyously, asked after his health and told him how she lived and fared. Prince Ivan spent three days with them and then he said: "I cannot stay with you longer. I must go to seek my wife, Marya Morevna, the fairest of queens." "It won't be easy to find her," Falcon told him. "Leave your silver spoon here just in case. We will look at it and think of you." Prince Ivan left his silver spoon with Falcon and set off on his way.

He rode for a day, and another day, and at dawn on the third day, standing before him, he saw a palace which was even more beautiful than Falcon's. Beside the palace there grew an oak and on its bough there sat an eagle. The eagle flew off the oak, struck the ground and turned into a handsome youth. "Come, Princess Olga, get up, for our own dear brother is here!" he cried. Princess Olga came running out of the palace. She embraced Prince Ivan, asked after his health and told him how she lived and fared. Prince Ivan spent three days with them and then he said: "I cannot stay with you longer. I must go to seek my wife, Marya Morevna, the fairest of queens." "It will not be easy to find her," said Eagle. "Leave your silver fork with us. We will look at it and think of you." So Prince Ivan left his silver fork with them and set off on his way.

He rode for a day, and another day, and at dawn on the third day, standing before him, he saw a palace which far surpassed the first two in beauty and splendor. Beside the palace there grew an oak and on its bough there sat a raven. The raven flew off the oak, struck the ground and turned into a handsome youth. "Come, Princess Anna, make haste and join me, for our own dear brother is here!" he cried. Princess Anna came running out of the palace.

She greeted Prince Ivan joyously, embraced and kissed him, asked after his health and told him how she lived and fared. Prince Ivan spent three days with them and then he said: "Farewell. I must go to seek my wife, Marya Morevna, the fairest of queens." "It will not be easy to find her," said Raven. "Leave your silver snuff-box with us. We will look at it and think of you." Prince Ivan gave Raven his silver snuff-box, and, taking leave of him and Princess Anna, set off on his way.

A day passed, and another day, but it was only on the third day that he found Marya Morevna. Seeing him, Marya Morevna threw her arms around Prince Ivan, burst into tears and said: "Ah, Prince Ivan, why did you not listen to me? Why did you let out Koshchei the Deathless?" "Forgive me, Marya Morevna, and hold no grudge against me," said Prince Ivan. "Come away with me while Koshchei the Deathless is nowhere to be seen and perhaps he will not overtake us." And the two of them made ready for the journey and rode away together. Now, Koshchei the Deathless was out hunting. It was evening by the time he turned his way homewards, and as he rode along his horse stumbled under him. "Why do you stumble, you old bag of bones?" he asked. "Is it that you sense some misfortune?" Said the horse in reply: "Prince Ivan has been in your house and he has carried off Marya Morevna."

"Can we catch them up?"

"If we were to sow some wheat, wait till it ripened, reap and thresh it and grind it into flour, bake five ovenfuls of bread and not go after them till we had eaten it all up, we should still catch them." So Koshchei the Deathless sent his horse into a gallop, and he caught up Prince Ivan. "I forgive you this first time," said he, "for you were kind to me and gave me water to drink, and perhaps I'll forgive you a second time. But if you dare to go against me a third time, beware, for I will hack you to pieces!" He took Marya Morevna away from him and rode away with her, and Prince Ivan sat down on a stone by the wayside and wept and sorrowed. Then, drying his tears, he went back again for Marya Morevna.

Koshchei the Deathless was away from home. "Come with me, Marya Morevna," said Prince Ivan. "Ah, Prince Ivan, Koshchei will overtake us again!" "Let him! We shall at least have spent an hour or two together." So the two of them made ready for the journey and away they rode. By and by Koshchei the Deathless turned his way homewards. He rode along, and his horse stumbled under him. "You old bag of bones you, why do you stumble? Is it that you sense some misfortune?" he asked. "Prince Ivan has been in your house and has carried off Marya Morevna." "Can we catch them?" "If we were to sow some barley, wait till it ripened, reap and thresh it, brew beer out of it, drink till we were drunk and not go after them till we had slept it off, we should still catch them." So Koshchei the Deathless put his horse into a gallop, and he caught up Prince Ivan. "I told you you would no more see Marya Morevna than your own ears," he said. And he took her away from Prince Ivan and carried her off with him.

Prince Ivan was left alone, he wept and sorrowed, and then he went back again for Marya Morevna. And Koshchei the Deathless happened to be away from home as before. "Come with me, Marya Morevna!" said Prince Ivan. "Ah, Prince Ivan, Koshchei will overtake us and hack you to pieces!"

"Let him! I cannot live without you." So the two of them made ready for the journey and away they rode. By and by Koshchei the Deathless turned his way homewards. He rode along, and his horse stumbled under him. "Why do you stumble? Is it that you sense some misfortune?" he asked. "Prince Ivan has been in your house and has carried off Marya Morevna."

Off Koshchei galloped after Prince Ivan, he caught him, hacked him to pieces, put the pieces in a tarred barrel, bound the barrel with iron hoops and cast it in the blue sea. And he carried Marya Morevna off with him again.

Now, at this selfsame time the silver things Prince Ivan had left with his brothers-in-law lost their lustre and turned dark. "Prince Ivan must have met with some misfortune," said the brothers-in-law. So down Eagle dropped to the blue sea, seized the barrel and carried it out on to the shore. Falcon flew for some living water, and Raven for some dead water, and the two of them came flying back to where Eagle was waiting for them. They broke the barrel, took out the pieces into which Prince Ivan's body had been hacked, washed them and put them all together again properly. Raven sprinkled the pieces with dead water, and they grew fast to one another, and then Falcon sprayed them with living water, and Prince Ivan started and rose to his feet. "Ah, what a long sleep I have had!" he said. "You would have slept longer if it were not for us," his brothers-in-law told him. "And now come and be our guest." "No, my brothers, I must go and seek Marya Morevna."

Back he went again to Koshchei's palace, and it was there he found her. "Ask Koshchei where it was he got himself such a fine horse," he said to her. Marya Morevna bided her time and then she asked Koshchei the Deathless about his horse. Said Koshchei the Deathless: "Beyond the thrice-nine lands, in the thrice-ten kingdom there lives Baba-Yaga the Witch. Her house stands in a forest beyond the Flaming River, and she has many fine mares, among them one on which she flies round the world every day. I tended them for three days, and she gave me a foal in reward." "How did you manage to cross the Flaming River?" "With the help of my magic kerchief. I have only to wave it three times with my right hand, and a bridge so tall will rise before me that no flames can reach it." Marya Morevna heard him out and passed on every word to Prince Ivan. And she carried off Koshchei's magic kerchief and gave it to him.

Prince Ivan crossed the Flaming River and made for Baba-Yaga's house. On and on he walked for a long time, and he had to do without food or drink. By and by he came upon a strange bird and her brood of chicks. "I think I shall eat one of the chicks," said he. "Please, Prince Ivan, do not touch my chicks," said the bird in pleading tones. "Who knows but you may have need of me some day!" Prince Ivan walked on, and he came upon a bee-hive. "I think I shall take some honey," said he. "Do not touch my honey, Prince Ivan," said the bee queen. "Who knows but you have need of me some day!" Prince Ivan walked on, and whom should he see coming toward him but a lioness and her cub. "I think I'll eat the cub," said Prince Ivan. "I'm weak with hunger." "Please, Prince Ivan, do not touch my cub," said the lioness in pleading tones. "Who knows but you may have need of me some day!" "Very well, then, let it be as you ask."

He walked on, as hungry as ever, and he came to Baba-Yaga's house. Stuck into the ground all around it were twelve poles, all save one of them crowned with human heads. "Good morrow, Grandma!" said Prince Ivan to Baba-Yaga. "Good morrow to you, Prince Ivan! What brings you here?" "I have come to serve you, and I hope to get one of your fine steeds in reward." "So be it, Prince Ivan! It is not for a year but for only three days that you must serve me. If you keep my mares safe you shall have a fine steed in reward. If you don't, then your head will crown the last pole of the twelve, and you'll have no one but yourself to blame." To this Prince Ivan agreed, and Baba-Yaga gave him food and drink and told him to set to work. Prince Ivan drove the mares to pasture, but no sooner had he done so than they lifted their tails and galloped off across the meadows. And before he had had time to bat an eye they were out of sight. Prince Ivan wept and sorrowed, and then he sat down on a stone and fell asleep. The sun had already set beyond the forest when the bird whose chick he had spared came flying up to him. "Wake up, Prince Ivan!" she called. "The mares are all back in their stalls." Prince Ivan went home, and there was Baba-Yaga making a great to-do and shouting at her mares. "Why did you come back home?" she demanded of them. "What else could we do! Birds from all over the world came flying at us and nearly pecked out our eyes." "Well, don't run over the meadows tomorrow but hide in the forests."

Prince Ivan slept the night through and woke to see Baba-Yaga standing over him. "It is morning and time for you to pasture the mares," said she. "And if you should lose even one of them your head shall crown the last pole of the twelve." Prince Ivan drove the mares to pasture, and they at once lifted their tails and ran away deep into the forests. He wept and he sorrowed and then he sat down on a stone and fell asleep. The sun had already sunk when the lioness came running up to him. "Wake up, Prince Ivan," she cried. "The mares are all back in the stalls." Prince Ivan went home, and there was Baba-Yaga making a great to-do and shouting at the mares. "Why did you come back home!" she demanded of them. "What else could we do! The fiercest beasts from all over the world set upon us and nearly tore us to pieces." "Well, then, you had better hide in the blue sea tomorrow."

Prince Ivan slept the night through, and in the morning Baba-Yaga sent him off to pasture her mares again. "If you lose even one of them your head shall crown the last pole of the twelve," said she. Prince Ivan drove the mares to pasture, and they at once lifted their tails and vanished from sight. Into the blue sea they ran and they stood up to their necks in the water. Prince Ivan sat down on a stone. He wept and sorrowed and then fell asleep. The sun had already sunk beyond the forest when the bee queen came flying up to him. "Get up, Prince Ivan!" she cried. "The mares are all back in their stalls. Only mind, when you get back to the house, do not let Baba-Yaga see you but go to the stable and hide behind the crib. There is a mangy colt there wallowing in the dung. Lead him out in the deep of night and ride away."

Prince Ivan made his way to Baba-Yaga's house. He stole into the stable and lay down behind the crib, and there was Baba-Yaga making a great to-do and shouting at her mares. "Why did you come back home?" she demanded of them. "What else could we do! Swarms of bees came flying at us and they stung us all over."

Baba-Yaga went to bed and to sleep, and on the stroke of midnight Prince Ivan saddled the mangiest of her colts, sprang on his back and rode to the Flaming River. And no sooner was he there than he waved his magic kerchief thrice with his right hand, and lo!—there before him, spanning the river, rose a fine, tall bridge. Prince Ivan rode across, he waved his kerchief twice with his left hand, and the fine tall bridge turned into a narrow, low one. Morning came, Baba-Yaga woke, and, seeing that her colt was gone, rushed off in pursuit. Like the wind she flew in her iron mortar, using her pestle for a whip and sweeping the tracks away with her broom.

She flew up to the Flaming River, and, seeing the bridge, started off across it. But just as she got to the middle of it, the bridge broke down under her, and she fell into the water and drowned.
Prince Ivan pastured his colt in the lush green meadows, and when the colt grew up to be a strong and handsome steed, he saddled him and made for the house of Koshchei the Deathless. Seeing him, Marya Morevna came running out of the house and threw her arms round him. "How did you come back to life?" she asked him. "God must have been watching over you." Prince Ivan told her of all that had passed. "And now you must come away with me," he said. "I'm afraid, Prince Ivan! If Koshchei overtakes us he'll hack you to pieces again." "He'll not overtake us this time, for my horse flies like the wind." And they mounted the horse and rode away.

By and by, Koshchei the Deathless, who had been out hunting, turned his way homewards. On he rode, and his horse stumbled under him. "Why do you stumble, you old bag of bones?" he asked him. "Is it that you sense some misfortune?" "Prince Ivan has been in your house and has carried off Marya Morevna." "Can we catch them?" "God knows! For now Prince Ivan has a horse as fine as I am or finer." "That isn't going to stop me," said Koshchei the Deathless. "I'll go after them!"

Whether a short or a long time passed, nobody knows, but he caught up with Prince Ivan, and, jumping to the ground, was about to pierce him with his sword. But before he could do it, Prince Ivan's horse struck him with his hoof with all his might and smashed his head, and Prince Ivan finished him off with his cudgel. After that Prince Ivan brought a heap of firewood and made a fire. He burnt the body of Koshchei the Deathless and cast his ashes into the wind.

Marya Morevna got on Koshchei's horse and Prince Ivan on his own, and away they rode. First they went to see Raven, then Falcon and then Eagle, and they were welcomed with joy by all three. "Ah, Prince Ivan, we had lost all hope of ever seeing you!" they said. "But greatly as you have suffered, it was worth it. For if you searched the world over you would never find a bride as lovely as Marya Morevna!"

Prince Ivan and Marya Morevna feasted and made merry, and then they went back to their own kingdom. And there they lived in good health and good cheer for many a long and prosperous year; they never knew hunger, they never knew need, and they drank their fill of ale and of mead.

## Interpretation

At the beginning of the folktale Maria Morevna[62] represents a soul consciousness that lives in fullness and breadth of the soul world but has not yet dealt with death – she gives Koshchei, the boneman,[63] nothing to drink. Into the early Middle Ages, the soul

---

62  Morevna means Daughter of the Sea
63  The Russian name for the villain of this tale is Кощей, which is not a standard Russian word. It is transliterated by the translator of this tale as *Koshchei* but is translated in other stories as *Boneman*. The Russian word for bone is *кость*. Friedel Lenz translates as *Knochenmann*, that is, *Boneman*.

was the Daughter of the Sea. Then began a radical change. The intellectual soul, whose development began in Greek age, was by then fully mature. Man, who had learned to think, pressed onward and sought to grasp heaven and earth with this thinking. The great geographic discoveries quickly widened his horizons. New laws of physics, mechanics and statics were found. Man researched the physical world. While he had previously seen in nature spiritual beings, he now understood it from the outside through laws. The onlooker consciousness prevailed.

Novalis wrote[64]: "Nature stands alone and lifeless. Hard number and rigorous mass constrain her. Dark words turn the unmeasurable blossom of life to dust and air." Even the cosmos, formerly inhabited by heavenly intelligences, rigidified into a grandiose celestial mechanics. In Man, the mechanic ruled but can only know the skeleton, the dead. Expressed in pictures, Koshchei, the Boneman, ruled. Throughout the art of the late Middle Ages he appears as the eerie emblem of this age. (Note also the death dance.)

At the beginning of the story, the boneman is chained. How he became chained, we are not told, but this condition would seem to point to the earlier, Graeco-Roman age. Quantitative thinking (the boneman) was there – recall Greek mathematics and Roman engineering – but it was well under control and did not threaten the life of the soul. It is precisely the Johannine I consciousness – Ivan Tsarevich – that sets the boneman free and thus allows him to carry off the human soul, Maria Morevna.

To rescue Maria Morevna, Ivan must develop a thinking (= get a horse) equal to that of the Boneman. The soul gets the kerchief: living in thoughts that apply to the sense world and can grasp what

---

64 "Einsam und leblos stand die Natur. Mit eiserner Kette band sie die dürre Zahl und das strenge Maß. Wie in Staub und Lüfte zerfiel in dunkle Worte die unermeßliche Blüte des Lebens." *Hymnen an die Nacht* - Kapitel 6. The author quotes apparently from memory and not quite exactly.

is dead but orderly, soul helps the seeking I. With the help of the gift from the soul, the I penetrates into that background where many-sided forces of understanding – the mares – wait in the realm of the soul. There the spirit seeker gets the mangy foal: a young horse, still afflicted with childhood diseases, but especially strong in potential for the future. He is lying on the manure pile: there where remnants of former life become the fertilizer for new seed. When Ivan – the Johannine spirit – has mastered the intellectual thinking (the horse) and this thinking has so matured in the realm of the living that it can overcome the Boneman, then the soul is rescued. She can now herself ride the horse – the thinking – that once served the Boneman.

## 22. Milk of Beasts (A 204)

Once upon a time there lived a king who had a son and a daughter. Over the neighboring kingdom came great disaster: the whole people died. Then Ivan Tsarevich asked: "Father, give me your blessing, I will go to that kingdom to live there." But the father did not want him to go and refused the blessing.

"Then I will go by myself," said the Tsarevich, preparing for the journey. But his sister did not want to be parted from him and accompanied him.

They went and went and came to a cleared field. Lo! there was a little house on chicken feet that turned and turned.

Ivan Tsarevich said, "House, house, stand in the old way, as the mother put you!"

The cottage stood still, and they entered. Inside lay Baba Yaga, her feet in one corner, her head in the other, her lips on the doorjamb, and her nose up on the ceiling. "Hail, Ivan Tsarevich, do you have an act before you, or do you have deeds behind you?"

"I've done all sorts of deeds, but I have deeds yet to do. I know a kingdom where the people have all died. I go to live there."

"That you go is good," said the Baba Yaga, "but you wrongly took your sister; she will do you great harm."

She gave them food and drink and put them to sleep.

The next morning, brother and sister set off. The Baba Yaga gave the Tsarevich a little dog and a blue ball: "Where the ball rolls, there goes your way!"

The ball rolled and rolled to another cottage standing on chicken feet. "House, house, put yourself in the old way, just as the mother has put you down!"

The little house stood still, and the tsarevich and the tsarevna entered.

Inside, Baba Yaga was lying, asking, "Ivan Tsarevich, are you doing something behind you, or are you doing something before you?"

He told her why and where he is going.

"That you go yourself is right," said the Baba Yaga, "but you wrongly took the sister, she will do you much harm."

The Baba Jaga gave the two something to eat and drink and put them to sleep. In the morning she gave the Tsarevich a dog and a towel. "On your way you will come to a big river, there you can not go over. Take this towel and wave one end; immediately a bridge will appear. Go over and wave the other end, so the bridge will disappear again. But be careful and wave the towel so your sister does not see it!"

Ivan Tsarevich went to where the ball rolled, and his sister went with him. They came to a wide, wide river." Brother," said the sister, "let's sit down to rest!"

She sat down, but Ivan Tsarevich secretly waved the towel, and immediately a bridge arose. "Come on, sister, come, God has given us a bridge so we can go to the other side." When they were over, the Tsarevich secretly waved the other end of the towel, and the bridge disappeared as if it had never been.

And now they were in the kingdom in which the people had died out. Nobody was there, everything was empty. They stayed there and began to settle in.

The brother went hunting and roamed with his dogs through forests and swamps.

Just then the dragon Gorynych flew to the other side of the river, landed on the damp earth and turned into a handsome youth such as you cannot imagine, only tell of it in a fairy tale. He attracted the tsarevna and shouted: "I almost passed away in longing for you, I cannot live without you!"

The tsarevna was seized with love and shouted to him: "Fly over the river to me!"

"I cannot go over there!"

"What could I do about it?"

"Your brother has a towel, take it, come to the river and wave one end!"

"He will not give it to me!"

"Well, deceive him, tell him you want to wash it!"

The tsarevna returned home to the castle, and at the same time her brother also returned from the hunt. He had brought all kinds of game and gave it to the sister for the next day for lunch.

"Brother, do you not have to do some laundry?"

"Go to my room, little sister. there you will find some things," said Ivan Tsarevich and forgot the towel of Baba Yaga, which she had forbidden him to show the tsarevna. The tsarevna, however, took the towel.

The next day the brother went hunting, but the sister went down to the river. She waved one end of the towel, and at the same moment the bridge came up. The dragon came over the bridge, they caressed each other, kissed each other and went into the castle together. "How could we destroy your brother?" said the dragon.

"I do not know, you must think how yourself," answered the tsarevna. "Well, pretend to be sick and ask your brother for wolf's milk. If your brother goes out to get it, he may lose his head." The brother returned. The sister lay on the bed pretending to be ill and saying, "Brother, in the dream I have seen that I have recovered from wolf's milk. Could not you find some somewhere? Otherwise I must die!"

The Tsarevich went into the forest; a she-wolf suckled her pups. He started to shoot her, but she shouted in a human voice: "Do not shoot, Ivan Tsarevich, do not kill me, do not make my children orphans! Tell me what you need."

"I need your milk!"

"Gladly, milk it, I'll give you also a pup, it will serve you faithfully and honestly." The Tsarevich milked the milk, took the wolf pup and went home. The dragon saw him and spoke to the tsarevna: "Your brother comes back and brings a little wolf. Tell him now that you need the milk of the bear."

The dragon spoke and changed himself into a brushwood broom. The Tsarevich entered the chamber, followed by his dogs. They sensed the unclean spirit and started to attack the brushwood broom and the twigs began to fly. "What does that mean, brother? Control your dogs or I have nothing with which I can sweep tomorrow!" Ivan Tsarevich call off the dogs and gave the tsarevna the milk of the she-wolf.

In the morning the brother asked, "How are you, little sister?"

"I feel a little better, but if you brought me bear's milk, I would be perfectly well."

The Tsarevich went into the forest and found a mother bear nursing her cubs. He prepared to shoot her, but she pleaded with a human voice: "Do not shoot me, Ivan Tsarevich, do not make my children orphans; rather say what you need!"

"I need your milk! "

"Gladly, and I'll give you a bear cub in addition."

The Tsarevich milked the bear, took the cub, and returned home.

The dragon saw him coming and spoke to the tsarevna, "Your brother is coming; he brings a bear cub. You must now ask for lion's milk." And turned himself into a stove broom, and the tsarevna put him under the stove.

Ivan came with his hounds. The dogs smelled the unclean spirit, scrambled under the stove, and began to bite the oven-broom. "Brother, control your hounds, or I have nothing to sweep the stove with tomorrow!"

The Tsarevich called off his dogs; they lay under the table and growled. In the morning, Ivan Tsarevich asked, "How are you feeling, little sister?"

"Oh, it did not help, but I dreamed tonight that if you gave me milk from a lioness, I would be well." The Tsarevich went into a dense, dense forest, searched long and everywhere. Finally he saw a lioness nursing her young. He started to shoot her, but the lioness shouted in a human voice: "Do not shoot, Ivan Tsarevich, do not make my children orphans, say what you need!"

"I need your milk!"

"I'll give you milk and a little lion in addition."

The Tsarevich milked the lioness, took a small lion and returned home. The dragon Gorynych saw him and said to the tsarevna, " Your brother comes and brings a little lion." And he began to ponder how to destroy the Tsarevich. He thought and thought and finally he had it. He decided to send the Tsarevich to the thrice-tenth empire. In this kingdom stands a mill, behind twelve iron doors. Once a year the mill is opened, but only for a short time. As soon as you look around, the doors close again. "Let him try to get the very best flour out of this mill!" said the dragon to the tsarevna and turned into a poker which the tsarevna threw it under the stove. The Tsarevich entered the room, greeted the sister and gave her the lion's milk.

Again the dogs scented the dragon, threw themselves under the stove and began to gnaw at the poker. "Oh, brother, calm down your pack or they will break something else!"

Ivan Tsarevich Johannes called off his dogs; they lay down under the table, looked menacingly at the poker and growling. Toward morning the tsarevna pretended to become even sicker, groaning and groaning." What about you, little sister," said the brother, "does not the milk help you?"

"Not in the least, brother." And she talked to him, Ivan Tsarevich dried himself some rusks, called his dogs and the other animals and made his way to the mill. He had to wait a long time until the time came and the twelve doors opened. Then he entered the mill and quickly ground the fine flour. No sooner had he stepped out than the doors closed behind him, but the animals remained trapped in the mill. The Tsarevich began to cry bitterly: "Now I see that death is close to me!"

He returned home. The dragon saw that he came alone, without the animals, and said, "Now I no longer fear him!" He sprang to meet him, opened his throat, and cried, "I have long tried to get to you, Ivan Tsarevich, and now finally I will eat you!"

"Wait a minute to eat me. Better for you if I first wash in the bath-house!"

The dragon agreed and ordered him to carry the water himself, to chop the wood and to heat the bath-house. Ivan Tsarevich began to chop wood and carry water. Then a raven came flying and croaked: "Krah, krah, Ivan Tsarevich, chop the wood, but do not hack too fast, your animals have already gnawed through four doors!" Ivan chopped the wood, but what he hacked, he threw into the water. However, time went by and there was nothing to do, he had to heat the stove.

The raven came flying again and croaked: "Krah, krah, Tsarevich Ivan, heat up the bath room, but do not heat too fast, your animals have already gnawed through eight doors!" Ivan heated the bath room, began to wash and had only one thought: "Oh, if my animals can only get here in time!"

Then a dog came running. "With two, death is not frightening!" Ivan thought. Then all the other animals leaped around him.

The dragon Gorynych had been waiting for the Tsarevich for a long time. Eventually his impatience seized him and he himself came to the bath house. Then the animals rushed at him and tore him into small pieces. Ivan Tsarevich collected all the pieces, burned them in the fire and scattered the ashes on the open field. Then he went into the castle, followed by his animals, to cut off the head of the tsarevna. But she threw herself on her knees before him, cried and begged the tsarevich not to kill her.

He led her out and put her in a circle of stone. Beside it he laid a bundle of hay and two pails. One was full of water, the other was empty. Then he said, "If you drink this water, eat this hay and fill this pail with your tears, then God forgives you and I will forgive you."

Ivan Tsarevich left his sister in the stone circle and walked with his animals three times behind the ninth country. He walked and walked and came to a handsome big city. And see, half of the people celebrated festivals and sang songs, the other wept bitter tears. Then he asked an old mother for lodging for the night and asked: "Say, grandmother, why half of your people celebrate and sing songs while the other half is crying?" "Ah," answered the old woman, "to our lake has come a twelve-headed dragon, who comes every night to eat a human. We have established a specific order from which end of the series and on which day one will be sacrificed to the dragon. Those who made their sacrifices celebrate festivals, but the others cry tears."

"And whose time is it now?"

"Now the lot has fallen on the tsarevna herself. The tsar has only one daughter, and he must give her to the dragon. He made an appeal: If anyone will kill the dragon, he would give him half of his kingdom and the tsarevna as his consort. But where are there still such heroes today? For our sins, they have all passed away."

The Tsarevich collected his animals and went out to the lake. On the shore stood the beautiful tsarevna and cried bitter tears." Fear not, O tsarevna, I am your protector!"

Then the lake stirred and moved, and the twelve-headed dragon appeared. "Ivan Tsarevich, you Russian bogatir, why did you come here? Are you looking for battle or peace?"

"Why peace? That's not why a Russian bogatir comes to you." And he set his animals on the dragon, the two dogs, the wolf, the bear, and the lion. The animals grabbed him and tore him to pieces straight away. Now Ivan Tsarevich cut out the tongues of all twelve dragon heads and put them in his pocket. Then he let the animals run, rested his head on the knees of the tsarevna, and fell asleep.

In the early morning, the water-carrier came with his barrel. He saw that the dragon had been killed, that the tsarevna was alive, and that a brave young man was sleeping on her knees. So he ran up, drew his sword, and cut off the Tsarevich's head. Then he forced the oath of the tsarevna to call him her liberator. He brought the dragon's heads to the king. But he did not notice that all heads were without tongues. But sooner or later the animals returned and found the Tsarevich lying without a head. Then the lion covered him with green grass and sat down beside it. Suddenly ravens came flying in with their sons to pick on the corpse. Cleverly, the lion caught a young raven and pretended to tear it in half.

"Do not kill my baby, it did not harm you! If you need something, just command, I'll fulfill everything."

"I need water of life and water of death, bring it to me, and I'll give you back the your young!"

The raven flew away, the sun had not yet set, Then he returned and brought two bottles, one of water of life and one of water of death. The lion tore the raven boy, sprinkled it with the water of death, and the pieces closed again. The he sprinkled it with the water of life and the young raven revived and flew after the old raven.

Now the lion sprinkled Ivan Tsarevich with the water of death and then with the water of life. The Tsarevich stood up and said, "How did I sleep so long?"

"You would sleep forever if I were not here," answered the lion. And he told how he had found him dead and given him back his life. When Ivan Tsarevich entered the city, all the people there were celebrating a feast, embracing, kissing, and singing songs.

"Tell me, Grandmother," he asked the old woman, "why are you all so happy?" "Look what has happened to us, the water-carrier has defeated the dragon and saved the tsarevna, and now the king gives him his daughter to wife."

"Is it permissible to watch the wedding? "

"If you can play music, go; all the minstrels invited."

"I know how to play the gusli."

"Go, the tsarevna loves so much the music of the gusli." Ivan Tsarevich bought a gusli and went to the castle. He began to play, and everyone who heard him was amazed. "Where does this wonderful minstrel come from?" The tsarevna filled a cup with wine and handed it to him with her own hand. She looked up, remembered her liberator, and tears fell from her eyes.

"Why are you crying?" asked the king, her father.

"I recognized my liberator." Ivan Tsarevich made himself known to the king. He told him how it had all happened, and took out the dragon's tongues from his pocket. The water bearer was seized, led away and killed. And Ivan Tsarevich took the beautiful tsarevna to wife.

In his joy he remembered his sister and returned to the ring of stone. The sister had eaten the hay, drunk the water, and the empty pail was full of her tears. Ivan Tsarevich forgave her and let her live. He and his bride began to live together, and they lived and prospered.

Interpretation

A great impulse of love works in the Johannine spiritual stream that flows through history. It works especially there "where all the people have died." If a human spirit is taken by this impulse, then it becomes an Ivan Tsarevich; and, to be sure, the sister soul is connected. But it matters whether this soul is also grasped by this impulse of love. In the realm of the second Baba Jaga, which formerly prepared the work of the intellectual soul, Ivan gets the linen towel; he can now control his thought life in freedom.

So equipped, brother and sister reach the sought-for realm. But while the spiritual seeker explores this realm and hunts for new knowledge, the passive soul falls to the dragon. In the sister's hand, the thinking that the brother won becomes a bridge for that power which appears as a seductively beautiful spiritual force but is really the dragon of vanity and pride. (Gorynych means Son of Grief.) Wooed by Lucifer, the soul betrays the brother.

But here also is Lucifer "a part of that power that always wants to do evil and always does good,"[65] for the spirit seeker finds gets not only the milk of the beasts but also a young one who serves

---

65 "Ein Teil von jener Macht die stets das Böse will und stets das Gute schafft" Mephistopheles's description of himself to Faust, Goethe's *Faust* Part I, lines 1335–6.

him faithfully and in the end destroys the dragon. Milk is created in the mature organism and is therefore not a direct product of the earth – it is cosmic nourishment. But it fills the young with forces to deal with the earth. To get the milk of the animals means to win for the soul certain instincts as cosmic nourishment. Thereby it is possible that the same instincts which, unmastered, become raging forces and destroy thee human being, will from now on serve the spirit seeker as new, young forces. There are three of them, the wolf, the bear and the lion.

It was not long ago that there were still tribes on South Sea islands which, during an eclipse of the sun would run crying in great fear, "The wolf is eating the sun!" They lived still in the old picture consciousness and saw the process from the inside. The being of darkness swallowed the being of light that is the source of all life. The wolf eats mainly flesh and knows how to procure it with great greed. He earns his status as the symbol of darkness.

In Germanic mythology, Fenris Wolf summons the Twilight of the Gods. The inner light world of supersensible truth, in which Man had lived, darkened; Man can no longer see the gods. Fenris wolf eats the inner sun. Thereupon the spiritual world darkens, the physical becomes the only one recognized, Delusion and lies take control of Man. In the folktales "Little Red Cap" (= Red Riding Hood) and "The Wolf and the Seven Kids" the wolf appears in this role.

The end of this role for the wolf and the beginning of a much more positive one was connected with a major event in human history: the rise of Rome. Through its conquests it broke up long-standing tribal structures and mixed peoples throughout the empire. Many tribes were broken up and exogamy more and more replaced endogamy. Clairvoyance based on in-breeding within the tribe faded. Rome itself did not have its own gods; its gods were borrowed. Nor was its art original; it was imitated. In the imperial cult, a man was declared a god and revered as divine.

The symbol of Rome is the nursing wolf. A whole old world went under in the jaws of that wolf. But a new world came out. An inner world went in; an outer world came out and became more and more important. The new form of the state for the first time gave the individual human being rights. The concept of human rights continues today. Even beyond death, the citizen had (and has) rights; the legal testament or will goes back to Rome. Man was recognized as an individual, as an I.

The nursing she-wolf gives the milk on which the young being can thrive: the new, young, upward-striving I consciousness. All this lies in the emblem: the founders of Rome, Romulus and Remus, twins, are nursed by the she-wolf.

In this connection, the picture of the bear must be taken from its other side. What works as dullness and heaviness in the blood and hinders the awakening in Man can conversely work in a good way. As we have noted, the bear can briefly stand vertically on its hind feet and even dance. But it always falls back into the horizontal position. This constant falling back to the earthly can be seen as strong determination to master earthly tasks, as being true to the earth. A certain earth-bound quality and dependability in coping with what the earth daily demands of us is part of this bear instinct, and as such it can serve the spiritual seeker wonderfully well.

These abilities are further enhanced by lion-like courage and lion-heartedness. (As Man began to develop such personal qualities, he liked to put these animals into his coat-of-arms.) With them he can tread the way to the mill in the thrice-tenth land, in which the grain of the earth, the fruit of all our experiences is processed. Only what is processed can become nourishment for our eternal being. Only what is fully known and recognized becomes the bread of life. As we go through the twelve months, we pass through the twelve signs of the zodiac as through doors in that mysterious mill. But if the instincts lag "behind" and are not "there" in earthly employment, then the human spirit will naturally and necessarily fall prey to the dragon. But whoever can stand over against this power so that through it he feels called to inner clensing – "Better for you if I first wash in the bath-house!" – he is truly already on the road to conquering the dragon. Chopping wood and hauling water are important steps along this way. [In the Karlstein castle, built by Emperor Karl IV (1316 – 1378) and standing about 40 kilometers southwest of Prague there are frescoes which clearly depict the Rosicrucian initiation of the the emperor. The last of the pictures shows him dressed in a star-covered coat with the sun on the right shoulder and the moon on the left shoulder. He is celebrating with bread and wine at an altar. In these pictures there is a youth cutting wood and carrying water.]

To care for the inner tree of life is the job of the inner gardener, but to cut and split hardened wood is the work of the wood chopper. In a folktale, to chop wood means to live in abstract concepts and theories, to deal with the lignified thought of a materialistic age. This is a an indispensable step along the way to recognizing the spirit in matter. The modern spiritual seeker must become a wood chopper. The opposite of the wood chopper is the water bearer. To be a water bearer means to draw from deep sources of etheric life forces, to bear within oneself living, flowing feeling to offset all hardening. One who takes on these two tasks for inner purification experiences the inner messenger of the spirit, the raven. In the next stage, what is lignified and hardened must be soften by contact with what is filled with life and soul: Ivan chops wood but throws into water.

One who thus defends himself against the dragon wins again mastery over those forces that needed their time in the heavenly mill. With their help, the dragon is cut to pieces and his ashes, strewn on open field, become fertilizer for new seed.

If, however, the feminine in Man, the soul, has at this point been freed, it is still not yet the Eternal Feminine. There still lurks a far more dangerous dragon, the twelve-headed one. While the sister soul drinks "water" and eats what was once living and growing but is now dried (hay) and repents, Ivan and his animals free the Eternal Feminine and the chemycal wedding is celebrated.

# 23. Ivashko-Medvedko and the Three Bogatirs (A 141)

In a realm, in an empire, once lived an old man with his wife; they had no children. One day he said to her: "Old woman, go and buy turnips for our midday meal!"

The old woman went and got two turnips. One they ate at once; the other they put it in the oven to steam. After a while a little voice called, "Granny, open the oven. It's too hot in here!" The woman opened the oven door, there was a live girl in the oven.

"What is that?" asked the man.

"Oh, Father, God gives us a girl!"

The two old people were very happy and called the child Turnipkin. Turnipkin grew up and up. Once the girls of the village came out and asked: "Babushka, let Turnipkin go with us into the forest for berries!"

"No, you would leave her in the forest."

"No, we would never leave her, Babushka."

The old woman let Turnipkin go with the girls into the forest. They went together and came into such a dense forest that nothing could be seen before their eyes. But look, there was a hut. They went in, and there was a bear sitting on a post.

"Good day, beautiful girls, I've been waiting for you for a long time." He told them to sit down at the table and brought them groats to eat. "Eat, beautiful girls. Whomever does not eat, I want to take to wife!"

Everyone except Turnipkin ate some of the porridge.

The bear let the girls go home but kept Turnipkin with him. He fetched a sled, fastened it to the roof pole with ropes, lay down, and ordered her to swing him. Turnipkin rocked him and sang:

"Bye, bye old horseradish."

"No," said the bear, "do not sing that, sing 'Bye, bye, my dearest friend!'"

There was nothing to do. She rocked and sang, "Bye, bye, my dearest friend!"

For almost a year, Turnipkin stayed with the bear and became rounder. She looked for an opportunity to escape. Once the bear went hunting and left her alone in the hut. He barred the door with oak logs, but Turnipkin forced her way through. She struggled and struggled, at last succeeded, and ran home.

The old man and his wife rejoiced when she returned. They lived together for a month, a second mont and a third. In the fourth month Turnipkin gave birth to a son who was half human, half bear. They baptized him and gave him the name of Ivashko-Bearson[66]. Ivashko started to grow, he did not grow by years, but by hours. No sooner had an hour passed than he had grown a hand's breadth, as if someone were pulling him up. At the age of fifteen, he played with other children but was too rough. He took a boy by the hand and tore off the hand. He grabbed another's head and threw it away, The peasants complained to the old man, "Neighbor, it would be good if your grandson left. His play is ruining our children."

Then the old man became very unhappy and sad. Ivashko noticed that and asked: "Grandfather, why are you so sad? Has anyone harmed you?"

---

66. Ивашко-Медведко. The Russian word for bear is медведь, literally "honey eater".

The old man sighed heavily: "Oh, dear, you were my breadwinner, and now they want to drive you out of the village."

"That's no misfortune, Grandfather. It's just a pity that I have no weapon. Make me an iron club that weighs twenty-five pood!"

The old man forged him a club weighing twenty-five pood. Ivashko grabbed the club, took leave of his mother and grandparents and went out into the wide world. He walked and walked wherever his eyes led him and came to a river three versts wide. On the shore stood a man who caught the river with his mouth: suddenly caught a fish with his mustache, roasted it on his tongue and ate it.

"Greetings, Bogatir Mustache!"

"Greetings, Ivashko-Medvedko! Where are you going?"

"I do not know. Wherever my eyes lead me."

"Take me with you!"

"Come, brother, I am glad to have a companion!"

The two went on together. There they met a bogatir who carried a mountain, threw it into a valley and made level paths. Ivashko-Medvedko was astonished and said: "O wonder, what a miracle! You're overly strong, Mountmover Bogatir! "

"Oh, brother, my strength is not too great. Ivashko-Medvedko walks around the world; he's really strong."

"That's me!"

"Where are you going?"

"Wherever my eyes lead me."

"Take me with you!"

"Gladly, we'll go together!"

They went on together. Then they saw a bogatir who made sure that the oak trees all grew to the same height. If a tree was too high, he would push it back into the earth; if it was too small, he would stretch it up. Ivashko was astonished and said: "Oh, what strength!"

"Oh, brothers, my strength is not so great. Ivashko-Medvedko walks around the world, he's really strong."

"That's me!"

"Where is God leading you?"

"I do not know, Bogatir Oakman, wherever my eyes lead me."

"Take me with you!"

"Good, I'm glad to have another companion."

Now they were four, and they went on together. Sooner or later, they came into a dense, dark forest. In the middle of the forest stood a little hut on chicken's feet, which kept turning this way and that. "Little hut, little hut," cried Ivashko, "turn your face to us and turn your back on the wood!" The little hut turned to them, and doors and windows sprang open of their own accord. The men entered the hut. There was no one inside. But there were plenty of ducks, geese, and turkeys in the yard. "Brothers," said Ivashko, "it's no good having everyone at home. Let us choose who should stay; the others should go hunting."

The lot fell to Bogatir Mustache. The others went hunting. Mustache prepared a splendid meal, washed his head, sat down at the window and combed his curls. Suddenly everything spun around, it grew dark, and he saw green and blue before his eyes. The earth opened, a stone broke out, and out of it came Baba Yaga Boney Leg. She rode in an iron mortar, drove it with an iron mallet, and behind her a little dog yapped. "Mustache, I get food and drink."

"As you please, Baba Yaga Bonebone!" He sat her down at the table and gave her a little bit of food. She ate it; he gave her more, but she tossed it to the dog.

"With such food you entertain me!" shouted the Baba Yaga. She grabbed her iron mallet and struck him, beating and beating until he rolled under the bed, Then she cut a strip from his back, ate all the food, and drove off.

When Mustache came to himself, he tied his head with a kerchief, sat down, and groaned. Ivashko-Medvedko came home with his brothers: "Well, Mustache, give us something to eat. What have you cooked!"

"Oh, you brothers, I did not cook anything and did not fry anything. I'm dizzy with coal fumes and the house is full of smoke."

The next day, Mountmover stayed home. He cooked and roasted, washed his head, sat down at the window and combed his locks with a comb. Suddenly everything spun around; it grew dim, and he saw green and blue before his eyes. The earth became the navel, a stone broke loose, and out came the Baba Yaga Boneny Leg. She rode in the mortar, drove it with the iron mallet, and behind her barked a little dog. "Mountmover, I get food and drink!" "As it pleases, Baba Yaga Boneny Leg!" He gave her a bite, she ate it, he gave her a second one, she gave it to the dog.

"So that's how you entertain me!" she shouted, grabbing her iron mallet and beating him until he lay under the bench. Then she cut a strap from his back, ate everything except the last crumb, and drove away.

When Mountmover got on his feet, he bandaged his head, walked around and moaned. Ivashko came home with the brothers and asked, "Well, Mountmover, what have you cooked for us?"

"Oh, brothers, I have not cooked anything. The wood is damp, the stove is smoking: I have fired it with great difficulty."

Oakman stayed home on the third day. He cooked and roasted, washed his head, sat down at the window and combed his curls. Suddenly everything turned, it became dim, and he saw green and blue before his eyes. The earth opened, a stone rolled out, out of it came the Baba Yaga Boneny Leg. She rode in the iron mortar, drove it with the mallet, and behind her a little dog yapped,

"Hey, Oakman, I get food and drink!"

"As it pleases you, Baba Yaga Boneny Leg!" She sat down and he gave her something, he gave her a second; she gave it to the dog.

"So that is how you entertain me?" She took the mallet, struck him, and struck him until he lay under the bench. Then she cut a strip from his back, ate everything and drove off. When Oakman had recovered, he tied a cloth around his head and went groaning around. Ivashcheko returned home: "Oakman, give us food!"

"I did not cook or roast. I burned myself and the haze fogged me. The hut was full of smoke."

The fourth day it was the turn of Ivashko. He cooked and roasted, washed his head, sat down at the window and combed his hair. Suddenly everything spun around, it became cloudy, and he saw green and blue before his eyes, the earth opened, a stone broke out and, fuh, out came out Baba Yaga Bonenyleg. She rode in her mortar, drove it with a mallet, and behind it the dog barked. "Ivashko, I get food and drink!"

"As you please, Baba Yaga Boney Leg." She sat down, and he gave her a piece; she ate it. He gave her another, that's what she accused the dog of. "So you keep me in check?" She grabbed the mallet and pressed it against him, wanting to hit him.

But Ivashko became angry, snatched it from her and began to beat her. He hit and hit again until she was half dead. Then he cut three straps from her back and locked them in a closet. After a while his companions came. "Iwashko, we want to eat!"

"Yes, dear friends, help yourselves!" They sat down and ate. Everything was abundant. The bogatirs were surprised and said to each other: "Surely he was spared by the Baba Yaga!"

After dinner, Ivashko heated the bath room, and everyone went in to take a steam bath, Mustache, Mountmover, and Oakman washed, but never turned their backs to Ivashko. "Brothers," Ivashko asked. "Why are you hiding your backs from me?" Then they had to admit that Baba Yaga had beaten them and had cut a strip from the back of each one.

"So you were stunned by the haze?" Ivaschko called, running to the little room. The Baba Yaga removed the three thongs and placed them on the backs of his companions, and everything was whole again.

Then Iwashko-Medvedko took a rope, tied it to Baba Yaga's leg and hung her at the gate. "Well, brothers, let's shoot, Whoever cuts the rope is victorious!" Mustache shot first, but did not hit. As the second Mountmover shot and came closer. Oakman's shot brushed the rope, but Ivashko shot it in half. The Baba Yaga fell down, ran to the stone and disappeared into the earth. The bogatirs chased after her, and wanted to roll the stone away. One tries, the other tries - they can not lift the stone. Ivashko came running, kicked it, and it flew away. A hollow opened. "Brothers, who is going down?" No one wanted to. "Then I must go down," said Ivashko-Medvedko.

He took a post, put it beside the hole, hung a bell on it, and tied a rope onto the bell so that pulling on the rope would ring the bell.. "Let me down into the earth, and if I ring, pull me up again!" The bogatirs let him down into the cave. He came to the end of the rope but was still far from the bottom. Then Ivashko-Medvedko took from his pocket the three thongs from Baba Yaga's back, knotted them together, tied them to the rope and went down to the lower world. He saw a well-trodden path, went on to it and came to a castle.

There were three beautiful maidens in the castle, who called out to him: "Oh, good young man, why did you come here? Our mother, the Baba Yaga, will devour you soon."

"Where is she?"

"She sleeps, and under her head lies a mighty sword. But do not touch it, otherwise she will awaken immediately and throw it at you! Here are two golden apples in a silver bowl. Take one, gently wake the old woman and ask her to taste the golden apples. If she raises her head to eat, grab the sword and slice her head off with one stroke. But do not hit a second blow, or she will come back to life and deal you cruel death!"

Ivashko did everything exactly as the maidens had said, and cut off the head of the Baba Yaga. Then he led the beautiful maidens to the hole where he had come down. He tied the eldest sister to the rope, pulled the bell and shouted: "Here, Mustache, is your wife!" The bogatirs drew the maiden up and let the rope down again. Ivashko tied the second sister to it, rang the bell and shouted: "Mountmover, here comes your your wife!" And they pulled her up. Ivashko then tied the youngest sister to the rope and shouted: "Here comes my wife!" Then Ivashko tied himself tightly and rang the bell. But Oakman was unhappy not to get a wife and and became angry. And as they pulled up Ivashko, he took a cudgel and broke the rope in half. Ivashko plummeted and hit the ground hard. When the brave hero regained consciousness, he did not know what to do.

One day he sat, a second and third, without food and drink, and became very weak with hunger. Then thought to himself, "I'll look for food in the chambers of Baba Yaga, maybe I'll find something to eat." He went into their chambers, found food and drink, and also found a passage in the ground leading upwards. He went along it and climbed up to the light of day.

There he came to a clear field and saw a beautiful maiden, who grazed her flock. As he approached, he recognized his bride. "Beautiful maiden, what are you doing?"

"I am guarding the herd. My sisters married the two bogatirs. But I did not want Oakman, so he lets me keep cows here." In the evening, the beautiful maiden drove the cows home, and Ivashko followed her. In the hut, Mustache, Mountmover and Oakman were sitting at the table celebrating.

"Good people, give me a cup of young wine!" said Ivashko. They poured him a cup, he drank it down and asked for a second cup. He finished that and asked for a third. As he drank the third mug, his heroic heart lit up. He seized his war club and killed the three bogatirs. Then he threw their corpses into the open field to feed the wild beasts. Ivashko took his chosen bride, returned with her to the old man and his wife and celebrated a happy wedding. There was a lot of food and drink.

I was at the wedding too, drinking honey mead and wine. It flooded my beard, but my mouth stayed dry. They gave me a jug of beer in my hands - so my story is over.[67]

## Interpretation

Here a young, wild force is depicted which grows out of the dullness of the blood and cannot yet fully overcome the "bear" in him. The iron forces in the blood which make Man awake and I-comscious work in him so that at first he becomes wild, unruly and self-assertive. Then, when he is fifteen, these forces are forged into the cudgel that he learns to use and control.

---

67 Who are the three bogatir companions? Why must they be killed and the two older soul forces left widows in a strange land? This question surely occurred to Friedel Lenz, but if she had an answer, she did not share it. Do you have an answer? If you do, please share it.

In this tale, the Baba Yaga is an atavistic power that does not want to let the three soul forces come to free, full development. One who strives for wide-awake, self-conscious individuality must overcome her so that his soul forces can rise up out of the depths and become free.

# 24. Ivan Tsarevich, his Sister, and the Ironskin Bear (A 202)

In an empire - not in our empire - lived once a Tsar who had two children: a son, Ivan Tsarevich, and a daughter, Elena the Beautiful. One day a bear with iron skin appeared and began to devour the people. The Tsar sat and thought how he might save his children. He ordered a tall, high pillar to be erected. On this pillar he put Ivan Tsarevich and Elena the Beautiful with food for five years.

When the bear had swallowed up all the people, he ran to the Tsar's castle, but because he could not find anything, he began to gnaw furiously at a bush.

"Do not eat me, you Bear Ironskin," said the bush, "rather go into the field. There you will see a high pillar, and on this pillar sit Ivan Tsarevich and Elena the Beautiful."

The bear ran to the pillar and began to shake it. Ivan Tsarevich was startled and threw down some food. The bear ate it up, lay down and fell asleep.

When he had fallen asleep, Ivan Tsarevich and Elena the Beautiful descended and ran away, walking without looking back. On the way stood a horse. "Horse, horse, save us!" When they had just sat down on the horse, the bear caught up with them. He tore the horse to pieces, took Ivan Tsarevich and Elena the Beautiful into his throat and brought them back to the pillar. They gave him some of their food again. He ate it up, lay down and fell asleep.

When the bear slept, Ivan Tsarevich and Elena the Beautiful ran away without looking back. Along the way geese ran. "Geese, geese, save us!" They sat on the geese and flew away. But the bear awoke, caught up with them, seared the geese with blazing flames, and brought the tsar's children back to the pillar. They fed him again, and he fell asleep again.

When the bear slept, Ivan Tsarevich and Elena the Beautiful ran away without looking back. On the way stood a three-year-old bull. "Bull, Taurus, save us; behind us pursues the bear Iron Skin!"

"Sit on me, children! But you, Ivan Tsarevich, turn your face to the tail, and if you see the bear, tell me!"

When the bear caught up with them, Ivan Tsarevich told the bull, and the bull lifted his tail and blinded the bear. Three times the bear caught up with them, and three times the bull plastered his eyes. Then they had to swim through a river. The bear swam after them and drowned.

Ivan Tsarevich and Elena the Beautiful had become hungry. Then the bull spoke to them: "You must slaughter and eat me! But you should collect my bones and beat them against each other. From my bones will come the little man Kulachok - small as a nail and with a beard down to the elbow.

Time passed; they had eaten the bull and become hungry again. They beat the bones of the bull together and the little man Kulachok appeared. Now they all went to the forest. In this forest stood a house, and this house belonged to robbers. The little man Kulachok slew the robbers and their captain and locked them all in a room. He forbade Elena the Beautiful to look into the room.

After a while, however, she could not stand it, looked inside and fell in love with the head of the captain. She asked Ivan Tsarevich to bring her water of life and water of death. And no sooner had Ivan brought her life and death water, than Elena woke the robber captain from death. The two agreed to destroy Ivan Tsarevich. First, they decided to do it by sending him for wolf's milk.

Ivan Tsarevich and the little man Kulachok went together in search of wolf's milk. Finally they found a she-wolf. "Wolf, give us some of your milk!"

"Only if," said the wolf, "you also take my little wolf pup, for he is not doing well. He just wets and dirties himself, eats but does not grow."

They took the wolf pup with them, returned and brought Elena the milk, but the wolf pup they kept for themselves.

Then Elena and the captain saw that nothing had come of their tricks, and they sent Ivan Tsarevitch again to fetch bear's milk.

So the two, Ivan Tsarevich and the little man Kulachok, left to look for bear's milk, and finally found a mother bear. "Bear, would you give us some of your milk?"

"Yes," said the bear, "I'll give it to you. But take my little bear, too, for it does not do anything, just wets and dirties himself, eats but does not grow."

They took the milk and the bear cub and returned. Elena the Beautiful got the milk, but the bear cub remained with Ivan Tsarevich and the little man Kulachok. So, again, was this ruse failed.

Now they sent Ivan Tsarevich away to get the lion's milk. Ivan and the little man Kulachok left to look for lion's milk, and finally found a lioness. "Lioness, give us your milk!"

"Gladly," said the lioness, "I'll give it to you, but take my baby too, for it does not do anything, just wets and dirties himself, eats but does not grow. "

They returned. When the captain and Elena the Beautiful saw that they had not succeeded in destroying Ivan, they sent Ivan Tsarevich to fetch the eggs of the firebird. Ivan Tsarevich and the little man Kulachok went out into the world to look for these eggs and finally found the firebird. But when they wanted to take her eggs, the firebird became angry and swallowed the little man Kulachok. Ivan Tsarevich had to return home without eggs. He came to Elena the Beautiful and told her that he could not get the eggs and that the firebird swallowed the little man Kulachok.

Elena the Beautiful and the robber-captain were glad, for they thought that without the little man Kulachok, Ivan Tsarevich could do nothing, and they gave orders to kill him. Ivan Tsarevich, however, had heard everything and asked his sister to heat the bathhouse because he wanted to wash himself again before he died. Elena the Beautiful gave the order to heat the bath-room efficiently, and Ivan Tsarevich went in. After a while she sent her messengers to say to hurry up with the washing, but Ivan Tsarevich did not listen and washed himself slowly and leisurely. Suddenly the little wolf, the little bear and the little lion came running and shouted to him that the little man Kulachok had freed himself from the power of the fire bird and would come to him at once.

Ivan Tsarevich told the animals to lie down on the threshold of the bathhouse and continued to wash himself. Elena the Beautiful again sent a messenger to hurry up with the washing, and if he did not come out soon, she would fetch him herself. But Ivan Tsarevich did not listen to it and washed himself further. Elena the Beautiful waited and waited, but eventually she became impatient and went with the robber chief to see what Ivan Tsarevich was doing. She came and saw that he was still washing himself and did not listen to her orders. She became angry and struck him in the face. Suddenly the little man Kulachok came back and ordered the wolf, the bear and the lion to to attack robber captain. They tore him to pieces. Elena the Beautiful he tied naked to a tree, so that her body was exposed to the flies and mosquitoes.

Then he and Ivan Tsarevich set out on the big wide road. As they passed, they saw a mighty palace. "Ivan Tsarevich, do you not want to marry?" asked the little man Kulachok. "There lives a heroine maiden in this palace, and she's looking for a hero who is stronger than she is." They headed for the palace. Not far away Ivan Tsarevich mounted a horse, and the little man Kulachok sat down behind him, and they challenged the bogatir-girl to fight.

The bogatir-girl came out, they fought and fought, and she struck Ivan Tsarevich on the chest. Ivan Tsarevich almost fell off his horse, but the little man Kulachok held him tight. At last Ivan Tsarevich hit the heroic maiden with a lance, and she immediately fell off the horse. When he had thrown her off the horse, she said: "Well, Ivan Tsarevich, now I want to marry to you!"

A tale is quickly told; not so quickly done the deed. Ivan Tsarevich married the bogatir-girl. "Ivan Tsarevich," said the little man Kulachok, "if you feel weak during the first night, come out quickly. I'll help you." Ivan Tsarevich went to bed with his bogatir-bride. Suddenly she put her hand on his chest and Ivan became weak. He asked if he could go out. And when he had gone out he called the little man Kulachok and whispered to him that the bogatir-girl wanted to crush him. The little man went in to the bogatir-girl, struck her and murmured: "Honor your husband, honor your husband!" From that time on Ivan Tsarevich and the bogatir-girl lived together happily and prospered.

*　*　*

When a time had passed, the bogatir-girl begged Ivan Tsarevich to untie Elena the Beautiful from the tree and bring her home to live with them. Ivan Tsarevich did so, had her untied and brought to them. Elena the Beautiful lived with them for a long time. One day Elena the Beautiful said to Ivan Tsarevich: "Come, little brother, I'll check your head!"[68]

She started to search, but pushed a dead tooth into him. Ivan began to die. The lion cub saw Ivan Tsarevich dying and pulled out the dead tooth. Ivan Tsarevich began to live, but the lion cub began

---

68  Presumably for lice.

to die. The bear cub saw that and pulled the dead tooth away from the lion cub. The lion cub began to live, and the bear began to die. So the fox ran up and saw that the bear cub was dying, and pulled out the dead tooth. And because a fox is smarter than any other animal, he immediately threw away the tooth. It fell on a hot frying pan and fell to pieces. For this, Ivan Tsarevich ordered that Elena the Beautiful be tied behind a mighty horse, dragged over a field and torn to bits.

## Interpretation

This folktale is also called The Milk of Beasts. It describes, however, a later development than was described by the previous tale of that name, Number 22. In this one, a drama of the consciousness soul age unfolds before the inner eye. At the beginning of the tale, the soul-spiritual being is still "up" and thereby protected from the "bear". But once it is discovered by the "bear", one cannot escape him by giving him his share. Entrusting themselves to the carrying capacity of the intellect (the horse) does not work. Daring the inner high flight (the geese) also fails, for the dullness of the blood becomes the smoldering fire of passion. Only the bull of strong, purposeful will power succeeds.

From the bones of the bull comes the little man Kulachok. *Kulak* means *fist* in Russian, so Kulachok is "little fist" or "fist high". The genuine Will force of the bull can become inner awakening forces. One who uses actively the Will forces – beats together the bones of the bull – releases a force that masters all. To the world, it looks like a tiny dwarf, but it significant force long ago laid into Man that now comes to the aid of Ivan Tsarevich as a new I-consciousness.

First of all, Kulachok kills the robbers in the forest. The robbers are those forces in us which experience and enjoy the sense world without thinking or taking any responsibility. The robber-captain, who uses all the experiences as booty is the sense-bound intellect. He is the great robber, but he holds together all his sense impressions and makes of them his treasure of knowledge. Now Elena the Beautiful falls in love with cut-off head of the robber captain. That means: the consciousness soul connects itself to the dead forces of the intellect. Indeed, she uses Johannine wisdom to bring back to life these dead forces to her own detriment. Therefore she cannot get the golden egg of the firebird, for the intellectual soul draws back from such forces that want them only out of vain greed. The golden eggs are the regenerative life kernels of an exalted supersensible sun wisdom – the phoenix wisdom.

Finally the robber intellect is overcome and the consciousness soul that fell for it must experience its own poverty and nakedness. On the advice of Kulachok, Ivan Tsarevich fights to win that part of the soul that has not become the robber wife but has remained the divine daughter. Like Siegfried, he fights for the hero-maiden. With the help of that small but yet so strong I-consciousness, he masters and marries this strong soul.

But the intellectual consciousness soul is still not transformed. Death forces radiate from her. She sticks the dead tooth (or in some versions, dragon tooth) into the head of Ivan Tsarevich. While the Johannine I has fought itself free and has won a heroic higher consciousness, it almost falls prey to its own one-sided fugitive understanding forces. It is rescued only by its good instincts, the animals.

The folktale shows the intellectual, cold, unloving consciousness soul which fights against the Johannine spirit.

## 25. The Clairvoyant Dream (A 240)

Once upon a time there was a merchant who had two sons, Demetrius and Ivan. Once, when he blessed them for the night, he said to them, "Children, what you will dream tonight, you shall entrust to me tomorrow morning; but he who keeps his dreams to himself, I will have him killed."

The next morning, the elder son came and said, "Father, I dreamed that Brother Ivan flew beneath the heavens on twelve eagles and that your favorite lamb perished."

"And what did you dream, Vanya?"

"I'm not telling," replied Ivan. And as his father pressed him, he remained firm and replied to all admonitions: "I'm not telling! I'm not telling!"

The merchant became angry, called his servants, and ordered that the disobedient son be stripped naked and tied to a post on the highway. The servants seized him and, as ordered, tied him firmly to a post. It was terrible for the good boy; the sun was scorching hot; hunger and thirst tortured him; and mosquitoes bit him.

Then came a young tsarevich along the road and saw the merchant's son. He took pity on him, had him untied and dressed in his own robe. Then he led him to his castle and began to ask him, "Who tied you to that post?"

"My own father; he was angry with me."

"What did you do?"

"I did not want to tell him what I dreamed."

"How stupid of your father to punish a trifle so harshly! What did you dream?"

"I'm not telling, tsarevich!"

"You do not tell, and I saved you from death?"

"I did not tell my father, I will not tell you either!"

The tsarevich became angry and ordered Ivan, the merchant's son, to be imprisoned. Immediately the soldiers came and put the servant of God in a stone dungeon.

A year passed, and the tsarevich wanted to marry. He prepared himself and rode away to a foreign kingdom to marry Elena the Beautiful.

Soon thereafter, his sister once passed the dungeon. Ivan, the merchant's son, beheld her from his little window, and called in a loud voice, "Have mercy, O tsarevna, and release me! Maybe I can be useful to you; I know that the Tsarevich is leaving to marry Elena the Beautiful. But without me he will not be able to marry her, and in the end even pay for his plans with his head. Perhaps you yourself have heard that Elena the Beautiful is very clever and because of her already many suitors have lost their heads."

"And you want to help the tsarevich?"

"I could, but the falcon's wings are tied."

The tsarevna gave orders to liberate him immediately from the dungeon. Now Ivan the merchant's son chose his companions. There were twelve of them, all very alike. The were all of the same height, and had the same voice and the same hair. They dressed in shirts of the same color and the same size. Then they mounted their good horses and rode off. They rode one day - two days - three days. On the fourth day they came into a dense forest. In this forest they heard loud shouts.

"Stop, brothers," said Ivan, "Wait here a moment. I'll follow that noise."

He jumped off the horse and ran into the woods. In a clearing he found three old men who fought violently.

"Greetings, you old ones! Why do you fight?"

"Oh, brave youth, we received three miraculous gifts from our father: a little hat of invisibility, a flying carpet, and a pair of self-running boots. We have been quarreling for seventy years, but we cannot agree on who should get what."

"Do you want me to distribute the gifts?"

"That would be great!"

Ivan, the merchant's son, strung his bow, laid three arrows on it, and shot the arrows in three different directions. He then told one old man to walk to the right, another to the left, and the third straight ahead. "To the one who first brings back the arrow belongs the hat of invisibility; to the next to bring back the arrow belongs the flying carpet, and to the last to bring back the arrow go the self-running boots." Then the old men ran after the arrows.

Ivan, the merchant's son, then took the three miraculous gifts and returned to his companions. "Brothers," he said, "let the horses run free; come and sit down with me on the flying carpet!" They sat down together on the flying carpet and flew into the realm of Elena the Beautiful. They came to the capital and came down at the gates. Then they began to seek the tsarevich who had come to marry Elena the Beautiful. Soon they found him.

"What do you want?" asked the tsarevich.

"Take us good lads into your service! We will make you glad and serve you well with pure hearts."

The tsarevich took them into his service and gave to one the job of a cook, to another the job of a groom – to each his special place.

On the same day, the tsarevich dressed in his most festive robe and rode to the castle to introduce himself to Elena the Beautiful. She met him in a friendly manner, entertained him with food and drink, and asked, "Tell me, Tsarevich, why have you come to visit me?"

"I have come to court you, Elena the Beautiful. Will you marry me?"

"Yes, gladly, but you must first perform three tasks. If you perform them, I am yours; if not, let your head be ready for a sharp ax."

"Give the first task!"

"I want to have something tomorrow – I do not say what. You must figure it out, O Tsarevich, and bring me exactly what I desire!"

The tsarevich returned to his entourage with great concern. "O Tsarevich," said Ivan the merchant's son, "why are you so sad? Did Elena the Beautiful hurt you? Tell me your grief, then it will be easier for you!"

The tsarevich answered, "Elena the Beautiful has given me a task that no sage in the world can solve." And he told Ivan the task.

"Well, that's not the worst evil yet. Pray to God and go to sleep: the morning is wiser than the evening. Tomorrow we will consider the matter." The tsarevich went to sleep.

Ivan the merchant's son put on the little hat of invisibility, put on his self-running boots and hurried to Elena the Beautiful, went straight into her room and listened. She gave her best maid a job: "Take this precious cloth and bring it to the shoemaker, he should make a shoe for my foot out of it as soon as possible!"

The maid hurried off with Ivan behind her. The shoemaker immediately set to work, quickly sewed the shoe and put it on the window sill. Ivan softly took the shoe and put it in his pocket. The poor shoemaker soon saw that the shoe was gone. He walked back and forth searching, but his work was gone. He searched and searched, rummaging through every little corner, but all in vain. "This is a miracle," he said, "or some devil is joking with me." There was nothing to be done, he had to reach for the needle again and sew another shoe.

"What kind of slow worker are you?" said Elena the Beautiful when he brought her the shoe. "You spent so much time on a single shoe!" She sat down at her work table and began to embroider the shoe with gold and to cover it with large pearls and wonderful gemstones. But Ivan was there too, taking out his shoe and doing the same. If she took a pebble, he chose exactly the same, if she attached a pearl, so did he. Elena the Beautiful finished her work, smiled, and said, "What will the Tsarevich show me tomorrow?"

"Just wait," thought Ivan, "you do not know who's smarter!" He returned to the inn and laid down to sleep. At the dawn, he got up, dressed, and went to wake the tsarevich. He woke him and gave him the shoe. "Go to Elena the Beautiful, and show her the shoe, that's the first task!"

The Tsarevich washed, dressed nicely, and went to the Elena. All rooms were full of guests: boyars, magnates and councilors. When the tsarevich came in, the music played, the guests sprang up from their seats, and the soldiers went to the front. Elena the Beautiful took out her shoe, decorated with pearls and jewels, looked at the royal suitor and smiled.

"That's a beautiful shoe," said the Tsarevich, "but if one does not have have another like it, it is of no use. Clearly you must want the mate!" With these words he took out of his pocket the shoe and put it on the table. Then all the guests clapped and shouted in a loud voice: "Hail to the Tsarevich, he is worthy to wed Elena the Beautiful, our mistress!"

"Well, we shall see. First he must complete the second task! I want to have something tomorrow – I do not say what. You must figure it out, O Tsarevich, and bring me exactly my unknown desire!"

Late in the evening the tsarevich returned to his entourage, still more gloomy than before. "Stop grieving," said Ivan the merchant's son. Pray to God and lie down to sleep. The morning is wiser than the evening!" He put the tsarevich to bed, put on the self-running boots, put on the little hat of invisibility and ran to Elena the Beautiful. She gave the following order to her favorite maid: "Go down to the poultry yard as fast as possible and get me a white duckling!"

The maid ran into the poultry yard, and Ivan was right behind her. She grabbed a duckling and Ivan took a drake, and both returned in the same way. Elena the Beautiful sat down at her work table, picked up the duckling and decorated her wings with silk ribbons and a bow of diamonds. Ivan the merchant's son watched and did exactly the same with his drake.

On the next day Elena the Beautiful had again gathered all the guests, and the music resounded. She let go of her duckling and asked the tsarevich: "Have you guessed my task?"

"Yes, Elena the Beautiful, here is the drake for your duckling!" With that he let go of it. All the boyars called out in unison: "Hail to the Tsarevich! He is worthy to wed Elena the Beautiful!"

"Wait; he must still solve the third task! Tomorrow I will have something, – I do not say what. You must figure it out, O Tsarevich, and bring me exactly the same thing!"

In the evening the tsarevich returned to his companions so sadly that he could not speak at all. "Do not worry, lie down to sleep and pray to God. Morning is wiser than the evening," said Ivan the merchant's son. He quickly put on the hat of invisibility, put on the self-running boots and hurried to Elena the Beautiful. She was getting ready to drive to the blue sea. She got into a carriage and drove off at great speed, but Ivan, the merchant's son, did not lag one step behind her. Elena came to the blue sea to call her grandfather. The waves rippled and swayed, and out of the sea rose the great old man. His hair was silver, his beard was gold. He came out to the shore: "Greetings, granddaughter, I have not seen you for a long, long time. Search my head and comb my hair!" He laid his head on her knees and fell asleep. Elena the Beautiful, searched his head. Ivan, the merchant's son, stood behind her. When she saw that the old man had fallen asleep, she pulled out three silver hairs. Ivan, the merchant's son, not only took three hairs, but grabbed a whole tuft.

"Ow!" exclaimed the grandfather, rising, "Are you out of your mind, that hurts me!"

"Forgive me, Grandfather," said Elena the Beautiful, "I have not yet combed your beard. The hair is all tangled." The old man calmed down and fell asleep again. Elena the Beautiful, pulled three golden hairs from his beard. Ivan, however, grasped the beard and almost tore it out completely. The old man cried out, jumped up and threw himself into the sea. "Now it's all over for the tsarevich," thought Elena the Beautiful, "because he cannot get that hair."

The next day the guests gathered, and the tsarevich also drove to the castle. Elena the Beautiful, showed him the three silver and three golden hairs. "Did you ever see such a miracle?" she asked him.

"You found something you can rightfully boast of if you want, I'll give you a handful of them!" He took out the silver and golden tufts and gave them to her. Then Elena the Beautiful became angry and ran to her bedchamber to check in her sorcerer's book whether the tsarevich had guessed everything himself, or whether someone had helped him. In this book she read that he was not the wise man, but that it was his servant Ivan, the merchant's son.

Then she returned to the guests and said to the tsarevich, "Send me your favorite servant!"

"I have twelve of them."

"Send me the one called Ivan!"

"They are all called Ivan."

"Good, so shall they all come!" for she hoped to find out the key party.

The tsarevich gave the order, and immediately the twelve fine lads, his faithful servants, all in the face completely alike, height like height, voice like voice, hair like hair.

"Who is the oldest among you?" asked Elena the Beautiful.

"I, I, I am the oldest!" all cried at the same time.

"I can learn nothing this way," thought Elena the Beautiful to herself, and she ordered her servants to bring eleven ordinary cups and as the twelfth, her own golden cup. She filled the twelve cups with fine wine and entertained the good lads, but none of them drank from an ordinary cup, all twelve reached out their hands for the golden one. Everyone wanted to take it, and the wine was spilled.

When Elena the Beautiful saw that she could not guess in this way which was the key one, she ordered the lads to take food and drink and lie down to sleep. In the night, when all were sleeping, she went to them with her magic book, looked into the book and immediately recognized the right one. She took a pair of scissors and cut off the hair on his temples. "By this sign I will recognize him tomorrow and have him killed."

In the morning, Ivan the merchant's son awoke first of all and found his temples sheared. Quickly he jumped up and woke his companions." You have slept enough," he cried, "evil is near. Take scissors and shear your temples!"

After an hour, Elena the Beautiful called everyone to find out the key one. But - oh wonder - whomever she looked at, everyone had sheared temples.

Having lost hope of escaping her promise to the tsarevich, she grabbed her spellbook and threw it into the fire. Now she could no longer refuse, she had to marry the tsarevich. The wedding was celebrated. For three days and three nights no one went to sleep, for three days and three nights all the inns were open and anyone could eat and drink for free as much as he wished. When the banquets were over, the tsarevich set out with his young wife to drive to his kingdom. He sent the twelve servants in advance.

They hurried out of the city, spread out the flying carpet, sat on it and rose in the air. They climbed high, higher than the clouds, flew and flew, until they reached that thick wood where they knew their fine horses were. Just as they were descending from their carpet, the first old man ran backwith his arrow, and Ivan, the merchant's son, handed him the little hat of invisibility. Behind him, the second old man appeared and immediately got the flying carpet, and at last the third ran up and received the self-running boots.

Then Ivan called his companions and said: "Now, brethren, saddle your horses, it is time for us to get up and be on the way!" They caught the horses, saddled them and rode into their homeland. When they arrived in their country, they immediately appeared before the king's daughter. The king's daughter rejoiced beyond all measure and asked about her brother, about his wedding and when he would returned.

"How can I reward your great services?" she asked.

"Put me back in the tower!" replied Ivan, the merchant's son. And despite all the king's daughter said against it, he insisted on his will. The soldiers took him and led him back to the prison.

After thirty days the tsarevich appeared with his young wife and was solemnly received: the bells rang, the guns fired, and the music played. So many people were together that one could have walked on their heads. The boyars and all the other estates came to introduce themselves. But the tsarevich looked around and asked, "Where is Ivan, my faithful servant?" "He is in prison." "Who dared to put him in it?" "You yourself, brother, have done it," said the tsarevna. "You were angry with him and had him put in the tower. Remember, you asked him to tell you his dream, and he would not tell you."

"Is my servant really Ivan, the merchant's son?"

"Yes, he is, "said the tsarevna, "I released him for a short time to help you."

The tsarevich had Ivan the merchant's son brought to him, fell on his neck and begged him not to remember the past evil.

"You must know, O Tsarevich," said Ivan "I foresaw everything that happened to you, for I saw all this in the dream. That's why I knew what to do and why I could not tell you the dream."

The tsarevich raised Ivan, the son of a merchant, to the rank of general, took him to his castle, and gave him great estates. Ivan sent for his father and Demetrius, his older brother, to be brought to him, and all of them lived and prospered together in peace and harmony.

## Interpretation

Demetrius dreamed that the father's favorite lamb perished. The Age of the Ram – the era when the sun is in the constellation Aries as it crosses the celestial equator in the spring – ended long ago[69] but this age of the great lawgivers lives on in the ten

---

69 Different astrologers assign different dates to the end of the age of Ares, but they range from about 100 BC to 1 AD.

commandments of Moses, Roman law, and in fact in everything rooted in Roman culture. But when the Johannine spiritual action begins, it is not laws and commandments that carry Man to spiritual heights but the eagle forces of thinking.

Ivan the Merchant's Son is surrounded by twelve comrades. Today the number twelve is no longer especially meaningful to most people, but in the Middle Ages, it was quite different. Many pictures showed how the twelve regions of the zodiac worked into the being of Man and built his form. For the consciousness of that time, Man was built up out of the whole twelve-fold cosmos. The forces that make thought possible can develop in a twelvefold way from this consciousness. As one twelvefold being they gather around the central spirit seeker, the thirteenth.

Elena the Beautiful poses questions to her suitors, and who cannot answer them loses his head. It is the Turandot motif.

On the way to her realm Ivan the Merchant's son and his companions encounter three old spiritual forces. They must be used together for a common purpose, but those who posses them cannot agree on how to do so. Ivan sets the owners the task of finding direction – the arrows – and himself makes use of the forces until that direction is found. To wear the cap of invisibility means to be able to move freely in a supersensible world as a supersensible being, that is, to win spiritual presence in the highest sense of the word. To go in the self-running boots means to make definite progress in one's spiritual development, to experience progress that goes ahead on it own because a certain point has been reached. The flying carpet is the power to lift up into the sphere of the spirit inner feelings which enliven the barren world of facts with colorful pictures, in other words, to form true imaginations.

Ivan gives the three old men an aim, a purpose. And because he used their wonderful spiritual inheritance in dealing with Elena the Beautiful, it can later be applied in the sense world.

Ivan Tsarevich must guess and produce three things: shoes, a duck, and silver and golden hair. Shoes enable us to move freely and purposefully on the earth. Ivan Tsarevich must first prove that he knows how important earthly activity is and is equipped for it.

The duck is a creature of water and air. On land it waddles awkwardly. In the water it moves with beautiful grace. Look at the flowing, swelling water element and feel the security with which the duck lets itself be carried. Then you will understand the Elena's second challenge: move in the etheric soul world with grace and self-assurance; don't go under but have the confidence to let yourself be carried like the innocent little duck. (On temples in India, the symbol of the duck appears beside that of the goose and the swan.)

The old grandfather of Elena is handled a bit disrespectfully by Ivan, but he represents a wisdom whose time is passed: the hair of his head is silver like the moon, and he rises out of the water. Of such wisdom Ivan has plenty, and this beard must off.

Elena still probes to see if the Johannine being has penetrated all the companions of Ivan Tsarevich, but all of them say "I" and all of them drink Wisdom like she herself.

# 26. Ivan Tsarevich, the Fire-Bird and the Grey Wolf (A 168)

Translation by Irina Zheleznova[70]

Once upon a time there was a Tsar named Berendei, and he had three sons, the youngest of whom was called Ivan.

Now the Tsar had a beautiful garden with an apple tree in it that bore golden apples. One day the Tsar found that somebody was visiting his garden and stealing his golden apples. The Tsar was very unhappy about this. He sent watchmen into the garden, but they were unable to catch the thief.

The Tsar was so grieved that he would not touch food or drink. His sons tried to cheer him.

"Do not grieve, Father dear," they said, "we shall keep watch over the garden ourselves."

Said the eldest son: "Today it is my turn to keep watch." And he went into the garden. He walked about for a long time but saw no one, so he flung himself down on the soft grass and went to sleep.

In the morning the Tsar said to him:

"Come, now, have you brought me good news? Have you discovered who the thief is?"

"No, Father dear. That the thief was not there I am ready to swear. I did not close my eyes all night, but I saw no one."

---

70 This translation is not from the Afanasyev version but apparently from the version of Aleksei Tolstoy (1883 – 1945) The differences are minor, and the reader may appreciate the cleaner, more Grimm-like style.

On the following night the middle son went out to keep watch, and he, too, went to sleep and in the morning said he had seen no one.

It was now the youngest son's turn to go and keep watch. Tsarevich Ivan went to watch his father's garden and he did not dare so much as to sit down, let alone lie down. If he felt that he was getting sleepy, he would wash his face in dew and become wide awake again.

Half the night passed by, and all of a sudden what should he see but a light shining in the garden. Brighter and brighter it grew, and it lit up everything around. Tsarevich Ivan looked, and there in the apple-tree he saw the Fire-Bird pecking at the golden apples.

Tsarevich Ivan crept up to the tree and caught the bird by the tail. But the Fire-Bird broke free of his grasp and flew away, leaving a feather from its tail in his hand.

In the morning Tsarevich Ivan went to his father.

"Well, my son, have you caught the thief?" asked the Tsar.

"No, Father," said Tsarevich Ivan, "I have not caught him, but I have discovered who he is. See, he sends you this feather as a keepsake. The Fire-Bird is the thief, Father."

The Tsar took the feather, and from that time he became cheerful again and began to eat and drink. But one fine day he fell to thinking about the Fire-Bird and, calling his sons to his side, said:

"My dear sons, I would have you saddle your trusty steeds and set out to see the wide world. If you search in all its far corners, perhaps you will come upon the Fire-Bird."

The sons bowed to their father, saddled their trusty steeds and set out. The eldest son took one road, the middle son another, and Tsarevich Ivan a third.

Whether Tsarevich Ivan was long on the way or not, no one can say, but one day, it being summer and very warm, he felt so tired that he got off his horse and, binding its feet so that it could not go very far, lay down to rest.

Whether he slept for a long time or a little time nobody knows, but when he woke up he found that his horse was gone. He went to look for it, he walked and he walked, and at last he found its remains: nothing but bones, picked clean. Tsarevich Ivan was greatly grieved. How could he continue on his journey without a horse?

"Ah, well," he thought, "it cannot be helped, and I must make the best of it."

And he went on on foot. He walked and walked for three days. On the third day he was so tired that he was ready to drop. He sat down on the soft grass, and he was very sad and woebegone. Suddenly, lo and behold! who should come running up to him but Grey Wolf.

"Why are you sitting here so sad and sorrowful, Tsarevich Ivan?" asked Grey Wolf.

"How can I help being sad, Grey Wolf! I have lost my trusty steed."

"It was I who ate up your horse, Tsarevich Ivan. But I am sorry for you. Come, tell me, what are you doing so far from home and where are you going?"

"My father has sent me out into the wide world to seek the Fire- Bird."

"Has he now? Well, you could not have reached the Fire-Bird on that horse in three years. I alone know where it lives. So be it—since I have eaten up your horse, I shall be your true and faithful servant. Get on my back and hold fast."

Tsarevich Ivan got on his back and Grey Wolf was off in a flash. Blue lakes skimmed past ever so fast, green forests swept by in the wink of an eye, and at last they came to a castle with a high wall round it.

"Listen carefully, Tsarevich Ivan," said Grey Wolf, "and remember what I say. Climb over that wall. You have nothing to fear—we have come at a lucky hour, all the guards are sleeping. In a chamber within the tower you will see a window, in that window hangs a golden cage, and in that cage is the Fire-Bird. Take the bird and hide it in your bosom, but mind you do not take the cage!"

Tsarevich Ivan climbed over the wall and saw the tower with the golden cage in the window and the Fire-Bird in the cage. He took the bird out and hid it in his bosom, but he could not tear his eyes away from the cage.

"Ah, what a handsome golden cage it is!" he thought longingly. "How can I leave it here!"

And he forgot all about the Wolf's warning. But the moment he lifted the cage, a great hue and cry arose within the castle—trumpets began to blow, drums began to beat, and the guards woke up, seized Tsarevich Ivan and marched him off to Tsar Afron.

"Who are you and whence do you hail?" Tsar Afron demanded angrily.

"I am Tsarevich Ivan, son of Tsar Berendei."

"Fie, shame on you! To think of the son of a tsar being a thief!"

"Well, you should not have let your bird steal apples from our garden."

"If you had come and told me about it in an honest way, I would have made you a present of the Bird out of respect for your father, Tsar Berendei. But now I shall spread the ill fame of your family far and wide. Or no—perhaps I will not, after all. If you do what I tell you, I shall forgive you. In a certain tsardom there is a Tsar named Kusman and he has a Horse with a Golden Mane. Bring me that Horse and I will make you a gift of the Fire-Bird and the cage besides."

Tsarevich Ivan felt very sad and crestfallen, and he went back to Grey Wolf.

"I told you not to touch the cage," said the Wolf. "Why did you not heed my warning?"

"I am sorry, Grey Wolf, please forgive me."

"You are sorry, are you ? Oh, well, get on my back again. I gave my word, and I must not go back on it. A truth that all good folk accept is that a promise must be kept."

And off went Grey Wolf with Tsarevich Ivan on his back. Whether they traveled for a long or a little time nobody knows, but at last they came to the castle where the Horse with the Golden Mane was kept.

"Climb over the wall, Tsarevich Ivan, the guards are asleep," said Grey Wolf. "Go to the stable and take the Horse, but do not touch the bridle."

Tsarevich Ivan climbed over the castle wall and, all the guards being asleep, he went to the stable and caught the Horse with the Golden Mane. But he could not help picking up the bridle—it was made of gold and set with precious stones—a fitting bridle for such a horse.

No sooner had Tsarevich Ivan touched the bridle than a hue and cry was raised within the castle. Trumpets began to blow, drums began to beat, and the guards woke up, seized Tsarevich Ivan and marched him off to Tsar Kusman.

"Who are you and whence do you hail?" the Tsar demanded.

"I am Tsarevich Ivan."

"A tsasrevich stealing horses! What a foolish thing to do! A common peasant would not stoop to it. But I shall forgive you, Tsarevich Ivan, if you do what I tell you. Tsar Dalmat has a daughter named Yelena the Fair. Steal her and bring her to me, and I shall make you a present of my Horse with the Golden Mane and of the bridle besides."

Tsarevich Ivan felt more sad and crestfallen than ever, and he went back to Grey Wolf.

"I told you not to touch the bridle, Tsarevich Ivan!" said the Wolf. "Why did you not heed my warning?"

"I am sorry, Grey Wolf, please forgive me."

"Being sorry won't do much good. Oh, well, get on my back again."

And off went Grey Wolf with Tsarevich Ivan. By and by they came to the tsardom of Tsar Dalmat, and in the garden of his castle Yelena the Fair was strolling with her women and maids.

"This time I shall do everything myself," said Grey Wolf. "You go back the way we came and I will soon catch up with you."

So Tsarevich Ivan went back the way he had come, and Grey Wolf jumped over the wall into the garden. He crouched behind a bush and peeped out, and there was Yelena the Fair strolling about with all her women and maids. After a time she fell behind them, and Grey Wolf at once seized her, tossed her across his back, jumped over the wall and took to his heels.

Tsarevich Ivan was walking back the way he had come, when all of a sudden his heart leapt with joy, for there was Grey Wolf with Yelena the Fair on his back! "You get on my back too, and be quick about it, or they may catch us," said Grey Wolf.

Grey Wolf sped down the path with Tsarevich Ivan and Yelena the Fair on his back. Blue lakes skimmed past ever so fast, green forests swept by in the wink of an eye. Whether they were long on the way or not nobody knows, but by and by they came to Tsar Kusman's tsardom.

"Why are you so silent and sad, Tsarevich Ivan?" asked Grey Wolf.

"How can I help being sad, Grey Wolf! It breaks my heart to part with such loveliness. To think that I must exchange Yelena the Fair for a horse!"

"You need not part with such loveliness, we shall hide her somewhere. I will turn myself into Yelena the Fair and you shall take me to the Tsar instead."

So they hid Yelena the Fair in a hut in the forest, and Grey Wolf turned a somersault, and was at once changed into Yelena the Fair. Tsarevich Ivan took him to Tsar Kusman, and the Tsar was delighted and thanked him over and over again.

"Thank you for bringing me a bride, Tsarevich Ivan," said he. "Now the Horse with the Golden Mane is yours, and the bridle too."

Tsarevich Ivan mounted the horse and went back for Yelena the Fair. He put her on the horse's back and away they rode!

Tsar Kusman held a wedding and feast to celebrate it and he feasted the whole day long, and when bedtime came he led his bride into the bedroom. But when he got into bed with her what should he see but the muzzle of a wolf instead of the face of his young wife! So frightened was the Tsar that he tumbled out of bed, and Grey Wolf sprang up and ran away.

He caught up with Tsarevich Ivan and said:

"Why are you sad, Tsarevich Ivan?"

"How can I help being sad! I cannot bear to think of exchanging the Horse with the Golden Mane for the Fire-Bird."

"Cheer up, I will help you," said the Wolf.

Soon they came to the tsardom of Tsar Afron.

"Hide the horse and Yelena the Fair," said the Wolf. "I will turn myself into Golden Mane and you shall take me to Tsar Afron."

So they hid Yelena the Fair and the Horse with the Golden Mane in the woods, and Grey Wolf turned a somersault and was changed into Golden Mane.

Tsarevich Ivan led him off to Tsar Afron, and the Tsar was delighted and gave him the Fire-Bird and the golden cage too.

Tsarevich Ivan went back to the woods, put Yelena the Fair on Golden Mane's back and, taking the golden cage with the Fire-Bird in it, set off homewards.

Meanwhile Tsar Afron had the gift horse brought to him, and he was just about to get on its back when it turned into a grey wolf. So frightened was the Tsar that he fell down where he stood, and Grey Wolf ran away and soon caught up with Tsarevich Ivan.

"And now I must say good-bye," said he, "for I can go no farther."

Tsarevich Ivan got off the horse, bowed low three times, and thanked Grey Wolf humbly.

"Do not say good-bye for good, for you may still have need of me," said Grey Wolf.

"Why should I need him again?" thought Tsarevich Ivan. "All my wishes have been fulfilled."

He got on Golden Mane's back and rode on with Yelena the Fair and the Fire-Bird. By and by they reached his own native land,

and Tsarevich Ivan decided to stop for a bite to eat. He had a little bread with him, so they ate the bread and drank fresh water from the spring, and then lay down to rest.

No sooner had Tsarevich Ivan fallen asleep than his brothers came riding up. They had been to other lands in search of the Fire-Bird, and were now coming home empty-handed.

When they saw that Tsarevich Ivan had got everything, they said: "Let us kill our brother Ivan, for then all his spoils will be ours." And with that they killed Tsarevich Ivan. Then they got on Golden Mane's back, took the Fire-Bird, seated Yelena the Fair on a horse and said:

"See that you say not a word about this at home!"

So there lay Tsarevich Ivan on the ground, with the ravens circling over his head. All of a sudden who should come running but Grey Wolf. He ran up and he seized a raven and her fledgling.

"Fly and fetch me dead and living water, Raven," said the Wolf. "If you do, I shall let your nestling go."

The Raven flew off—what else could she do?—while the Wolf held her fledgling. Whether a long time passed by or a little time nobody knows, but at last she came back with the dead and living water. Grey Wolf sprinkled the dead water on Tsarevich Ivan's wounds, and the wounds healed. Then he sprinkled him with the living water, and Tsarevich Ivan came back to life.

"Oh, how soundly I slept!" said he.

"Aye," said Grey Wolf, "and but for me you would never have wakened. Your own brothers killed you and took away all your treasures. Get on my back, quick."

They went off in hot pursuit, and they soon caught up the two brothers, and Grey Wolf tore them to bits and scattered the bits over the field.

Tsarevich Ivan bowed to Grey Wolf and took leave of him for good.

He rode home on the Horse with the Golden Mane, and he brought his father the Fire-Bird and himself a bride—Yelena the Fair.

Tsar Berendei was overjoyed and asked his son all about everything. Tsarevich Ivan told him how Grey Wolf had helped him, and how his brothers had killed him while he slept and Grey Wolf had torn them to bits.

At first Tsar Berendei was sorely grieved, but he soon got over it. And Tsarevich Ivan married Yelena the Fair and

They lived together in health and cheer
For many a long and prosperous year.[71]

Interpretation

In Richard Wagner's *Der Ring der Nibelungen* the Wälsingen are also called the Wölfinge. They are the beloved sons of Wotan that wear the wolf skin. They have the "glowing worm" in their eyes; that means, in them lives the serpent of Luciferic self-awareness, of Luciferic striving for freedom. They fall out of the tribe as the first to "go it on their own". Also they no longer say "we" but "I". But this lower I-consciousness was experienced only on the margin, in the sheaths of the soul (the wolf's pelt). It was a long time before it was fully felt, and still longer before it could become the unselfish carrying force: our Grey Wolf.

---

71 This nice conclusion is the translator's flight of Russian fantasy. The Russian in the Afanasyev version is also unique: и начал с нею жить дружно, полюбовно, так что один без другого ниже единой минуты пробыть не могли. "and began to live with her friendlyly and lovingly so that one without the other could not exist a single minute."

First Ivan's horse falls prey to this wolf and is torn in two[72]. The understanding (the horse) becomes split; it doubts[73] and cannot carry the hero to his goal. The spirit seeker must take the doubt on himself. After three days he meets the wolf. The force that led to doubt must necessarily become sustaining, carrying strength when advancement of knowledge is sought. "Get on me, the Grey Wolf." The lower I consciousness as a powerful instinct now serves the spirit seeker. It is because of wolf that the spirit seeker can now step by step penetrate into the inner realms which still live from old forces.

To get the firebird means to win the phoenix, the bird that after a certain length of time throws itself into the fire to burn to ashes from which it arises to new life. The phoenix was the pictorial expression of a very particular mystery wisdom. The old Man must die in order that a new, higher one can be born. The mystery is described in the Chymical Wedding of Christian Rosenkreuz.

| Und so lang du das nicht hast, | And so long as you don't have |
| Dieses: Stirb und werde! | This: Die and become! |
| Bist du nur ein trüber Gast | You are but a murky guest |
| Auf der dunklen Erde. [74] | On the dark earth. |

"Do not take the cage!" and "Do not take the bridle!" counsels the Grey Wolf. The cage represents the ability to hold the phoenix consciousness (the firebird) while in earthly existence; the bridle represents the ability to wisely guide the powerful intellect that can rise to lofty objects (the horse with the golden mane). The Grey Wolf knows that he himself cannot develop either ability and that

---

72 In the Afanasyev version, the wolf attacks the horse in the presence of Ivan Tsarevich and tears it in two.
73 The German word for to doubt, *zweifeln,* has as its root *zwei,* two. In Russian, however, there is no connection between the word for *doubt* and the word for *two*.
74 From Goethe's poem "Selige Sehnsucht".

Ivan Tsarevich has not yet so developed. He does not yet have Elena the Beautiful. To attempt what one is not yet prepared for invites disaster.

On the back of the wolf – and so not in heights above the earth but borne by the instinct of his lower I consciousness and in the earthly itself – the spirit seeker learns to know and love the pure consciousness soul in its glorious perfection. Now Ivan can safely take the bridle and the cage.

But a final test remains. How does one carry the what has been won back into the realm of the father? The confrontation with the older, also inherited forces that have not been through this development demands the highest wakefulness of the spirit. But because the earth-bound lower I thinks it does not need to be on the job, the higher I cannot stay awake. The soul and everything that has been won falls to the forces that have remained back, and the higher I cannot preserve itself whole. It is cut to pieces. The instinctive lower I consciousness (the wolf) cannot itself repair the harm, but it can send a messenger, and the messenger brings new life forces won from the spiritual world. And now, after resurrection from the dead, the Johannine spirit enters realm of the father and the consciousness soul is forever bound with him.

## 27. The Tale of the Frog and Ivan Bogatir (A 570)

In a realm, in a kingdom once lived a king[75] who had three sons. One day he called his sons to him and said, "My dear sons, you are now grown, and it is time for you to think of brides. Take bows and arrows and get ready to shoot! Go to the royal courts and shoot in different directions. In the house where the arrow falls, there get your bride!"

The princes each took an arrow, went to the royal courts, and shot the arrow: the eldest to the right, the middle to the left, and the youngest, Ivan Bogatir, straight ahead. Then each one went to seek his arrow. The eldest brother found his arrow in the house of a minister of state, and the middle son found his in the house of a general, and they married their beautiful daughters. But Ivan Bogatir could not find his arrow for a long time and was very sad. For two days he wandered through forests and over mountains, and on the third day he came to a swamp and saw in it a large frog. The frog held in its mouth the arrow he had shot. Ivan Bogatir wanted to run and get away from what he had found, but the frog called to him:

"Kva, kva, kva, Ivan Bogatir, come to me and take your arrow, otherwise you will never get out of the marsh." When the frog had said this, it did a somersault and at once a nicely decorated arbor appeared. Ivan Bogatir went into the arbor.

"I know," said the frog, "that you have not eaten for three days. Do not you want to eat something?" It did another

---

75 This tale is somewhat unusual in that in the Russian the old ruler is called a *король*, a king, not a tsar, and his son is a king's son or prince, not a tsarevich. The frog, *лягушка,* is grammatically feminine in Russian and so uses feminine pronouns which I have kept. In German, *Frosch* is masculine, so Friedel Lenz had to use masculine pronouns for a definitely feminine figure.

somersault, and at the same moment a table appeared with all kinds of food and drink. Ivan Bogatir sat down at the table and ate and drank until he was satisfied.

"Listen," said the frog, "your arrow flew to me, you must take me to wife, and if you do not take me, you will never get out of this swamp!"

Ivan Bogatir became sad and did not know what to do. He thought for a long time, but then he took the frog with him and brought it into his kingdom. The brothers and their women laughed at the two of them.

The day came when Ivan Bogatir had to marry. He drove to the wedding in a carriage, and the frog was carried on a gold plate. When night came, and the bridegroom and the bride went into their chambers in the castle, the frog took off its frog skin and turned into a wonderful beauty. During the day she became a frog again. Ivan Bogatir lived happily with his wife.

After some time, the king called his sons to him and said to them, "My dear sons, you are all married now. I wish to wear a shirt that your women, my daughters-in-law, sewed." He gave each one a piece of cloth and demanded that the shirts should be ready by the next day.

The two older brothers brought the cloth to their wives. The women called their maids and servants to help them sew the shirts. The maids and servants hurried and set to work, some to cut, others to sew. In the meantime, the two sister-in-laws sent their lowest maid to see how the frog would sew the shirt. Just as the maids entered the chambers of Ivan Bogatir, he came with the cloth and laid it sadly on the table.

"Ivan Bogatir, why are you so sad?" asked the frog.

"How could I not be sad," answered the prince, "my father orders you to make a shirt out of this cloth by tomorrow!"

"Do not cry, do not grieve," said the frog, "lie down to sleep, the morning is wiser than the evening, everything will be done right!" She took a pair of scissors and cut the cloth into small pieces, then opened the window, threw them into the wind and shouted, "Blowing wind, carry off the bits and make a shirt for my father-in-law!"

The maid went home and told the royal daughters-in-law that the frog had cut the cloth in little pieces and thrown them out of the window. They laughed a lot at the frog and said, "What will her husband bring to the king tomorrow?"

The next morning the bogatir woke up, and the frog handed him a shirt. "Ivan Bogatir, bring this shirt to your father!" The king's son took it and carried it to his father. The older brothers also brought their shirts.

The king looked at the eldest brother's shirt and said, "This shirt is sewn as shirts are usually sewn." Then he took the second son's shirt and said that it was no better. But when the youngest son handed him his shirt, he could not wonder enough. There was not a single seam on it, it was all in one piece and he said: "I will wear this shirt on the most important occasions."

A second time the king called his sons to him and said, "Beloved sons, I would like to know if your women know how to embroider with gold and silver. Take silk, silver, and gold, and let each embroider a rug by tomorrow!"

The wives of the two older sons summoned their maids and servants to embroider the rugs. Immediately the maids and servants began embroidering the rugs, some with gold, some with silver, and the others with silk. Again they sent the lowest maid to see what the frog would do. Ivan Bogatir brought home gold, silver and silk and was very sad.

The frog sat in a chair and asked, "Kva, kva, kva, Ivan Bogatir, why are you so sad?"

"How could I not be sad," he replied, "Father ordered you to embroider a rug with gold, silver and silk by tomorrow!"

"Do not cry, do not grieve," said the frog, "lie down to sleep. The morning is wiser than the evening!" Then she took a pair of scissors, cut the silk and tore the gold and silver to bits, threw everything out the window and said, "You blowing winds, bring the rug with which my father-in-law will covers his windows!"

When the daughters-in-law heard about it through their maid, they thought they could do it that way. They waited a long time. But as the winds did not bring them carpets, they sent to buy silk, silver, and gold, and began embroidering the rugs, as they had done before.

Early in the morning, when Ivan Bogatir had risen, the frog handed him the rug. All three brothers brought their rugs to the father. The king first took the eldest's rug and said, "This rug is fit only to cover the horses in rainy weather."

Then he took the rug of the middle son: "This one can be spread out in the antechamber for people to wipe their feet on."

Then he took the rug of his youngest son and marveled, saying, "This shall be spread over my table on festive occasions!" He ordered that carpet to be kept carefully and well. But he gave the other sons their rugs saying, "Take them to your wives and tell them to keep them for themselves!"

A third time the king said to his sons: "Now, dear sons, I want bread made by the hands of your wives."

When the daughters-in-law heard that, they immediately sent the maid to investigate how the frog would do it. At the same time, Ivan Bogatir came home very sad.

"Kva, kva, kva, Ivan Bogatir, why are you so sad?"

"How am I not to be sad? Father orders you to bake a loaf of bread for him."

"Do not cry, do not grieve," said the frog, "I can do anything!" She ordered sourdough starter, flour, and water. She sprinkled flour on the sour dough, added water, and threw in flour, Then she poured everything into a pan and put it into a cold oven, closed the oven door, and said: "Bake, bread, pure, light, and white as snow!"

The maid returned to the daughters-in-law and said: "I do not understand why the king so praises the frog. She does everything wrong!" But the daughters-in-law thought to do the same. They mixed flour and cold water and poured the mixture into a pan and set it in a cold oven. But when they saw that everything was flowing apart, they brought flour again, mixed it with hot water, and put the dough in a heated oven. They were afraid of being late, and hurried so that one's bread burned and the other's was not done.

The frog took her bread out of the oven and it was pure, light and white as snow.

The brothers went to the father and brought him their bread. The father received the eldest's bread, looked at it and said: "Such bread can only be eaten in times of famine." He looked at the bread of the middle son and said: "This is not any better!" Then he took the bread of the youngest and commanded the servants that they should put it on the table for the royal guests.

"Beloved children," continued the king, "your wives have done everything for me that I have asked of them, so I invite you to come tomorrow with them to my castle for dinner."

The sons went home and told their wives. Ivan Bogatir was saddened and thought to himself: "How shall I bring the frog to the king?"

The frog sat on the chair and said, "Kva, kva, kva! Ivan Bogatir, why are you so sad?"

"Why should I not to be sad?" said Ivan. "Father has ordered us to come to his castle tomorrow with our wives. How am I to take you there?"

"Do not cry, do not grieve," said the frog, "Lie down and sleep; the morning is wiser than the evening!"

The next morning Ivan got ready and went to the castle without the frog. The daughters-in-law again sent their maid to see how the frog would go. The frog opened the window and shouted in a loud voice: "Oh blowing wind, fly into my kingdom and say that a richly decorated coach should come, with all that belongs with it, with servants, pages, runners and outriders!" She closed the window and sat in her chair.

When everyone was gathered in the castle, they were waiting for the frog when suddenly they saw that runners had run up, riders had ridden ahead, and an elaborately decorated coach was coming. The king thought that a foreign king or prince had come, and started to go to meet him.

"Do not bother, Father" said Ivan Bogatir, "that's just my little frog, who's dragging herself here in a box!" The carriage drove up, and out came the wife of Ivan Bogatir – a gorgeous beauty – and everyone was astonished.

They sat down to the meal. The frog-wife drank, and what she did not drink she poured into one sleeve. She ate and put the bones in the other sleeve. The daughters-in-law did the same: what they did not drink, they poured into one sleeve, what they did not eat, put them in the other.

When they got up from the meal, the music played, and the frog-wife went to the dance. She waved her left sleeve, and a lake appeared, an arshin[76] deep. She waved her right sleeve, and there

---

76  The arshin is the traditional Russian cubit standardized by Peter the Great as 1 arshin = 28 inches.

were geese and swans swimming on the water, and everyone who saw them was amazed by their charm. When the frog-woman stopped dancing, everything disappeared, the water, the geese and the swans. Then the other daughters-in-law went to dance. As they waved their sleeves, they only splashed themselves and nearly knocked their eyes out with the bones.

Ivan Bogatir went home, took the frog skin and burned it. When his wife came, she searched for her skin everywhere, but she did not find it. "Ah," she said, "Ivan Bogatir, if only you had had patience for a little while longer! Because you could not be patient, you must now go out to look for me. Seek me beyond three times nine lands, in the three times tenth kingdom, in the Kingdom under the Sun, and know that my name is Vasilisa the Wise. "

She spoke and disappeared.

Ivan Bogatir wept inconsolably. Then he set out.

Whether it was a short time or a long time, whether it was near or far, a tale is quickly told, not so quickly done is the deed. Eventually he came to a cottage that stood on chicken feet and turned around unceasingly. "Little hut, little hut," he said, "turn your back to the forest and your front to me!"

At his words the little hut faced him and stopped turning. Ivan Bogatir went inside. In the front corner sat the Baba Yaga. In an angry voice she exclaimed: "To this day I have not seen the Russian spirit with my eyes, I have not heard it with my ears, but now the Russian spirit appears before my eyes! How do you come, Ivan Bogatir, voluntarily or out of compulsion?"

"I come voluntarily but twice as much involuntarily," replied Ivan Bogatir, and told all that had happened. "I am sorry," said the Baba Yaga. "If you allow, I will serve you and show you Vasilisa the Wise. Every day she comes to me to rest here. If she comes up, try to grab her by the head. If you catch her, she'll turn into a frog, a toad, a snake and all sorts of worms, and finally into an arrow.

Take this arrow and break it in the middle, then she will be forever yours. But be sure that you hold onto her – do not let her go."

With that Baba Yaga hid the king's son, and she had scarcely hidden him when Vasilisa the Wise flew in. Ivan Bogatir stepped up softly and took her by the head. She turned into a frog, a toad and finally a snake. But Ivan Bogatir was startled and let the serpent out of his hand. Instantly Vasilisa the Wise vanished.

"Because you could not hold onto her," said the Baba Yaga, "you'll never find her here again. But if you like, go to my sister. Vasilisa the Wise also flies there to rest!"

The king's son went to the next Baba Yaga. But again he was not able to hold Vasilisa. He came to the third Baba Yaga sister: "If you now let go of Vasilisa the Wise, you will never ever find her!" When Vasilisa the Wise came, Ivan Bogatir stepped up and took her by the head, and no matter what she did or what she turned into, Ivan Bogatir did not let her out of his grip. Finally she became an arrow. He took the arrow and broke it right in the middle into two pieces. At the same moment Vasilisa appeared before him, saying: "Well, Ivan Bogatir, I surrender to your will!"

The Baba Yaga gave them a flying carpet, they sat on it and flew home to their kingdom. After three days, on the fourth day, the carpet settled in front of the castle. The king received his son and daughter-in-law with great joy. He made a great banquet and made Ivan king in his stead.

## Interpretation

Let us build up the picture of the frog. Its evolution from egg to tadpole and further from a gill-breathing water creature to a lung-breathing land or even tree inhabitant shows it to be a creature of exceptional capacity for transformation. It lives on land but is not warm-blooded and therefore does not have the passions and desires of the warm-blooded creatures. And it lives in water and through its cold blood is one with this element. But it is no fish; it needs air to breathe. In fact, it has a special relation to the air and is very sensitive to every change in the atmosphere and is therefore the best weather prophet.[77] As a symbol of metamorphosis the frog appears in many cult images and sarcophagi.

*"Weather-frogs (tree-frogs) were kept in preserve glasses with some water in the bottom and a small ladder. If the weather was changing for the better the frog would climb the ladder; if rain was imminent the frog descended the ladder."* Iain Galbraith, in an endnote to W. G. Sebald's Across the Land and the Water: Selected Poems, 1964–2001. Quoted on the Internet.

Man once had a similar consciousness when in the distant past he went through this stage of development. It is now deeply buried inside us but in the Aquarian Age (when the sun is in the constellation of Aquarius at the spring equinox) new forces will awaken.

---

77 At the approach of rain, tree frogs descend to mate near puddles and ponds that will make good homes for their offspring in their early stages. The captive frogs, lacking a tree, climb the ladder at the approach of fair weather and descend when they sense coming rain. To attract mates, many frogs croak loudly at the approach of rain.

The frog woman in this folktale is the symbol of the future soul consciousness. Ivan's arrow – the arrow of evolution – flies to her, but Ivan is at first shocked. It takes great resolution and will power to completely say "yes" to this future. During day consciousness, when Man is occupied with sense perceptions and absorbed by his own thoughts and judgments, he experiences this being only dimly as a sort of instinct. At night, asleep, when he dips into the world of supersensible beings, he recognizes it in its true form. But in the morning, this being is again lost. It becomes an instinct again.

The king sets aims and tasks and supplies the substance. The prince transmits; the frog woman transforms. What does the shirt mean in myth and folktale? We have looked at the soul and spiritual structure of Man. But if we start from the soul-spiritual part as the kernel of Man, then the lower members, physical body, life or etheric body and sentient body can be considered sheaths. The first sheath is the etheric body, the life forces that stream through the mineral body and give it form and force during life but leave it at death. In the picture language it is the shirt. The shirt being of woven cloth – and one can follow this motif through the European folktales – points to the fact that this etheric body is the bearer of our subconscious thought life. Of course, Man forms thoughts in the brain – there he "spins the threads" – but the forces streaming through the etheric body the thoughts. Their thoughts combine into a subconscious fabric, to linen. The Johannine I and the soul consciousness should form a new life body. The medieval soul lived and wove comfortably in itself. The soul of the future cuts what it has inherited to bits and throws them to the wind. The atmosphere of the earth that has been transformed by the resurrection deed of the Christ should live within the fabric of the shirt.

The king demands the decoration of the carpet. The hard reality of facts should be enlivened with rich inner feeling. Sun wisdom (gold), moon beauty (silver) and shimmering light (silk) should play in this picture-rich life of feeling. Such an inner life is turned to the world and resurrection forces work within it. (There is a variant in which the king says, "This carpet shall cover my table on Easter."

Thirdly, the king demands that the wives make bread. This time he does not give the substance; the soul must provide it. What out of feeling, thinking and willing has been won as the extract of all true knowledge becomes nourishment for the spirit. One who can bring spiritual knowledge, bread, transforms himself.

At last the long hidden soul being reveals herself in the light of day. When the soul in the course of its development has brought her relation to the heavenly and to the earthly, to the above and to the below, into perfect balance, when she has overcome weight and moves with grace and rhythm – then the folktale says the maiden dances.

"The frog-wife drank, and what she did not drink she poured into one sleeve. She ate and put the bones in the other sleeve." Then, as she danced, "She waved her left sleeve, and a lake appeared, an arshin[78] deep. She waved her right sleeve, and there were geese and swans swimming on the water." This picture becomes more easily understood in a variant: "She ate of the swan and put the bones into the *right* sleeve; the remainder of the drink, into the *left*."

The wine the frog princess pours into the heart sphere (the left) becomes a whole soul-etheric world. And what reigns therein as forces of awakening won by her higher (swan) consciousness becomes many-fold enlivened.

But the development is still not so far advanced that the soul is entirely freed from the instinctive nature. With the will alone it is not done, for this will burns the instinctive nature all too soon in its

---

78  The arshin is the traditional Russian cubit standardized by Peter the Great as 1 arshin = 28 inches.

own fire. The soul being must be *recognized* as the royal highway out of the Kingdom under the Sun. The way must be trod which she herself flew along. Every deception must be seen through and she herself as the main thing[79] held onto by the head. Then she becomes objective-finding, target-striving force – the arrow. And of this force the Johannine being takes his share; he breaks the arrow in half. And thereby is the soul consciousness lifted from the sphere of the instinctive to the clarity of the spirit, to the Sun Kingdom.

Already in 1847 this folktale appeared in print in Moscow. The language is modern, but the content agrees completely with the folk tradition. Afanasyev therefore included it in the explanatory material. At the point where the maids of the wives of the other brothers have watched how the frog made the bread and gone home, it continues "but the frog had just deceived them. As soon as they were gone, she took the dough out of the oven, discarded it as if nothing had been done, went out of the house, laid the frog skin aside and called, "Ye nurses and maids, make me such bread as my father ate on Sundays and holidays." Here also the bread – spiritual knowledge – is formed from the atmosphere.

---

79 Untranslatable German word play: the German word translated as "main thing" is *Hauptsache*, "head thing."

# 28. Rejuvenating Apples, and Living Water (A 173)

In an empire, in a realm once lived a tsar who had three sons. Two were clever; the third, a simpleton.

Once the tsar had a dream. [80]He dreamed that beyond three times nine countries, in the thrice-tenth realm, there lived a beautiful maiden from whose hands and feet flowed water. Anyone who drinks from this water will become thirty years younger. The tsar was very old. Then he called his sons to him and all his counsel and said to them, "Can anyone interpret my dream?"

The councilors answered the tsar: "High tsar, we have not seen it with our eyes, we have not heard with our ears that there is such a beautiful maiden. We do not know how to get to her."

Then the eldest son of the tsar, Demetrius, said: "Father, give me your blessing, I will ride in all four directions, look at people, show myself and find the beautiful maiden."

The tsar gave him his father's blessing. "Take money with you as much as you like, and also of provisions and troops as much as you need!"

Demetrius, the tsasrevich, took a hundred thousand warriors and set off. He rode a day, a week, a month - and two and three. No matter whom he asked, no one knew anything about the beautiful maiden. At last he came to barren regions, there was nothing to see, only heaven and earth. He drove his horse on, and suddenly a high, high mountain stood in front of him. Scarcely could the eyes measure its height. Somehow he climbed the mountain and found an ancient, gray man there. "Greetings, Father!"

---

80  There is a simpler variant in which the tsar just says to his sons, "Go to the hero-virgin Sophia to get living and dead water to heal my eyes."

"Greetings, brave young man! Are you avoiding a deed or do you want to accomplish one?"

"I seek a deed."

"What do you seek to do?"

"I have heard that behind three times nine countries, in the thrice-tenth empire, there lives a beautiful maiden, from whose hands and feet healing water flows. Whoever wins and drinks this water will be thirty years younger."

"Well, brother, you will not reach her!"

"Why not?"

"Because on the way there are three broad streams and three ferries. On the first they will cut off your right hand, on the second your left foot, on the third your head."

Demetrius Tsarevich was very saddened. He lowered his bold head, deeper than his mighty shoulders, and thought to himself: Either I must have pity on my father's head, or my own! Better, I'll turn back! He went down the hill, came back to his father and said: "No, Father, I could not find anything. Nobody has heard of this maiden."

Then the middle son, Basil, asked his father, "Father, give me your blessing, perhaps I will find the maiden!"

"Go, my son!"

The tsasrevich Basilius took a hundred thousand warriors and set off.

He rode a day, a week, a month - and two and three - and came into a desert of forests and swamps. There he found the Baba Yaga with the Bony Leg. "Greetings, Baba Yaga with the Bony Leg!"

"Greetings, brave young man! Do you avoid a deed or do you want to accomplish one?"

"I'm seek a deed. I have heard that behind three times nine countries, in the thrice-tenth empire, lives a beautiful maiden, from whose hands and feet healing water flows."

"There is, there is, but you will not succeed in getting there."

"Why not?"

"Because on the way there are three broad streams, three ferries. On the first you will cut off your right hand, on the second your left foot and on the third your head."

Basil, the tsasrevich, became thoughtful: either I must have pity on the head of my father or guard my own head. I prefer to go home safe and sound.

He returned home and said to the father, "No, dear father, I could not find anything, no one has heard of this maiden."

Now the youngest, Ivan Tsarevich, asked: "Father, bless me, perhaps I will find the wonderful maiden!"

The father blessed him: "Go, my beloved son! Take money and warriors as much as you need!"

"I do not need anything, just give me a good horse and a bogatir's sword made of fine steel!"

Ivan Tsarevich mounted the steed, took the sword of fine steel and set out on his way. He rode a day, a week, he rode a month and two and three. And he came to an area where his horse sank to his knees in the water, up to his breast in the grass. But he, the brave young man, had nothing left to eat. Then he saw a house that stood on chicken feet, and he stepped inside. In the cottage sat the Baba Yaga with the bony leg. "Greetings, grandmother!"

"Hail, Ivan Tsarevich! Do you avoid a deed or do you want to accomplish one?"

"And what a deed! I ride into the thrice-tenth empire. There, it is said, is a beautiful maiden, from whose hands and feet healing water flows."

"There is something like that! Even though I have not seen her with my eyes, I heard tell of her with my ears. But you will not reach her."

"Why not?"

"Because on the way there are three broad streams and three ferries: on the first one they will cut off your right hand, on the second your left foot, on the third head."

"Well, babushka, one less head does not make me poor. I will ride as God directs."

"Oh, Ivan Tsarevich, return home! You are still so young; you have never been in dangerous places; you have not had any great fears yet."

"No, whoever starts something must also finish it."

The tsarevich bid farewell to the Baba Yaga and rode on. He rode one day, a second and third and came to the first ferry. The ferrymen slept on the other side. "What should I do?" thought Ivan Tsarevich, "If I call, I will deafen him forever; if I whistle, I will sink the ferry. He whistled with a soft whistle. The ferrymen immediately awoke and took him across the river. "What do you want for your work, brothers?"

"Give us your right hand!"

"No, I need my hand myself." The tsasrevich waved his sword to the right and to the left and killed all the ferrymen. Then he mounted his horse and rode away. He did the same on the other two ferries. And soon he approached the thrice-tenth empire. At the frontier stood a wild man, as tall as the forest, as broad as a haystack, and holding in his hands an oak he had pulled up by the roots. "Where are you riding, you worm?" the giant shouted.

"I ride into the thrice-tenth empire. I want to see the beautiful maiden from whose hands and feet the healing water flows."

"Whither indeed, shorty! For a hundred years I have guarded her realm. She is not for for you. Many powerful heroes have come here and have fallen by my strong hand. And what are you? Nothing but a worm!"

The tsasrevich saw that he could not cope with the giant and moved aside. He rode and rode and entered a dark forest. There was a cottage in the woods and an old woman was sitting in the cottage. She saw the brave young man and said, "Greetings, Ivan Tsarevich, why did God bring you to me?"

He told her everything without concealing anything. Then the old woman gave him a magic herb and a little ball of yarn. "Go to the open field," she told him. "Light a fire and throw this herb in it! But be sure that you yourself are upwind from the fire. The smoke of this magic herb will make the giant fall into a deep sleep. Cut off his head. Then let the ball roll and ride after it. The little ball will take you to where the beautiful maiden rules. She lives in a large, golden castle, and often she rides with her army out to the green meadows to enjoy themselves. They enjoy nine days, then for nine days and nine nights they sleep the sleep of bogatirs."

Ivan Tsarevich thanked the old woman and rode into the open field. In the open field he lit a brushwood fire and threw the magic herb into the flame. A strong wind carried the smoke to where the giant stood guard. Soon all became black before the giant's eyes. He lay down on the damp earth and fell fast asleep. Ivan Tsarevich cut off his head and then let the ball roll and followed where it went. He rode and rode, and already in the distance the golden castle shone. He turned off the path, let his horse graze, and hid in the bushes. No sooner had he managed to hide than a huge cloud of dust rose from the golden castle. The beautiful maiden rode with her hosts to enjoy the green meadows. Ivan Tsarevich saw that the whole army was made up of virgins; if one was beautiful, the next was more beautiful, but the queen was most beautiful. She spent nine days in the green meadows. The tsasrevich did not turn a blind eye to her; he could not see enough of her. On the tenth day she entered the golden castle; she lay on the down bed and she slept the sleep of a bogatir. From from her hands and feet the healing water dripped. With her slept the whole faithful army. Ivan Tsarevich filled two vials with healing water. But his young heart could not bear it - he hugged the virgin beauty. Then he left the castle, mounted his good horse, and dashed homeward.

The beautiful maiden slept for some days. When she awoke, she became angry, stamped her feet, and exclaimed in a loud voice, "What worthless one was here? Who drank my kvass[81] and did not cover it?" She swung herself on her fast-footed mare, and in a swift pursuit pursued the tsarevich. The mare runs; the earth shakes. The maiden catches up with the brave youth; she swings her sword and hits him in the chest. The tsarevich sinks to the raw earth, the clear eyes close, the red blood flows and cakes. The beautiful maiden looks at him, and deep pity grabs her. Another youth of such beauty cannot be found anywhere in the world. She places her hand on his wound and wets it with the healing water. Then the wound closes, and Ivan Tsarevich rises up sound and whole.

"Will you take me to wife?"

"I will take you, beautiful maiden!"

"Well, ride home and expect me after three years!"

Ivan Tsarevich took leave of his betrothed bride and continued on his way. He came near to his kingdom, but the older brothers

---

81  Kvass, a fermented drink made from bread, raisins, sugar and water. (Note by the author.)

had set guards everywhere so as not to let him go to the father, and the guards announced his arrival. The older brothers rushed to meet him on the way and gave him a drink until he was intoxicated. Then they took away the two bottles of healing water and threw him into a deep abyss.

Ivan Tsarevich was suddenly in the other world.[82] He walked and walked. Suddenly a violent storm arose; the lightning flashed, the thunder rumbled, and the rain poured. He came to a tree and wanted to hide under it. Then he saw some young birds sitting on the tree; they were soaking wet. He took off his clothes, covered the birds with them, and sat under the tree. Suddenly a huge bird came flying. It was so big that it covered the sky with its wings. It was already dusk, but now it grew very dark. The big bird was the mother of the little birds that the tsarevich had covered. When the bird saw that her nestlings were covered, she asked, "Who has covered my little birds?" And when she saw the tsarevich, she cried, "You did, thank you. Ask me what you like, I will do everything for you!"

Then the tsarevich answered, "Carry me up into that other world!"

"Make a very big double sack, catch all kinds of game, and put it in one half, in the other pour water so that you have food asnd drink for me!" The tsasrevich did as he was told. Then the bird took the sack on his back, the tsasrevich sat down in the middle, and off they flew. And sooner or later the bird carried him up to the other world. They took leave of each other, and the bird flew back into her realm.

---

82  At this point, A 173 breaks off in the middle of a sentence. I have not found the Russian corresponding to the German text between here and the next footnote. It is not in any of the seven stories A 172 – A 178 which all have the same name. It was necessary to get Ivan Tsarevich back to this world, and Friedel Lenz seems to have borrowed this section from some other story. Accordingly, this section is translated from the German, not the Russsian.

[83]Ivan Tsarevich returned home, but the father no longer loved him and banished him from his eyes. For three years he was at home and yet not at home and lived everywhere. When three years had passed, the royal maiden came riding on her ship. She sent a letter to the tsar, demanding that he should give the guilty party; if he refused, she would beat up and burn the whole empire, leaving nothing behind. The tsar sent his eldest son to the ship. The two sons of the royal virgin saw him coming and asked their mother: "Is that perhaps our father?" "No, that is your uncle." "How shall we receive him?" "Take a whip and drive him back!" The eldest tsarevich went home defeated, as if he had eaten salt, so he went.

But the royal maiden threatened and demanded further, and the tsar sent out his second son. However, the same thing happened to him. So the tsar ordered to seek the youngest son, and when he was found, the tsar wanted to send him to the royal maiden's ship. But the Ivan Tsarevich said: "I only go there when there is a crystal bridge to the ships, and there are precious foods and fine wines on this bridge."

There was nothing to do; they built the crystal bridge and prepared the food and wine and honey. The tsarevich gathered his friends and said: "Come all of you, accompany me, eat and drink and do not be sorrowful!"

As he crossed the bridge, the boys shouted, "Mother, who is that?" " That's your father!" " How shall we receive him?" "Take him by the hand and lead him to me!" They hugged each other, caressed and kissed each other. Then they went to the tsar and told him all that had happened. Then the tsar drove the two elder sons from his court, and began to live together with the youngest, and they lived and lived and prospered.

---

83  From this point on, the story is from the end of A 172.

## Interpretation

The consciousness stemming from the past has grown old and helpless. It dreams of sources of life, but can no longer interpret the dreams. The development of the understanding has begun; the way to the spirit must be entered up "on horseback." That lasts three ages. The true spirit seeker knows that one must undergo grave dangers, that one can simply just go to the thrice tenth realm. Three times one must cross the fateful river – the Greeks called it the Styx or sometimes the Lethe. In his thinking, feeling and willing, Man comes to an inner boundary and must get across. Many become inactive and passive and loose all initiative for action in dealing with spiritual matters: he looses the right hand. Man slack off in the transformation of their lives, no longer follow the voice of their hearts, and make no further moral progress; they loose their left foot. And finally, one can also loose ones head: without gaining any real spiritual consciousness, the old consciousness looses its validity. The Johannine Man, however, *grasps* life actively out of the Will of the I, *strides* forward in the inner transformation of himself, and makes steady *head*way as a seeker of knowledge on the way to the spirit.

At the boundary of the spiritual world awaits his severest test, the wild man, a giant with a strong-rooted earth tree in his hand. He is the natural force that over and over drives Man back when he wants to enter this realm without proper preparation – it is his own nature that rises up to protect him from premature entry.[84] Many heroes have done battle with this giant and been defeated. Throughout the Middle Ages, he was fought by mortification and asceticism. Ivan, however, knows that it is senseless to go directly against this giant, so he goes to the side. Note how he over and over seeks advice and help in the soul world. One who ignites the

---

[84] Presumably the Lesser Guardian of the Threshold as described by Rudolf Steiner in his *Knowledge of Higher Worlds and its Attainment.*

fire of the Will out of inner freedom is through with this giant and a new development can begin.

For nine days the spirit seek beholds in mystic vision the eternal soul and the host of serving forces. Then nine days and nights she lies in holy sleep, but the I (Ivan) is awake and acquires heavenly wisdom. What is the meaning of this mysterious embrace? The relation of the human spirit to the soul has changed in the course of human evolution as in the course of life. Out of naturally given connection, the soul is the sister of the spirit. But if the Spirit dips into a higher world, then it will work creatively on the soul. It will fructify the soul. – And she becomes bride and wife. In the golden age the human spirit was totally one with its soul. It was itself still "above", rooted in the spiritual world. If it dipped into this world *seeing*, it fructified the soul. The spring of spiritual revelation[85] flowed. (For the ancient Egyptian, this was the time when Osiris ruled the earth with his sister and wife Isis.) As Man mastered the sense world, this spring closed for all but a few. In the *Song of Solomon*, the highest dialogue of the human spirit with the soul bride, we find (4:12 and 15) "My sister, my bride, thou art a closed garden, a closed spring, a sealed fountain. ... Thou art a garden spring, a fount of living water that flows from Lebanon."[86]

The turning point was the deed of Christ. He gives streams of living water. Johannine deeds unseal the springs and open for all who seek the source of wisdom which enlivens and rejuvenates: the spring is no longer closed. This act of free, exalted divine will the eternal had the eternal soul never experienced. She did not yet

---

85  *Uroffenbarung.*
86  The text above is my translation of German used by Friedel Lenz. There are scores of different English translations, The King James Version is (4:12) *A garden enclosed is my sister, my spouse, a spring shut up, a fountain sealed. (4:15) a fountain of gardens, a well of living waters, and streams from Lebanon.*

know the words, "the kingdom of suffereth violence."[87] What was previous given by grace must from now on be actively sought.

Over and over the spirit seeker who would lead mankind to true wisdom is repulsed. To be sure, those who have remained behind grab his knowledge to enliven and renew themselves, but the impulse itself is never grasped. Ivan must descend into the depths of the earth, into the realm of the elements. Meanwhile ripens the fruit of the mysterious embrace. It is a twin being that comes to life. In the "soldier's sons" we have already met these twins. From that tale we know that one seeks knowledge for earthly action; the other is totally turned heavenward. But in that story in the end they went under; the sphere of freedom was not mastered. Now, as offspring of the royal maiden and the royal I that has attained freedom, a new I is born, also a double being. It is turned heavenward in knowledge and earthward in action. But the heavenly is also recognized in the earthly and action is also directed to the heavenly. Whosoever wishes to approach unclensed the eternal soul is driven back by this young I.

The spirit seeker, who has opened the fountain of wisdom for all humanity does not go alone to the royal maiden. First he builds the crystal bridge – are not crystal clear thoughts the bridge to the eternal soul? Treading this way feeds the hungry and gives drink to those that thirst.

---

87 "And from the days of John the Baptist until now the kingdom of heaven suffereth violence, and the violent take it by force." (Matthew 11:12)

# 29 The Water of Life and the Sweet Apples of Youth (A 174)

Once there lived a tsar who had three sons, Theodore, George and Ivan. Ivan, however, was not exactly smart. The tsar sent the eldest son to fetch the water of life and the sweet apples of youth. The son rode away and came to a crossroads. There stood a post, and on it was written, "Go to the right – Eat and Drink; Go to the left – lose your little head." The tsarevich rode to the right. Soon he came to a house and entered. There was a maiden inside who said to him, "Tsarevich Theodore, go to sleep with me!" He did so and lay down. But then she shoved him and pushed him away, God knows where. For a long time the tsar waited for his eldest son. Finally he sent out the second. He made his way to the same place and entered the house. But the maiden also pushed him away, God knows where. Now the tsar sent the third son into the world and said: "You ride, too!"

The youngest rode out, came to the same crosssroads, and said, "For my father I'll risk my head!" and rode to the left. Sooner or later he came to a little hut and went inside. Inside sat the Baba Yaga spinning with her golden spindle. "You Russian bones, Ivan Tsarevich, where are you going?" she asked.

"Give me a drink, give me food," he answered, "Then you may ask me anything!" She gave him something to drink, she gave him something to eat, she asked him to tell her everything.

He answered, "I have gone out to seek the water of life and the sweet apples of youth, where the white swan lives, the swan daughter of Zacharias."

"You are not likely to achieve that, but perhaps you can if I help you," said the Baba Yaga and gave him her horse.

He swung himself onto this horse, rode and rode and came to the sister of Baba Yaga. He entered the hut and the old woman shouted, "Foo, foo, Russian bones! My ear has never heard him, my eye has seen him, and now he suddenly appears in my yard by himself! Ivan Tsarevich, where are you riding?"

"Give me something to drink, give me something to eat, then you may ask me!" She gave him something to drink, she gave him food, and he said: "I have ridden forth to seek the water of life and the sweet apples of youth, where the white swan lives, the swan daughter of Zacharias."

"You will scarcely attain that," replied the Baba Yaga and gave him her horse.

The tsasrevich rode and rode, and came to the third Baba Yaga. He went into the hut, and the old woman shouted: "Foo, foo, Russian bones, no ear has heard of him, no eye has seen him, and now he himself appears in the yard! Ivan Tsarevich, where are you riding? "

"Give me something to drink, give me something to eat, then you may ask me!" She gave him a drink, she gave him food, she asked everything, and he said, "I am am seeking the water of life and the sweet apples of youth, where the white swan lives, the swan daughter of Zacharias."

"It will be hard, O tsasrevich, and you will scarcely reach it!" She gave him her horse and club with the power of seven hundred and advised him: "If you come to the city of the white swan, then strike the horse with this club, and it will jump over the castle wall!"

He did exactly so, jumped over the wall, tied his Horse to a post and entered the chambers of the white swan, the swan daughter of Zacharias. The servants wanted to hold him back, but he pushed ahead saying, "I'm bringing the white swan a letter!" And he got into her room. She lay in a deep sleep on the bed of swan-fluff, lying with relaxed limbs, and the water of life was at her head. He took the water, kissed the maiden and caressed her.[88] Then he took the apples of youth and rode home again.

But when his horse jumped over the palace wall, it struck it with its hoofs, and all the bells began to toll, and the whole city awoke. The white swan, daughter of Zaharias awoke and franticly called out to the maids, beat one and whacked another, and shouted: "Someone has been in the house, drunk of the water, has not closed the well!" Meanwhile, the tsasrevich rode so quickly that he came to the Baba Yaga and changed his horse. But the white swan chased after him and came to the same Baba Yaga: "Baba Yaga, where have you ridden? Your horse is wet with sweat!"

"I rode into the field to drive the cattle out."

Ivan Tsarevich reached the next Baba Yaga and changed his horse again. But the white swan chased after him: "Baba Yaga, where have you ridden? Your horse is wet with sweat!"

"I rode into the field to drive out the cattle, so my horse is wet with sweat."

Ivan Tsarevich came to the last Baba Yaga and changed his horse again. But the white swan also followed him here and asked: "Baba Yaga, why is your horse wet with sweat?"

"I was in the field, drove out the cattle, so my horse is so wet with sweat."

Then the white swan returned home. But the tsasrevich rode on to his brothers and came to the hut where the maiden lived. She jumped to the threshold, welcomed him, and called him to sleep with her, but the tsarevich said, "Give me a drink, give me food, then I'll go to sleep!" She gave him a drink, she gave him food and said, "Lie down with me!"

---

88  The literal translation would be "he joked a little," but it later turns out that she has two children from this encounter.

"You lie first," answered the tsasrevich.

She lay down and he pushed her down - she fell, God knows where. The tsasrevich thought to himself: "I want to open this trapdoor; perhaps my brothers are trapped down there." He opened the trapdoor, and in fact, down there sat the brothers.

He said to them, "Come out brothers! What are you doing there? Are you not ashamed?" They pulled themselves together and made their way home to their father. But on the way, the older brothers decided to kill the youngest. Ivan guessed their thoughts and said to them, "Do not kill me, I will give you everything!" But the brothers did not respond and killed him. They threw his bones over the open field and rode away. The horse of Ivan Tsarevich, however, gathered all the bones together and sprinkled them with the water of life. Then they grew together, the joints joined, and the tsasrevich came to life again. "I slept for a long time, I quickly rose!" He came home to his father in an old fur coat.

"Where have you been?" asked the father, "go and clean the pits!"

Meanwhile the white swan, the swan daughter of the Zacharias, returned to her royal courts and sent from there a letter to the tsar demanding that he should give her the guilty party. The tsar sent the eldest son out.

"Here comes our father," cried the white swan's children when they saw him. "What shall we serve him with?"

"No, it is not your father," said the mother, "it is father's brother. Serve him with what you hold in your hands!" Each of them had a cudgel in his hand, and they beat him hard so that he could barely get home.

Then the father then sent her the second son. "Here comes our father" the children called and rejoiced.

"No," said the mother," this is Father's brother."

"What shall we serve him with?"

"Serve him with what you hold in his hands!" and they beat him as they had beaten the eldest brother.

Again the white swan sent to the tsar and asked him to give her the guilty party. At last the tsar sent his youngest son. Slowly he crept along with his feet in tattered bast shoes wearing a tattered fur coat. "Look, there comes a beggar!" cried the children. "No, that's your father," said the mother. "What shall we serve him with?"

"With what God sends!"

When Ivan Tsarevich approached, the maiden, the swan daughter of Zacharias, clothed him in splendid garments, and they went together to the tsar. Ivan Tsarevich told all his adventures, how he had freed his brothers from the trap, and how they had killed him. Then the father became angry, stripped the brothers of all honors and rights, and employed them in lowly services. And he made Ivan his heir.

Interpretation

The apple is in the rose family, but unlike the fruits of most members of that family, it is juicy. In most other members of the family, as the ovaries swell and ripen, they also dry out. In plants with juicy fruits something exceptional and quite wonderful happens. The ovary, this being of light and warmth sinks itself deep into the receptacle to gain access to the stem where water and root forces work from below upwards. (In botany, this is called an "inferior" ovary, and the fruit that is then formed, mostly from the receptacle – rather than the ovary – is called an "accessory" fruit, or in older terms, a pseudofruit. Apples, pears, bananas, and strawberries are common accessory fruits.) Thus the apple, as representative of juicy fruits, besides its relation to light and warmth that all fruits have, has also an special connection to the earthy element. The Latin word for apple is *malum* – which also means *evil*.

As Man, emerging from paradise under the influence of Luciferic beings, dissolved the ties that bound him to the spiritual world and fell into a separate existence, he involved himself more and more with the sense world which surrounded him. His consciousness became more and concerned with it. In this way, he developed an I-consciousness that was more concerned with the sense world than with the supersensible -- an egoistic I-consciousness. This egoistic I is – like the apple – a pseudo fruit. Therefore the apple became the symbol for certain forces connected with the Fall of Man; it became the apple of Eve. The fruit from the tree of knowledge of good and evil makes Man I-conscious and creative in the earthly. But it also drives him too deeply into the earthly. In that way, the forces of death gain power over him – recall Snow White. The reversal of this fall would be that Man finds his supersensible I and becomes creative in the spirit. The fruit of the tree of knowledge would then become fruit of the tree of life. The human being then rejuvenates itself in that it again experiences the divine forces that work in him. In the Edda it is told of the goddess Idun that she kept apples in a vessel and from time to time the gods ate of them to become young again. When in this story the sweet apples of youth are kept where the water of life flows, then we know that they are like the apples of Idun. The two elder brothers lie down in the sense world; one could also say that they eat the apple of Eve. The youngest, not blinded by the intellect, knows his way.

The higher being of Man, that is pure, beautiful and innocent and can rise to spiritual heights is like a swan. We Germans also have an expression, "it swans me" meaning "I am afraid." ... The name Zacharias brings to mind the father of John the Baptist. "The swan daughter of Zacharias" may mean what of the nature of the Baptist lives on working secretly within the soul that seeks the hero of this folktale.

## 30. The Sea Tsar and Vasilisa the All-wise (A 222)

Translation by Irina Zheleznova

Beyond the thrice-nine lands, in the thrice-tenth kingdom there once lived a king and queen who had no children. One day the king went traveling to distant lands and was away from home for a long time, and in his absence the queen gave birth to a son whom she named Prince Ivan. Of this the king knew nothing. He was on his way back to his own realm and was not far from it, when, the day being very, very hot, he felt so thirsty that he would have given anything for a drink of water! He looked about him, and, seeing a large lake ahead, rode up to it, got off his horse, lay down on the ground on his belly and began taking great gulps of the icy lake water. He drank and he drank and did not know there was anything to fear when all of a sudden someone clutched him by the beard! "Let go of my beard!" he cried. "No, I won't! How dared you drink this water without my permission?" said the King of the Sea, for it was he who was clutching the beard. "Take any ransom you want of me, only let me go!" "Promise to give me that which you have in your house but do not know about." The king thought it over, and, being quite sure that there was nothing in his house he did not know about, agreed. He felt his beard, saw that no one was clutching it any more, and, getting to his feet, mounted his horse and rode away.

He came home, and there was the queen, as happy as could be, welcoming him back! She was holding the baby in her arms, and when the king learned that he had a son, he burst into tears. He told the queen about the King of the Sea, and she wept with him, but what could they do! And as for Prince Ivan, he grew and grew, not by the day but by the hour, as fast as dough with yeast added to it, and before long was quite grown. "I can't keep him with me forever, I'm afraid," thought the king. "The day will come when I'll have to give him up to the King of the Sea, there's no avoiding it!" He took Prince Ivan by the hand and led him to the lake. "Look for my ring, I dropped it here somewhere the other day," said he, and, leaving Prince Ivan all by himself, turned his way homewards.

Prince Ivan began looking for the ring, and as he walked along the shore, he met an old woman coming toward him. "Where are you going, Prince Ivan?" she asked. "Leave me alone, you old witch, I have trouble enough as it is!" Prince Ivan said. "Oh, all right, then, and may God be with you!" And the old woman left him and turned off the road. But Prince Ivan regretted having behaved so badly. "Now, why was I so rude to the old woman?" he asked himself. "I'd better go after her and get her to come back. Old people are wise; she may be able to tell me something that will be of help to me." And he called to the old woman, begging her to forgive him for his foolish words and come back. "It was because I was troubled that I was so rude," said he. "My father told me to look for his ring, but though I have looked and looked I cannot find it anywhere." "It isn't because of the ring that your father brought you here," the old woman said, "but because he promised the King of the Sea that you would be his. The King of the Sea will soon appear and take you away with him to his underwater kingdom."

Prince Ivan burst into tears. "Do not grieve, Prince Ivan, luck will yet come your way," said the old woman. "Only you must listen to me. Hide behind that currant bush there and keep very quiet. By and by twelve doves, fair maids all, will come flying here, and a thirteenth will follow them. They will bathe and splash about in the water, and while they are at it, you must carry off the thirteenth maid's shift and not give it back to her till she gives you her ring. If you fail to do this, you are lost, for the King of the Sea has a high fence a full ten miles long round his palace, with a human head crowning every paling. One paling only has no head on it, so beware lest it be crowned with yours!" Prince Ivan thanked the old woman and hid behind the currant bush.

All of a sudden twelve doves came flying to the lake shore. They struck the ground and turned into maids so fair as pen cannot write or tongue tell! They flung off their gowns and rushed into the water, and they played and splashed about there merrily. Then the thirteenth dove came flying up. It struck the ground and turned into a maid, and of them all, fair as they were, she was the fairest! She took off her gown and shift and stepped into the water, and Prince Ivan could not take his eyes from her so smitten was he, but then, recalling what the old woman had told him, he crept out from behind the bush and carried off the shift.

The maid came out off the water and looked about for her shift. It was not there, and though she and her sisters searched and searched for it, they could not find it. "Do not search for it any longer but fly home!" said the maid to her sisters. "It's my fault that I did not keep an eye on it and I must be the one to answer for it." And the twelve maids, her sisters, struck the ground, and, turning into doves, flapped their wings and flew away. The maid was left alone, and she looked all around her and said: "You, whoever you are, who have my shift, come out and show yourself! If you are old, you shall be as my own father to me; if you are in your middle years, you shall be as a brother to me; if you are of an age with me, you shall be my own dear love!" And she no sooner uttered the last word than Prince Ivan appeared before her. She gave him her gold ring and said: "Ah, Prince Ivan, why did you not come here sooner? The King of the Sea is sorely vexed with you. Yonder lies the road that leads to his underwater kingdom. Follow it without fear and you will find me at the end of it! For I am Vasilisa the Wise, daughter of the King of the Sea." Vasilisa the Wise turned into a dove and flew away, and Prince Ivan set out for the underwater kingdom which, when he got there, he found to be, what with the sun shining overhead and green fields, meadows and groves everywhere, very much like any kingdom on earth. He came into the presence of the King of the Sea, and the King of the Sea roared at the top of his voice: "What made you tarry so long? Why did you not come here sooner? I shall punish you for it by setting you a task! I have a waste plot of land thirty miles long and thirty wide, which is all ditches, gullies and sharp stones and grows only thorns and thistles. Now, I want this to be made as smooth as the palm of a man's hand and sown with rye, and the rye to be high enough by tomorrow morning for a jackdaw to hide in. And if you do not do it, I'll have your head cut off!"

Prince Ivan left the King of the Sea, and the tears poured from his eyes. And Vasilisa the Wise, sitting at the window of her chamber, saw him and said: "Good morrow, Prince Ivan! Why do you weep?" "How can I help it!" said Prince Ivan. "The King of the Sea bids me level his waste plot of land which is all ditches, gullies and sharp stones and grows only thorns and thistles, to sow it with rye and to have the rye grow high enough by morning for a jackdaw to hide in." "That is no great misfortune, there is worse to come. Go to bed and to sleep with God's help. Night is the mother of wisdom, and all will be done for you!" Prince Ivan went to bed, and Vasilisa the Wise stepped out on the porch and called in a loud voice: "Come, my faithful servants, fill in the ditches and gullies, bear off the sharp stones, cast out the thorns and thistles, plow up the plot and sow it with rye, and have it all done by tomorrow morning!"

Prince Ivan woke with the dawn, he looked about him, and lo! — everything had been done: not a ditch or a gully was there, the ground had all been leveled, the plot sown with rye, and the rye had grown high enough for a jackdaw to hide in. He went and told the King of the Sea about it, and the King of the Sea said: "Thank you for doing as I bade. And now here is another task for you. I have three hundred stacks of wheat, with three hundred sheaves in each, and you are to thresh it all for me to the last grain and yet leave every single one of the sheaves and stacks whole, and if this is not done by morning, I'll have your head cut off!" "I will do as you bid, Your Majesty!" said Prince Ivan, and as he walked out of the palace and across the courtyard the tears poured from his eyes.

"Why do you weep?" Vasilisa the Wise asked him. "How can I help it! The King of the Sea bids me thresh all of his wheat in the space of one night, and I am not to lose a single grain and keep all of the stacks and sheaves whole." "That is no great misfortune, there is worse to come! Go to bed and to sleep, and may God be with you. Night is the mother of wisdom, remember!"

Prince Ivan went to bed, and Vasilisa the Wise stepped out on to the porch and called in a loud voice: "Come, ants, crawl here, all of you, as many as there are in the world, pick out the grains from my father's stacks of wheat and do not leave a single grain behind!" Morning came, and the King of the Sea summoned Prince Ivan. "Have you done as I bade?" he asked. "I have, Your Majesty!" "Come along, then, I wish to see it for myself." They came to the threshing floor, and there were all the stacks whole and of a piece; they came to the granary, and it was filled to the top with grain. "Thank you, my lad!" said the King of the Sea. "Just build me a church out of wax and have it ready by morning, and I will ask you to do nothing more." Off went Prince Ivan, and as he crossed the courtyard the tears poured from his eyes. "Why do you weep?" Vasilisa the Wise, sitting at the window of her chamber high up in the palace, asked him. "How can I help it! The King of the Sea bids me build him a church out of wax in the space of one night." "That is no great misfortune, there is worse to come. Go to bed and to sleep; night is the mother of wisdom, remember!"

Prince Ivan went to bed, and Vasilisa the Wise stepped out on to the porch and called in a loud voice: "Come, bees, all of you, from all over the world, fly here and build a church of wax in the space of one night!"

Morning came, Prince Ivan rose, and there stood the church before him, made of the purest wax! He went and told the King of the Sea about it, and the King of the Sea said: "I thank you, Prince Ivan! Many are the servants I have had, but not one of them pleased me as you have. Be my heir and the defender of my realm!

And you can take to wife whichever one you choose of my thirteen daughters." Prince Ivan chose Vasilisa the Wise, they were at once married, there was great joy in the palace, and a feast was held which went on for three days.

Whether a short or a long time passed nobody knows, but Prince Ivan missed his parents and badly wanted to go back to Russ. "Why so sad, Prince Ivan?" Vasilisa the Wise asked him. "It is that I miss my mother and father and wish to go back to Russ," said Prince Ivan. "Ah, now there is indeed great misfortune ahead! For if we leave this realm, many men will be sent after us to try to bring us back, and the King of the Sea will be greatly angered and have us put to death. But we may yet outwit them all!" And she went and sprayed three of the corners of their sleeping chamber with water, and, leaving it and locking the door behind her, rode away together with Prince Ivan.

Early on the following morning the servants of the King of the Sea came to rouse the young couple and summon them into the King's presence, and they knocked at the door of their chamber and called: "Wake up! Wake up! The King wishes to see you." "It's much too early, come a little later!" the drops of water called back in Vasilisa's own voice. The servants went away, but they came back again in an hour or so and knocked at the door again. "Time to get up!" they called. "Wait a little while, we have to get dressed!" the drops of water called back. Another hour passed, and the servants came back for the third time. "The King of the Sea is vexed with you, you must not dawdle any longer!" they called. "We'll be with him in a moment!" the drops of water called back.

The servants waited a while longer and began knocking at the door again, but there was no reply, so they broke down the door, and lo!— the chamber was empty. They told the King that the young couple had run away, and he flew into a temper and sent many men after them to bring them back.
By then Vasilisa the Wise and Prince Ivan had left the palace far

behind them. They galloped on their fleet-footed steeds and never so much as stopped for a rest. "Come, Prince Ivan, put your ear to the ground and see if you can hear anything," said Vasilisa the Wise. Prince Ivan jumped down from his horse's back and put his ear to the ground. "I can hear men calling and hooves pounding," he said. "That means the King's men are after us!" said Vasilisa the Wise, and she at once turned the horses into a green meadow, Prince Ivan into a shepherd and herself into a sheep.

The King's men were soon upon them. "Tell us, shepherd," they called, "have you seen a youth and a maid riding past here?" "No, kind folk, I have not," replied Prince Ivan. "I have been grazing sheep here for forty years, and never has a bird flown past or a beast run by in all that time." The King's men went back to the palace. "We have not seen anyone on the way, Your Majesty, save a shepherd and a sheep," said they. "And you should have seized them, for they were the ones I sent you after!" roared the King, and he sent more of his men after the runaways. Prince Ivan and Vasilisa the Wise were far away by then, and Vasilisa the Wise said: "Come, Prince Ivan, put your ear to the ground and see if you can hear anything." Prince Ivan jumped down from his horse's back and put his ear to the ground. "I can hear men calling and hooves pounding," said he. "The King's men are coming after us!" said Vasilisa the Wise, and she turned herself into a church, Prince Ivan into a priest and the horses into trees.

The King's men were soon upon them. "Tell us, Father, have you seen a shepherd passing by here with a flock of sheep?" they called. "No, kind folk, I have not," said Prince Ivan. "I have been with this church for forty years, but never has a bird flown past or a beast run by in all that time." The men went back to the palace. "We have seen no shepherd or sheep on the way, Your Majesty," said they. "We only saw a church and a priest standing by it." "Why didn't you pull down the church and seize the priest? They were the ones I sent you after!" roared the King, and he got on his horse and, followed by his men, set out after the runaways himself.

By then Prince Ivan and Vasilisa the Wise were far away. "Come, Prince Ivan, put your ear to the ground and see if you can hear anything," Vasilisa the Wise said. Prince Ivan climbed off his horse's back and put his ear to the ground. "I can hear men calling and hooves pounding more loudly than ever," said he. "That is the King himself coming after us with his men!" Vasilisa the Wise cried, and she turned the horses into a lake, Prince Ivan into a drake and herself took the shape of a duck. The King of the Sea came galloping up to the lake, and he at once guessed who the duck and the drake were. He struck the ground, turned into an eagle and swooped down upon them from above, but though he did this again and again the drake and the duck were too quick for him and dived into the water before he could get at them! By and by, seeing that he could do nothing, he gave up and galloped away, back to his underwater kingdom. And Vasilisa the Wise and Prince Ivan waited awhile and then set off for Russ.

Whether a short or a long time passed nobody knows, but by and by they came to Russ. "Wait for me in this wood," said Prince Ivan to Vasilisa the Wise, "and I'll go on ahead and show myself to my mother and father." "You will forget me, Prince Ivan!" "I won't." "You will, I know it! But you must try and remember me when you see two doves beating against a window pane." Prince Ivan came into the palace, and, seeing him, his parents threw their arms around him and held him close, and in his joy Prince Ivan forgot all about Vasilisa the Wise. He lived with his mother and father for a day and another day, and on the third day bethought him of marrying a princess he had met in the palace.

And Vasilisa the Wise went into town and took up service with a priest's widow who made wafers for a living. They began making wafers, and she took two pieces of dough, fashioned two doves out of them and put them in the oven. "Do you know what will happen to these doves, mistress?" asked she. "No, for what can happen to them? We'll eat them, that's all." "Do you really think so?" And Vasilisa the Wise opened the oven and then the window, and lo!—the doves started up and flew straight to the palace. They began beating at the windows there, and try as the king's servants might they could not chase them away. Then it was that Prince Ivan remembered Vasilisa the Wise and sent envoys to all corners of the realm to try and find her. She was soon found and brought to the palace, and he took her snow-white hands in his, kissed her on her sugar-sweet lips and led her to his mother and father. And from that day on, all the four of them

> Knew no woe, shed never a tear,
> And prospered more from year to year.[89]

---

89  Again this skillful translator lifts the rhyming conclusion which in the original is "жить да поживать да добра наживать" literally, "to live, yea, live on (and) acquire goods."

## Interpretation

Ivan's relation to water is very varied from one folktale to another. One must distinguish whether it is an old relation or a new or future one. Generally where Ivan fights against opponents from the water, especially dragons, forces are meant that are connected with the soul life of the past that was filled with imaginations of a dream-like nature. This tale is different. It tells how this consciousness transformed onto a higher plane comes again as an imaginative consciousness that developed from thinking – the thought-vision of the future. The tale describes the development of this future consciousness.

Vasilisa the All-Wise is the thirteenth dove, the thirteenth maiden. For many people a strange feeling is connected to the number thirteen, a sort of superstition. We must go far back to understand this superstition.

For Man of an earlier age the twelve-fold working of the zodiac on humans was an open secret. Today this knowledge reappears in decadent form. One hears of Leo types, of Taurus types, and so on. In former times, a Man was to some extent formed and shaped by his constellation and was much influenced by this forming. In the course of time there formed a consciousness that began to free itself from these twelve archetypes – the I-consciousness. It was unfamiliar and – as most people opposed it – scary. One who had it fell out of the usual groups and types. This new consciousness also brought an impoverishment with it. As long as Man experiences his lower I – and this is the necessary step – this impoverishment lasts. And with it, thirteen becomes an unlucky number. The Briar Rose[90] sleep, brought on by the thirteenth wise woman, depicts such a consciousness.

But an I-consciousness that grows beyond all twelve types is like the sun that traverses the zodiac and warms, enlightens and

---

90  Briar Rose = Sleeping beauty

awakens all twelve cosmic realms. In the Christ Jesus as the thirteenth among the twelve this highest, all encompassing consciousness was revealed. Vasilisa, the thirteenth, is that soul being that unites all twelve heavenly directions in herself and has brought them all into harmony. She is the all-wise higher soul permeated by the Christ.

Once Ivan is in the realm of the Sea King, the first task that must be accomplished is to make cultivatable soul ground that has become hard and unworkable materialism so that it bears only "thorns and thistles".

The second task is to bring in the harvest: to gather all that has ripened in the soul as a result of earthly experience so that it can become the bread of experience or seed for future harvests. Also Mankind as the fruit of the earth could be meant. It must be brought in, but it must be done without any application of force, without destroying the existing binding and associations, only through the wise action of that high soul that uses only diligence – the ants.

The third task is to build the church of wax. Bees live in a society in which the individual selflessly serves the community. Together they gather the nectar from the flowers and transform it into the sun-food of honey. They are in their whole life and work subject to the sun. And so – out of unselfish social cooperation, out of the force of the inner sun – love – the church of the future builds itself.

To do all of this in the soul world is the one task; the other is to bring it into the Slavic culture of Russ[91]. For that the development of the intellect must be undertaken. That happens in three steps.

---

91 Russ (Русь) was not the same as modern Russia. It extended from a little south of Kiev (the capital) in the south to a little north of Novgorod in the north; from somewhere in Poland in the west to Vladimir and Murom in the east.

First appear pursuing forces that would confine the Johannine wisdom to the soul world, that would keep it "in the sea" with Ivan as the shepherd and Vasilisa as a lamb that he protects (echos of the age of Aries the Ram). Next Ivan works as priest in the soul, but the preparation continues in stillness – "never has a bird flown past or a beast run by". In the third step, the stage of the white duck is reached. The horses turn to water: the intellectual thinking, long practiced on the sense world, becomes fluid, mobile, and adaptable. It becomes imaginative. Even when the pursuer feigns the thought power of the eagle, the I-spirit and the soul being evade the attacks by the imaginative thinking they have won – they have created a new sea kingdom. But before they can make this a reality in Russ, one more transformation must occur: Vasilisa the All-wise goes into the city to work in social endeavors. The tale says that she works for the woman who bakes bread for communion. But hearers would have known that in old Russ this bread could be baked only by women and that the women who baked it also cared for the sick, laid out the dead, and were respected as wise and good. Vasilisa transforms the spirituality of the dove into the life-bread of knowledge. And knowledge that has become the bread of life leads to the final union of the eternal I-being with the eternal soul and to the new founding of Johannine Christianity on the soil of Russ.